India and China

India and China: Retrospective Views on Development

Dipak Basu
and
Victoria W. Miroshnik

LEXINGTON BOOKS
Lanham • Boulder • New York • London

Published by Lexington Books
An imprint of The Rowman & Littlefield Publishing Group, Inc.
4501 Forbes Boulevard, Suite 200, Lanham, Maryland 20706
www.rowman.com

86–90 Paul Street, London EC2A 4NE

British Library Cataloguing in Publication Information Available

Library of Congress Cataloging-in-Publication Data

Names: Basu, Dipak, author. | Miroshnik, Victoria W., author.
Title: India and China : retrospective views on development / Dipak Basu and Victoria W. Miroshnik.
Description: Lanham : Lexington Books, [2023] | Includes bibliographical references and index.
Identifiers: LCCN 2022044350 (print) | LCCN 2022044351 (ebook) | ISBN 9781666921922 (cloth) | ISBN 9781666921939 (ebook)
Subjects: LCSH: Economic development—China. | Economic development—India. | China—Economic conditions—2000– | India—Economic conditions—21st century. | China—Politics and government—21st century. | India—Politics and government—21st century.
Classification: LCC HC427.95 B38 2023 (print) | LCC HC427.95 (ebook) | DDC 330.951—dc23/eng/20221026
LC record available at https://lccn.loc.gov/2022044350
LC ebook record available at https://lccn.loc.gov/2022044351

This book is dedicated to our uncle Nishith Ranjan Mitra, Managing Director of the leading publishing house in India Dev Sahitya Kuthir, who is the constant source of encouragement for us.

Contents

Introduction

India and China are two of the oldest civilizations. Up to the eighteenth century, for the Europeans, these two countries were depository of immense wealth and mystery. However, that idea has undergone serious change between the mid-eighteenth and early nineteenth centuries. These countries became synonymous for poverty, backwardness, and stagnant nations, in the words of James Mill "rude" nations, dark and dismal countries. Since 1992 this was being reversed. Both countries are called "emerging economies." China, with the destruction of the Soviet Union, became the darling of the West and "strategic partner." India, in contrast, still is the "slumdog millionaire" and receives extreme hostility from the West.

At least for more than 750 years the Indian economy was larger and grew faster than the economy of China; and it was ahead of China until 1750 AD (Maddison 2007a,b, 2001, 1998). China began to develop faster and was able to close the gap gradually with India, particularly since the Islamic invasion of northern India in 1192 AD. China then became ahead of India in terms of the size of the economy and its growth of gross domestic product (GDP). Due to the arrival on the throne of India of the English East India Company in the middle of the eighteenth century, India became deindustrialized; its resources were used for the British industrial revolution. China under the Manchus went ahead (Chermokhin et al. 2015).

After 1947, India had followed the Soviet system of five-year planning half-heartedly but also at the same time promoted crony capitalism and faced a famine-like situation (1965–1968) and a crippling foreign exchange crisis (1990–1991) due to the disappearance of the Soviet Union, which used to provide all necessary imports with 50 years' interest-free credit payable in Indian currency or by exports from India. India not only became self-sufficient in food grains, but it also achieved respectable growth rate per year under the control of the IMF-World Bank with significant change in the character of the economy where the public sector is disappearing (Ahluwalia 2002; Bardhan 2010).

By 1978, per capita income of China was $979 and of India $966. Agricultural productivity per worker was almost identical in 1975 in the two countries: China 2.3 and India 1.9 (relative to the United States = 100) and in per hectare terms 218.2 and 212.4, respectively, again relative to the United States as 100 (Maddison 1998).

China and India are the two emerging economies in the world. As of 2021, China and India are the second and fifth largest economies in the world, respectively, on a nominal basis. On a purchasing power parity (PPP) basis, China is at first and India is at third place. Both countries share 21 percent and 26 percent of the total global wealth in nominal and PPP terms, respectively. Among Asian countries, China and India together contribute more than half of Asia's GDP. In 1987, the GDP (nominal) of both countries was almost equal. Now in 2021, China's GDP is 5.46 times higher than India. On a PPP basis, the GDP of China is 2.61 times that of India. China obtained the GDP of $1 trillion in 1998, while India obtained that only after nine years in 2007 on an exchange rate basis. Both countries have been neck and neck in GDP per capita terms till 1990. As per both methods, nominal and PPP India was richer than China in 1990. In 2021, China is almost 5.4 times richer than India on the nominal and 2.58 times richer in the PPP method. The per capita rank of China and India is 63rd and 147th, respectively, in nominal GDP. The per capita rank of China and India is 76th and 130th, respectively, in PPP (Wu 2016; Weber 2021; ten Brink 2019; Narlikar 2019).

China attained a maximum GDP growth rate of 19.30 percent in 1970 and a minimum of −27.27 percent in 1961. India reached an all-time high of 9.63 percent in 1988 and a record low of −5.24 percent in 1979. From 1961 to 2019, China grew by more than 10 percent in 22 years while India never had achieved that yet. The sector-wise GDP compositions of India in 2017 are as follows: Agriculture (15.4 percent), Industry (23 percent), and Services (61.5 percent). The sector-wise GDP compositions of China in 2017 are as follows: Agriculture (8.3 percent), Industry (39.5 percent), and Services (52.2 percent). China was the most populous country with approximately 1.42 billion people in 2018. India was the second largest country by population with approximately 1.35 billion inhabitants in 2018. China and India together account for 36.28 percent of total world population, 7,632,819,325 (Nolke et al. 2019; Wu 2016; Weber 2021).

A regular feature in almost every global journal and publication has been a comparison of India's slow economic growth and, until recently, China's rapid progress. China was a "poorer" country than India in terms of GDP per capita till 1990. In 2019, the Chinese per capita GDP is 4.6 times of India's.

Proponents of India talk of the democratic and inclusive nature of the country's growth while ignoring the slow pace of change. China's backers point to unprecedented poverty eradication, urbanization, and infrastructure improvements while ignoring the social and environmental costs these efforts have incurred (Nolke et al. 2019; Wu 2016; Weber 2021).

Table 0.1 Dynamic Comparison of China and India

Year	*Nominal GDP of China (Billions $)*	*Nominal GDP of India (Billions $)*	*Per Capita GDP*		*Growth Rate (%)*	
			China	*India*	*China*	*India*
2020	14,722.70	2,622.98	10,500	1,901	2.300	–7.965
2019	14,279.90	2,870.50	10,217	2,101	5.950	4.042
2018	13,894.80	2,701.11	9,977	1,997	6.750	6.533
2017	12,310.40	2,651.47	8,879	1,981	6.947	6.795
2016	11,233.30	2,294.80	8,148	1,733	6.849	8.256
2015	11,061.60	2,103.59	8,067	1,606	7.041	7.996
2014	10,475.70	2,039.13	7,679	1,574	7.426	7.410
2013	9,570.41	1,856.72	7,051	1,450	7.766	6.386
2012	8,532.23	1,827.64	6,317	1,444	7.864	5.456
2011	7,551.50	1,823.05	5,618	1,458	9.551	5.241
2010	6,087.16	1,675.62	4,550	1,358	10.636	8.498
2009	5,101.70	1,341.89	3,832	1,102	9.399	7.862
2008	4,594.31	1,198.90	3,468	999	9.651	3.087
2007	3,550.34	1,216.74	2,694	1,028	14.231	7.661
2006	2,752.13	940.26	2,099	807	12.721	8.061
2005	2,285.97	820.38	1,753	715	11.395	7.923
2004	1,955.35	709.15	1,509	628	10.114	7.923
2003	1,660.29	607.70	1,289	547	10.038	7.860
2002	1,470.55	514.94	1,149	471	9.134	3.804
2001	1,339.40	485.44	1,053	452	8.336	4.824
2000	1,211.35	468.40	959	443	8.490	3.841
1999	1,094.00	458.82	873	442	7.662	8.846
1998	1,029.04	421.35	829	413	7.846	6.184
1997	961.60	415.87	782	415	9.237	4.050
1996	863.75	392.90	709	400	9.923	7.550
1995	734.55	360.28	610	374	10.954	7.574
1994	564.33	327.28	473	346	13.037	6.659
1993	444.73	279.30	377	301	13.884	4.751
1992	426.92	288.21	366	317	14.225	5.482
1991	383.37	270.11	333	303	9.263	1.057
1990	360.86	320.98	318	368	3.920	5.533
1989	347.77	296.04	311	346	4.206	5.947
1988	312.35	296.59	284	354	11.223	9.628
1987	272.97	279.03	252	340	11.657	3.965

(Continued)

Table 0.1 (Continued)

Year	Nominal GDP of China (Billions $)	Nominal GDP of India (Billions $)	Per Capita GDP		Growth Rate (%)	
			China	India	China	India
1986	300.76	248.99	282	310	8.950	4.777
1985	309.49	232.51	294	296	13.431	5.254
1984	259.95	212.16	251	277	15.192	3.821
1983	230.69	218.26	225	291	10.770	7.289
1982	205.09	200.72	203	274	9.017	3.476
1981	195.87	193.49	197	270	5.113	6.006
1980	191.15	186.33	195	267	7.834	6.736
1979	178.28	152.99	184	224	7.591	–5.238
1978	149.54	137.30	156	206	11.326	5.713
1977	174.94	121.49	185	186	7.570	7.255
1976	153.94	102.72	165	161	–1.570	1.663
1975	163.43	98.47	178	158	8.720	9.150
1974	144.18	99.53	160	163	2.310	1.185
1973	138.54	85.52	157	144	7.760	3.296
1972	113.69	71.46	132	123	3.810	–0.553
1970	92.60	62.42	113	112	19.300	5.157
1971	99.80	67.35	119	119	7.060	1.643
1969	79.71	58.45	100	108	16.940	6.540
1968	70.85	53.09	91	100	–4.100	3.388
1967	72.88	50.13	97	96	–5.770	7.826
1966	76.72	45.87	104	90	10.650	–0.055
1965	70.44	59.55	98	119	16.950	–2.636
1964	59.71	56.48	85	116	18.180	7.453
1963	50.71	48.42	74	101	10.300	5.994
1962	47.21	42.16	71	90	–5.580	2.931
1961	50.06	39.23	76	85	–27.270	3.723
1960	59.72	37.03	90	82		

Source: World Bank.

China's economic reforms started with Deng Xiaoping's fang-shou ("letting go" and "tightening up") efforts between 1978 and 1989 (see Table 0.1). The reforms then accelerated in a sustained manner, be it the Family Responsibility System that transformed agriculture, the opening up of the industrial sector for the growth of local enterprises, or the substantial effort to make state-owned enterprises more efficient (Chow 2004; Cheung 2014).

India started reforming more than a decade later, in 1992 with the instruction of the International Monetary Fund (IMF) to implement the Washington Consensus (see Table 0.1). China's had a trebling of its per capita income in the first 25 years of its reform efforts, whereas India's per capita income "only" doubled during those years. As a result, India has almost tracked China's growth pattern in terms of absolute real GDP growth after 13 years. India's real GDP in 2014 was $1.55 trillion, which is close to China's 2001 real GDP of $1.56 trillion at 2005 prices. By 2030, India could increase its workforce by 200 million, which is a problem given the level of unemployment in the country. Thus, having a younger population is not an unqualified blessing.

A closer look suggests that India must gain ground on two counts: better work quality and working conditions. As per the Economic Survey 2014, 92 percent of the labor force is either self-employed or employed in the unorganized sector. This means inferior work quality, poor working conditions, and lower than organized sector wages, all of which significantly hampers productivity. Second, a large percentage of India's labor force is unskilled or uneducated. Although the workforce is growing and getting younger, this lack of skill and education would not only mean a massive loss of opportunity but also lead to significant socioeconomic challenges (Ramesh 2017; Stephen and Parizck 2019; Wang 2013).

India's GDP growth rate in the previous 17 years from 2017 has averaged 6.61 percent while China's GDP growth rate has averaged 9.28 percent. China's capital investment as a percentage of GDP has averaged 43 percent while India's investment as a percentage of GDP has averaged 34.2 percent in the previous 17 years from 2017. India's GDP per capita has lagged to China's GDP per capita. India grew its GDP per capita at 5.31 percent between 2000 and 2017 while China grew its GDP per capita at 8.71 percent. The GDP of India is about $1.5 trillion in 2018, compared with about $7 trillion for China at the same time. China's nominal GDP per capita was $9,580 compared with India's nominal GDP per capita of $2,038 in 2018 (Wu 2016; Weber 2021; ten Brink 2019).

China still gives tremendous importance in investing in infrastructure. It is evident in its One Belt One Road (OBOR) initiative, which is designed to export China's unemployed materials and labor forces in foreign countries by offering cheap loans. India's average investment in infrastructure in the first 50 years after independence was 3 percent of the GDP when the recommended investment should be over 6.5 percent of the GDP. China, on the other hand, invested nearly 9 percent of GDP in infrastructure.

China created special economic zones to encourage manufacturing and export-oriented industries, particularly by foreign companies. The general rules of business are relaxed in these zones. Indian special economic zones that came up decades later lacked such push and better incentives to attract foreign investors in numbers and size to give China a competition.

China's GDP growth was supported by massive export surplus while India is still having massive trade deficit mainly due to China. China's export as a percentage of GDP reached 36 percent in 2006; since then it declined to 19.7 percent in 2018. Twenty-one percent of China's exports are of high-technology products, compared with only 6.4 percent for India over the last 25 years.

The Indian manufacturing sector is now overwhelmed by Chinese products since China joined the World Trade Organization. At least 50 percent of the employments in the Indian manufacturing industry are being lost due to Chinese competition. India's trade deficits with China exceeded $100 billion in 2021. Problems of India include slow and expensive transport systems, erratic electricity supply, as well as lack of skills of the Indian labor force.

Higher productivity of the Chinese labor force can be explained by efficient rail and road networks, modern infrastructure and port facilities, and skill development since 1978. India still has backward infrastructure in every category. Costs of energy are serious impediments for India's industrial development.

Energy is very important for the economic progress of a country. China has made a serious improvement in promoting solar power. China is now the second largest solar energy producer. China with the help of Elon Musk's company Tesla increased the production of electric vehicles; India is trying to follow it.

The Indian economy has a clear strategic advantage, which does not exist in China. The Indian education system as created by the British promotes English and as a result Indians can work all over the world. They can work in the information technology sector and higher level of management for the international companies, which the Chinese cannot do because of their lack of English language and non-English education, which has no market value in the world.

China is still more or less a communist country, which means most organizations are under the control of the state whether at the central or town-municipal level. This has the obvious advantages that wishes of the central leadership can be implemented all over the country. On the other hand, the Indian economy can be handicapped by democracy with layers of different political parties with conflicting policies, individual and provincial jealousy, judicial system that takes decades to settle any issue, and changing policies of the central government along with elections at the central and state levels.

An authoritarian political system is a definite advantage as demonstrated by China. Indian democracy is an obstacle for economic development. Physical infrastructure, such as electricity, railways, roads, ports, and airports, has not kept pace with the growth of the Indian economy because land disputes can stop any plan for development for decades. Any political party because of its jealousy can start a dispute and destroy a plan. In the state of West Bengal in 2010 the plans to create a special economic zone supported by Japan and an automobile factory of Tata motors, planned by the Marxist Communist party of India, were destroyed by very jealous politicians of the opposition party, Trinamul Congress. As a result, economic development of West Bengal was ruined for several decades in future. These kinds of situation cannot be created in China.

Since 2016, India's growth rate declined steadily; in the financial year 2019–2020, even before the attack of coronavirus pandemic, India's GDP growth rate went down to 4 percent. For 2020–2021 it would be minus 5 percent as estimated. Between 1980 and 2004, the calculating at the PPP rate, average growth rate was 86 percent for China. In 1952, China's population was 57 percent higher than that of India. At present, China's population growth rate is less than 1 percent per year. For India, the rate of growth of population is 1.7 percent per year.

Higher growth rate of China was possible because of very high rate of growth of gross domestic investment as a ratio of GDP, which was about 70 percent more than that of India. However, regarding productivity, India's performance is not that bad compared with China. Agriculture value added per agricultural worker is just 17 percent less in India compared to China. In information technology, China has defeated India in hardware items. But India has defeated China in software.

Chinese banks provide credit, which is two and a half times as a ratio of GDP, compared to that in India. In China, marginal tax rate on corporate incomes is at 30 percent, while in India it is 40 percent. In China, central government transfers 51.4 percent of the tax revenue to the provinces, while in India the equivalent transfer is 36.1 percent (Wang 2013; Alder et al. 2016; Bosworth and Collins 2007; Coase and Wang 2016; Zhu 2012).

Surprisingly, the GINI index of income inequality was also higher in China than India. China's modernization is urban oriented. Economic reforms in China had the result of having sharp increases in urban incomes in the eastern sea-side cities, when the rural and western provinces were kept backward. India is one of the most unequal countries in the world with the top 10 percent controlling 55 percent of the total wealth according to the 2018 World Inequality Report. The bottom 50 percent control only 15.3 percent of the total wealth.

Public expenditure on health in China as ratio of GDP was three times more than that in India. If India plans to double its economy to $5 trillion it will need to invest more in health and education. India's public health expenditure is among the lowest in the world at 1.02 percent of GDP (in 2015), far behind the 5 percent recommended by the United Nations Development Program (UNDP). A universal basic income (UBI) through cash payment was proposed in the Economic Survey of India in 2016–2017; however, it is not economically feasible, according to the government (Naughton 2007; Ramesh 2017; Zhu 2012).

The World Economic Forum's Global Competitiveness Report (GCR) in 2018 and 2019 evaluates human capital on two criteria: health and skills. The health criteria have one component, life expectancy, whereas the skills criteria have four components: two for the current workforce and two for the future workforce. According to the Global Circularity Gap Report (GCR 2018), China has a score of 87 for the health criteria and a score of 64 for the skills criteria. India's scores are dismal, respectively, 59 and 54. The scores in the GCR 2019 are similar: China: 88 and 64; India: 61 and 50. Road connectivity and electricity are the two key fields where India is far behind China in the rankings. India's road connectivity score is 75.8, whereas China's score is 95.7

We can identify some important characteristics of the period 1980–2020 that are responsible for China's superior economic performance:

(a) Major reforms in China started many years earlier in 1978; India had started its reforms in 1992 after the collapse of the Soviet Union.
(b) In China, the leaders were determined to lift up the country from the dismal position created by Mao Tse-Tung. In the case of India, the reforms of 1991 were imposed by the IMF-World Bank.
(c) Foreign investments and introduction of modern technology from Japan, Taiwan, Singapore, South Korea, and particularly Russia have pulled up China. In India, foreign investments were not welcomed by the Indian business oligarchs who made their fortunes in the government's policy of cronyism in the guise of socialist planning.
(d) Foreign companies from the countries mentioned above and many Western companies supported China's export drive by setting up their production bases in China taking advantage of the very low wages of the Chinese workforce in the beginning. In India both the private sector oligarchs and the British system of bureaucracy created massive obstacles for foreign investments, with very slow growth of exports.
(e) The Chinese government improved its infrastructure and electricity supply system in a very significant way to provide supports for industrial development. India was very slow until recently. Its electricity supply is still erratic.
(f) Indian politicians are in most cases are very corrupt, and they do not think about their country but they think about their personal fortunes and provincial developments. Corruption is there in China but they are determined to defeat everyone in both economic development and military power. India has limited determination.

We have to mention some subsidiary reasons for the differences between China and India. These are as follows:

(a) Mass production and dumping

    Chinese companies observe the local market and import similar popular items in bulk but on much cheaper price so that the local industry cannot compete. This is how the smartphone industry in India, along with small electrical components industry, is severely affected negatively. India-made smartphones such as Micromax, Lava, and Intex once had nearly 54 percent share of the Indian market; today these are reduced to only 10 percent of the market share and may close down soon.

(b) Competitive pricing, exchange rate manipulation with reverse manufacturing

Chinese manufacturers copy the technology from advanced countries like Japan, the United States, France, and Russia and start making their own products copying foreign products. It saves their cost and resources on innovations. Chinese government supports these activities by keeping the exchange rate artificially low and through repressive policy toward the labor force. For instance, iPhone X costs around Rs. 70,000 in India, while GooPhoneX, a Chinese clone of the same, will cost Rs. 6,500. Chinese high-speed trains are direct copies of Japanese Kawasaki trains. Chinese aircrafts particularly those in the military sector are direct copies of their corresponding Russian aircrafts. On the contrary, the Indian business community lacks in global exposure. They still believe in traditional way of doing business; although their sons and daughters go to the United States to study MBA, but they learn nothing about technology or new business strategy as the Chinese do.

(c) Trained labor

China has a competitive advantage due to cheap labor owing to a big population and absence of trade unions. The Chinese government supports the skill development of the labor force and helps them to discipline the labor force if there is any demonstration against the repressive policy of the employer. As a result, the productivity of Chinese laborers is much higher than that of Indian laborers. On the contrary, India although has the largest number of young people in the world, only an insignificant portion of them has undergone formal skill training as Periodic Labour Force Survey (PLFS) of 2018 demonstrated. Indian government has created several plans for skill development programs but failed to implement these effectively due to mismanagement, provincial jealousy of the bureaucrats and politicians, nonavailability of funds, and mindless official paperwork. As a result, the labor force in India is either unproductive or less educated compared with that in China.

(d) Stability of government policy

Political stability, due to lack of any democracy, is the prime reason behind China's emergence as a popular destination for manufacturing. In India due to its democratic system there are layers of government bureaucracy at both central and state levels. The political powers can change in some dramatic ways causing chaos and confusion to start or manage a business. That is the main reason why international investors are reluctant to come to India but prefer to go to China or Vietnam or Thailand.

(e) Education

Education system is the most important factor behind how China became economic superpower. Chinese education system also encourages vocational and practical courses. The Indian education system still is affected by the British legacy with emphasis on academic studies. China literacy rate for 2018 was 96.84 percent while India's was 74.37 percent (UNESCO).

(f) Industrial network clustering

China has established a vast network of industrial clusters for manufacturing industries. The examples are: provincial municipal-level industry; Shanghai-based chemicals, pharmaceutical, automobile, electronic apparatus, and financial networks; Shenzhen-based IT, semiconductors, communications, and electronics information systems; Beijing-based IT, communications, and electronics systems; Guangzhou-based automobiles, electronic appliances, textiles, apparel, toys, and petrochemical-based industries. In India, politicians and bureaucrats at the state levels are promoting themselves and trying to draw investors to their state, harming the prospect of other states.

(g) Government and industry partnership

Chinese government works in collaboration with the corporate sector and in most cases controls these corporate entities directly in expanding their economic activities in foreign countries. China's the Belt and Road Initiative (BRI), a global infrastructure development strategy, was initiated by the Chinese government in 2013. Now China has 138 countries and 30 international organizations in the BRI infrastructure projects of mainly ports, railways, highways, power stations, aviation, and telecommunications. Through project like these China can export its surplus steel, glass, building materials, and labor to these countries by offering loans, which other international aid organizations and banks will not be interested due to their nonviability and the lack of repayment ability of the borrowing countries. Seven out of ten biggest construction firms in the world are now Chinese. These companies are helping China to expand its empire by taking over land, mines, sea ports, and airports in different developing countries (Edith et al. 2015; Deng 2000; Gordon and Gupta 2003).

China, already supported by several American presidents starting with Bill Clinton, became the alternative superpower. India has no such ambition or support from the American power, although India is following since 1992 a pure capitalistic method of development with extreme inequality and high unemployment, whereas China is still following the national economic planning, which is the clue to its success.

Due to the trade war with China initiated by former U.S. president Donald Trump and the onset of the COVID-19 pandemic, it has been widely argued that Western multinationals ought to resettle away from China to their home countries or to some friendly countries nearby to ensure the safety and reliability of production. Reliance on global value chains (GVCs) as is necessary for reasons of cost and scale should be diversified away from China toward other Asian partners. In theory, democratic and law-governed India, with a large workforce, should be an ideal partner.

The reality, however, does not match the rhetoric. Despite wages that are almost three times as high as in India, production costs in China are only 5 percent higher than in India as China's vastly larger economies of scale allow it to remain competitive.

Apart from the United States, India is the only major country that has not joined the region's trade groupings: the Western-controlled Comprehensive and Progressive Trans-Pacific Partnership and the China-controlled Regional Comprehensive Economic Partnership.

Thus, it is difficult for India to break into any of these GVCs that might be relocating away from China. Indian companies do not show much interest in the preferential accesses that already exist through bilateral free trade agreements of India, because they are not aware of the relevant details of these treaties.

These two nations, India and China, have totally different systems of political administration. India is a parliamentary democracy, while China is a one-party fascist dictatorship. Reforms of India have reduced the dominance of the state-run industries, while China's reforms have formed a command economy that depends on foreign investments and foreign markets. India has accepted the control of the ideology of the capitalist Western countries while China has resisted that. China's public sector enterprises remain an important part of the economy, and the government is expanding its control as one can see from the temporary arrest and disappearance of Jack Ma of the highly successful internet marketing organization Alibaba. China has indeed retained much of its planned economy. China uses the market system when it is useful and discards it when it wants. Unlike China, India since independence has remained a mixed economic system until 1992. In 1992 collapsed. The Soviet Union used to supply all that India needed payable with Indian rupees; there is no need for any foreign exchange to pay for India's imports. After emergency loans from the IMF, India decided to float its currency, devalued the rupee, privatized the state-owned enterprises, and relaxed the conditions for the entry of foreign direct investment. Of a labor force of

520 million, only 1.2 million now still work for state-owned firms. The result is increasing unemployment and pessimism. The alternative to IMF was there in 1992. India could have asked its temples to release the vast amount of gold they have to the government in exchange for bonds, and there would be no need to go to the IMF to accept harmful economic policy of privatization. China never accepted IMF recommendation but it used its own mind. China's so-called inefficient state-owned industries still exist and expanding, whereas India is either closing these down or selling these to private owners at massive discounts. The private owners are more interested to buy palaces in London with these surplus money than to invest in India (Herd and Dougherty 2007; Heston and Sicular 2007; Kroeber 2016).

The lessons for India is that following the economic policy as suggested by the "Washington consensus" will not help to revive India's weak economy to compete with China and a stronger medicine is needed. Policymakers should try to create demand in the economy, and India needs to infuse money into the economy, especially toward the poor to create their purchasing power. India needs to take measures to support the public sector to create new jobs. India should not close down or privatize its public sector industries. India should promote urbanizations. That would promote rapid delivery of civic services to improve quality of life and create new jobs (Kohli 2006; Krueger 2002; Weber 2021).

Chapter 1

Indian Economy until 1990

India has adopted in 1951 the Soviet planning system but without having socialism. At the height of the planned economy of India, only 14 percent of the economy was under the public ownership. The rest of the economy was used to be controlled by various permits and quotas for the private sector industries and various incentives like subsidies for the agriculture. Justification for this capitalist economy, not of a socialist planned economy, was provided by Mahalanobis (1952, 1953, 1955, 1956; Taylor 1979; Basu and Miroshnik 2015).

THE MIXED ECONOMIC PLANNING, 1951–1991

Economic planning was introduced in 1951. However, in 1966 it was halted for three years when India had to import food grain from the United States, which forced India to borrow from the IMF and India had to accept IMF policies. Planning had started in 1969 with vigorous direction under Indira Gandhi with nationalization of major banks, coal and other mines, and foreign trade. The war with China in 1962 and with Pakistan in 1965 and 1971 diverted resources from the economy to defense but made India's relationship with the Soviet Union very close. While the Soviet Union encouraged Indian planning, the Western countries particularly the United States and the United Kingdom were hostile to the idea of industrialization of India (Mellor 1976).

All major industries, particularly in the defense-space-aircraft-nuclear sector, were developed in India with the help of the Soviet Union. The Soviet Union helped India to develop its oil and gas sector with significant discoveries of oil and gas fields in India while the Western countries dismissed India. The Soviet Union used to supply every kind of products and equipment with

50 years' interest-free credits payable by India's exports. All these facilities came to a halt in 1991 when the Soviet Union disappeared and India went into a serious economic crisis. India had to pay in terms of international currency from 1991 onward, whereas it used to pay in terms of its own currency before 1991. Rather than using the enormous amount of gold kept in the temples, Indian government went to the IMF and the economic reform to dismantle the planning system in India started in 1992.

Progress during the Planned Period

In 1951, India's dream was to create a "socialistic pattern of society through planning in a mixed economy and to achieve a reasonable standard of living." At that time after about 200 years of British rule, Indian economy was in a devastating condition with millions of refugees from Pakistan, created by the British. Between 1900 and 1946, India experienced total stagnation and continuous transfer of money, gold, and silver from India to the United Kingdom. Gross national product (GNP) grew more slowly than population. Food production virtually stood still, and the result was extreme hardship and poverty. Britain used to take away food grains whenever it needed. In 1943 during the Second World War, at least 5 million people starved to death in Bengal when the British took away the food grains from Bengal.

In 1951, India started its first Five-Year Plan (1951–1955) to industrialize the economy against the background of acute shortages of food and raw materials in general and rehabilitation problems of millions of refugees after the partition of the country. It was decided that the private sector could not pull up the economy from the pathetic economic situation that prevailed at that time. The Soviet Union was the model for India. However, most part of the economy left in the hands of the private sector. There was not much effort to mobilize primary source of surplus, that is, agricultural surplus, as the Soviet Union did. The deficit in the public budget was financed by increased taxation and domestic borrowings. This period was characterized by price stability and high industrial and agricultural growth despite evidence of inflationary financing through budget deficits.

The second Five-Year Plan (1956–1960) was a bold attempt to industrialize the country through massive investments in heavy industry using import control measures. GNP grew in real terms by 4.96 percent in 1956–1957, by 6.97 percent in 1958–1959, and 7.33 percent in 1960–1961. The total foreign borrowing during that period of the second plan was 9.06 billion rupees, when foreign aid was very limited. Inflation went up from 2.29 percent in 1957 to 6.6 percent in 1960. New finance minister Morarji Desai, after the departure of the previous finance minister Krishnamachari on charges of corruption, was instrumental for the ouster of the architect of that success of the second plan, P. C. Mahalanobis, from the Planning Commission in 1959 for that inflation and balance of payment problem of India during the third plan, of 1962 to 1967 (Basu and Lazaridis 1983). However, Morarji Desai himself was responsible for the balance of payment problem during the second plan. He insisted that in order to be an honest nonaligned country, when the Soviet Union was constructing a steel plant, India must invite Western countries to do the same and invited Germany and Britain to construct two other steel plants, thus increasing the cost of the second plan, which had caused severe balance of payments problem for India.

The success of the second plan of Mahalanobis was demonstrated in 1962 and 1963, when the growth rate of the real GDP was 5.33 and 7.05 percent, respectively. The failure of Morarji Desai became obvious from the facts that both public expenditures went up from 14.37 billion rupees in 1960–1961 to 23.89 billion rupees in 1962–1963 and foreign borrowings went up from 2.51 billion rupees in 1960–1961 to 3.74 billion rupees in 1962–1963. Inflation during the third plan became worse. Annual percentage change of price was 3.7 in 1959–1960, became 12.8 in 1964–1965 and 15.9 in 1966–1967. The third plan, presided by Morarji Desai, failed and in 1965 India was in serious economic crisis.

Through the 1956 Industrial Policy extensive series of license, quotas, and permit systems were arranged to control output, investments, location, and direction of the private sector's efforts. Natural advantages of the Eastern India in industrial raw materials were ignored to promote industrial development of the Southern, Western, and Northern India by giving subsidies on the prices of industrial raw materials to equalize these throughout India.

Disaster struck India during the 1960s during the third plan of 1961 to 1966. The Chinese invasion of 1962 and Pakistani invasion of 1965 had destroyed the certainty of the old conception that India did not have to worry about defense and it could devote all resources on development. Defense expenditures as a percentage of GDP rose from 2 percent before 1962 to 4 percent between 1962 and 1972. Foreign aid from the United States was suspended. That was followed by a severe drought in 1965–1966, and the United States only had the ability to supply wheat. India was forced by the United States to go to the IMF and borrow money, devalue the rupee, and stop the planning for three years.

Most of the major private sector industries in West Bengal were ruined by the Finance Minister Morarji Desai at that time. The private sector industries used to depend on the public sector contracts. When the public sector investments were reduced drastically by the government, these private sector industries had nowhere to sell their products as exports of their products, mainly capital goods, were not permitted by the government. Morarji Desai actively induced the private sector industries and banks to move away from

West Bengal. Violent and irresponsible trade unionists also have contributed to the movement of industries and banks to the Western India and South India. That has increased the cost of subsidy, as the Eastern India was the natural source of major industrial raw materials. According to the Industrial Freight Equalization Act of 1956 of the Finance Minister Krishnamachari, from Tamil Nadu, the prices of all industrial raw materials were equalized throughout India by using subsidies. These subsidies were wasteful particularly when India did not have enough revenues to increase investments. That discrimination against the Eastern India continued even after 1992, when the Minister for Industries Maran actively moved the private sector car industry Hindustan Motors from West Bengal to Tamil Nadu, gradually during 1990s.

During the fourth plan of 1970 to 1974, India had escaped from the stranglehold of the IMF in 1969 when public investments were released from the restrictions, coal and other mining industries were nationalized, leading to the dramatic improvement of the standard of living for the laborers of the coal and other mining industries. The major private commercial banks were also nationalized leading to significant increase in rural banking. Green Revolution also took place at the same time when the wheat production went up, from 1967 to 1971, by 50 percent. However, that good fortune, of higher than expected growth rate of the GDP of 5.6 percent during 1970–1971 and good harvests, could not last long. The year 1971 was the beginning of the conflicts in East Pakistan, when Pakistan government refused to obey the verdicts of the election of 1970 and started killing the people of East Pakistan. More than 10 million refugees came to India, and public expenditure rose by 22 percent. The government had to resort to deficit financing, and money supply rose rapidly. The result was the runaway inflation of about 25 percent in 1972–1973.

On top of that the "Oil Price Shock" of 1974 came when the Organization of the Petroleum Exporting Countries (OPEC) increased the price of crude oil by 400 percent. India was spending about 75 percent of its export earnings just to import crude oil. From a surplus of 280 million rupees in 1972–1973, balance of payments went for a deficit of 9.6 billion in 1974–1975. India had lost about 2.1 percent of its GNP during the period of 1974–1976 due to that oil price shock.

However, that crisis also had a blessing. Middle East countries were flushed with money, and Indian companies got contracts for the massive construction projects in the Middle East and Libya in North Africa. Large number of people from India got jobs in various countries of the Middle East. At the same time, export of consumption goods from India to the Middle East increased by many folds. Between 1974 and 1976, exports rose by 60 percent in money terms and 39 percent in volume terms. However, that opportunity was lost due to the lack of dynamism of the industrial sector in India due to bureaucratic controls and corruptions, and very soon Japan, Korea, and China took over that market.

During the second oil price shock in 1979, Indian exports could not grow but costs of imports went up rapidly. Balance of payments deficits rose up by 4.3 billion rupees in 1979–1980. The GDP was affected adversely by 3 percent in 1978–1979. International political situation went against India as well when India supported the Soviet action to defend Afghanistan from the Pakistani-CIA joint invasion in 1979. Pakistan was receiving massive amount of defense equipment freely from both the Western and the Muslim countries. To combat that India also got to import defense equipment and debt service to export earnings rose to 40 percent in 1988.

After the murder of Mrs. Indira Gandhi in 1984, the economic policy of India had a dramatic change under the new prime minister Rajiv Gandhi, who initiated a more outward-oriented economic policy. Western economists suggested a wholesale reform of the economic policy. The government borrowed vast amount of money from Western commercial banks to spend on Western defense equipment and aircrafts. Foreign borrowings went up from 13.08 billion rupees in 1984 to 29.9 billion rupees in 1989. Balance of payments deficits went up from $2,343 million in 1984 to $7,148 million in 1988. Nominal exchange rate declined from Rs. 7.5 in 1970 for one dollar to Rs. 7.86 for one dollar in 1980 and to Rs. 17.50 for one dollar in 1990.

Domestic debt as a percentage of GNP rose from 0.37 in 1980 to 0.47 in 1989. Public expenditure went up from Rs. 430.7 billion in 1985 to Rs 769.8 billion in 1989. Government expenditure went up giving a false impression of very high rate of growth of the GDP. That had created a bubble in the most irresponsible fiscal policy of Rajiv Gandhi, which was busted in 1991, when the Soviet Union collapsed.

During the days of the Soviet Union, India had no worries about foreign exchange as the Soviet Union used to supply all industrial materials and capital goods for industrial developments with long-term loans over 50 years payable by Indian rupees, which the Soviet Union could use to buy products from India. It had dual advantages that India did not need to have hard currency to import capital goods or defense equipment from the Soviet Union. India had the captive export market in the Soviet Union. All these facilities collapsed in 1991.

India had an anti-Soviet government of Morarji Desai in 1977–1979 during which the industrial development of India was restricted but after 1980, it was revived under Mrs. Indira Gandhi, who was both a socialist and pro-Soviet. That industrial development collapsed when in 1991, India, due to acute foreign exchange problem created by the collapse of the Soviet Union, had to borrow from the IMF. Although Indian temples had massive stocks of gold, which India could use, the government decided to go to the IMF.

ANALYSIS OF MAHALANOBIS DOCTRINE

The two-sector model formulated by Mahalanobis played an important role in the development of major ideas relating to economic planning in India. As against the Harrod–Domar model, the Mahalanobis model laid considerable emphasis on the possibility that the overall rate of real investment in the economy might be constrained by the level of output in the capital goods industry within the economy (Kaushal 2004). In such a situation, since the overall rate of growth over a given period of time tended to vary directly with the overall rate of investment in the economy, the Mahalanobis model suggested the allocation of a higher proportion of total investment to capital goods industries rather than to consumer goods industries. Feldman model (Fel'dman 1928, 1929), which lay at the back of Stalinist model, was constructed as early as in 1928, but it remained in obscurity till its discovery (even after the publication of Mahalanobis model) claimed by the Polish-American Evsey Domar in his book, *Essays in the Theory of Economic Growth*, published in 1957 (Domar 1957). We suspect Domar has never seen the Feldman model because the model he passed on as the Feldman model was the Mahalanobis model, extended to make it highly complicated, but without adding any substance, losing the elegancy of the Mahalanobis model in the process. As he was a Polish, brought up in Poland and Manchuria before his emigration to the United States, he might not know any Russian at all.

The real Feldman model was translated by Spulber (1964) where Feldman, to prove his theory, that higher allocation of investment can make growth of the national income higher, gave a series of numerical examples. Mahalanobis instead gave a series of algebraic proofs in some closed-form solutions. In Feldman model, the output of wage goods and agricultural commodities was kept constant. This pattern emphasized the network of building heavy industry for erstwhile USSR. Mahalanobis produced a model similar to that of Feldman only in philosophical sense. This Mahalanobis type of industrialization strategy was adopted for the Indian economy even after the ouster of Mahalanobis from the Planning Commission in 1959, at least until 1992, when IMF started directing economic policy of India.

Feldman used his model in the third Five-Year Plan for the USSR, and Mahalanobis used the model in India's second Five-Year Plan. Mahalanobis model is based on the following assumptions: The economy is a closed one: there are no exports or there are severe constraints on the growth of exports. This leads to a strategy of maximizing investment in the capital goods industries, and this, it was thought, will maximize the growth of productivity in the economy as a whole (Rudra 1975).

The capital or machinery once installed in a particular industry cannot be shifted to another. The economy is divided into two sectors—the consumer goods sector and the investment goods sector. Growth rate of aggregate investment in the economy is exactly equal to the growth rate of output in the capital goods sector within the economy.

The model assumes away the possibilities of acquiring additional capital goods through imports. There is no excess capital in either of the two sectors and whatever is produced by the capital goods sector is fully used for the purpose of capital formation in the economy. Mahalanobis assumes that relative prices are constant. Thus, he assumes away the problems of the terms of trade debate between the two sectors (Rudra 1975).

Rationale of Mahalanobis Growth Model

According to him, if large investment is not made in the basic heavy industries producing capital goods, the country will forever remain dependent on foreign countries for the imports of steel and capital goods like machinery for real capital formation (Kaushal 2004).

Since it is not possible for India to earn sufficient foreign exchange by increasing exports, the capital goods cannot be imported in sufficient quantities owing to foreign exchange constraint. The result will be that the rate of real capital formation and the rate of economic growth in the country will remain low (Karmakar 2012).

Thus, Mahalanobis was of the opinion that without adequate investment in basic heavy industries, it would not be possible to achieve rapid self-reliant economic growth. Therefore, according to him, to achieve rapid economic growth and self-reliance, it would be necessary to give the highest priority to basic capital goods industries in the development strategy of a plan.

Employment Generation in Mahalanobis Model

It is necessary in this connection to mention Mahalanobis' views on increasing employment opportunities and to achieve a stage of full employment. According to him, productive employment can be increased only by increasing the production of capital goods like steel, electricity, machinery, fertilizers, and so on. Whether it is increase in employment in the industrial sector or in the agricultural sector, it cannot be achieved without increasing the output of capital goods (Karmakar 2012). To quote him, "The only way of eliminating unemployment in India is to build up a sufficiently large stock of capital which will enable all unemployed persons being absorbed into productive capacity. Increasing the rate of investment is, therefore, the only fundamental remedy for unemployment in India" (Mahalanobis 1955).

Thus, in Mahalanobis' opinion, not only to achieve the objective of rapid economic growth but also to achieve the goal of full employment, it is necessary to accord high priority to capital goods industries in the development strategy (Kaushal 2004).

IMPORT-SUBSTITUTING INDUSTRIALIZATION

Mahalanobis' emphasis on basic heavy industries was also due to his objective of meeting the requirements of higher rate of capital accumulation from within the economy and therefore enabling the economy to stop imports of foreign capital equipment and machines (Karmakar 2012)

To quote him,

> The proper strategy would be to bring about a rapid development of the industries producing investment goods in the beginning by increasing appreciably the proportion of investment in the basic heavy industries. As the capacity to manufacture both heavy and light machinery and other capital goods increases, the capacity to invest by using domestically produced capital goods would also increase steadily and India would become more and more independent of the imports of foreign machinery and capital. (Mahalanobis 1953)

In fact, Mahalanobis growth model advocates import substitution type of industrial development strategy. It is important to note that Mahalanobis assumed, though implicitly, that export earnings of India cannot be sufficiently increased. If this assumption is not valid, as has been pointed out by several critics, then he could not justifiably identify rate of investment in the economy with the domestic output of capital goods (Karmakar 2012).

If exports of a country can be adequately raised, the various capital goods can be imported in exchange for exports. In that case, rate of investment or rate of capital accumulation in the economy can be stepped up without giving high priority to the basic heavy industries provided the exports can be adequately increased. Thus, the assumption of stagnant exports is crucial in the Mahalanobis growth model for providing the rationale for a general shift in the investment pattern to the domestic production of capital goods (Rudra 1975).

Second Five-Year Plan, based as it was on Mahalanobis growth model, proposed an explicit strategy of development, which gave top priority to basic heavy industries. Not only the objectives of rapid rate of economic growth and employment generation but also the aim of self-reliant and self-generating economy were sought to be achieved by "the building up of economic and social overheads, exploration and development of minerals and the promotion of basic industries like steel, machine building, coal and heavy chemicals." To quote from second plan again,

> Low or static standards of living, under-employment and unemployment and to a certain extent even the gap between the average incomes and the highest incomes are all manifestations of the basic under-development which characterizes an economy depending mainly on agriculture. Rapid industrialization and diversification of the economy is thus the core of development. But if industrialization is to be rapid enough, the country must aim at developing basic industries and industries which make machines to make the machines needed for further development.(Mahalanobis 1956)

It is clear from above that in the second plan there was clear shift of priorities from agriculture to industries and within industries to basic heavy industries. As mentioned above, the logic of Mahalanobis in emphasizing heavy industries was that the growth of basic heavy industries would enable the economy to accelerate the rate of capital formation and therefore economic growth. In fact, he identified the rate of growth of investment in the economy with the rate of growth of output in the capital goods (sector) industries within the economy (Karmakar 2012).

MAHALANOBIS' FOUR-SECTOR MODEL

Mahalanobis realized that the basic heavy industries being capital intensive will not ensure rapid expansion of employment opportunities. Thus, he put forward a four-sector growth model in which he kept heavy industry sector (i.e., K-sector) intact but divided the C-sector (i.e., consumption goods sector) into three subsectors: C1, C2, and C3. Sector C1 represented factory enterprises using mechanized techniques and producing consumer goods, Sector C2 represented the household and small-scale enterprises also producing consumer goods, and Sector C3 represented provision of services. Mahalanobis model then had the aim of increasing supply of consumer goods to meet their rising demand. It also had the aim to ensure, consumer goods being labor intensive, expansion of employment opportunities (Rudra 1975; Mahalanobis 1955).

In keeping with this approach, second Five-Year Plan put restrictions on the growth of capacity in factory enterprises engaged in commodity production. However, since for these household or cottage enterprises, adequate resources were not provided, nor any effort was made to improve their productivity, they could fulfill neither their largest of production of consumer goods nor of generating enough employment opportunities (Karmakar 2012; Kaushal 2004).

In the third plan (1961–1966) also the strategy of second plan was continued as is clear from the following: "In the Third Plan, as in the Second, the development of basic industries such as steel, fuel and power and machine building and chemical industries is fundamental to rapid economic growth" (Mahalanobis 1956).

These industries largely determine the pace at which the economy can become self-reliant and self-generating. Though, "to achieve self-sufficiency in food-grains and increase agricultural production to meet the requirements of industry and exports" was stated to be one of the objectives of the third plan, actual allocation of resources between agriculture and other sectors did not exhibit any difference from that of the second plan (Rudra 1975).

The term "long-run economic growth model" is used for a model that describes how an economy grows in the long run. This growth may be measured via growth in index such as gross domestic product or via growth in total values of assets (land, capital, human capital). They may also be used to make long-run forecasts about the growth of specific economies, but this need not be their primary purpose (Kaushal 2004).

Long-run economic growth models differ from each other in terms of the extent to which they account for and the extent to which they make population growth endogenous, human capital improvements, accumulation of physical capital, and technological progress. They also differ in terms of the level and nature of their micro-foundations.

Long-run economic growth models differ from short-run models that generally focus more on the role of fiscal and monetary policy, animal spirits, and regime uncertainty. Inputs, such as labor, capital, and technology, that could vary from year to year, determine outputs at a given point of time or in a given year, via a fixed functional relationship, called a production function. The production function itself is fixed (Karmakar 2012).

The inputs themselves can change from year to year. Part of this change is through feedback from the output: some of the output are allocated to investment such as investment in physical capital, investment in human capital (either through population growth or through improving the skill level of the existing population), or investment in technological improvement. The extent to which this happens depends on the economy's savings rate. However, there could also be changes to inputs arising from other factors (such as discovery of new technology, or discovery of new natural resources, or other "random chance" factors).

The criticism of the World Bank and neoliberal economists against Mahalanobis strategy has always been that they underestimated the trade prospects available to the economy. Because of their "inward-looking" nature it missed out on the growth opportunity that being linked to the world economy offered at that time. By contrast, the East Asian economies, which seized this opportunity, performed better than India prior to India's abandoning this "inward-looking strategy" (Hazra 1985; Kaushal 2004; Ramesh 2017).

Likewise, the criticism of others has been that it is not the "machine-making sector" but agriculture that was the real bottleneck sector for the Indian economy, so by emphasizing the former and ignoring the latter, this strategy caused an increase in food grain prices and perpetuated poverty.

Both these criticisms have been countered by the defenders of the strategy. Against the first criticism, it has been argued that the idea behind the strategy, as Mahalanobis himself had stated explicitly, was not to promote autarky but to engage in world trade on the basis of an altered (less agro-based) production structure compared to the one that prevailed at the time of independence, which would actually lead to a higher rate of export growth. This was because world trade, in the sort of goods whose production the strategy would be promoting, grew faster than in the goods that the country predominantly produced at independence (Karmakar 2012).

Against the second criticism, it has been argued that while emphasizing investment allocation in favor of heavy and basic industry, the strategy did not actually ignore agriculture but sought to increase its output through other means, notably through increasing the *effectiveness* of investment (i.e., through an increase in the output-capital ratio). "Of course, the most potent way of doing so was through land reforms, which the strategy did not properly address, but that relates not to any conceptual flaw in the strategy *per se* but rather to the class character of the state, that is, the need to placate the landed interests" (Rudra 1982).

India's production structure at independence was dominated by its export structure, where "manufacturing" exports took the form primarily of jute and cotton textiles. Emphasizing export growth as a means of raising the growth rate of the economy in such a situation would necessarily have meant *at best*, if at all notable export growth could have been achieved, pushing out more agro-based products, which would have jeopardized the country's food security by diverting land away from the production of food grains (Karmakar 2012; Rudra 1982).

It may, of course, be argued that being "outward-looking" would have drawn foreign capital to set up manufacturing units for exports, as had happened in East Asia, but there are two obvious problems with this argument, even leaving aside all questions of whether this was a *desirable* way for India to have followed (because of the constraints on labor and other democratic rights that such a path entails). Direct foreign investment for locating plants in low-wage Third World countries, with the objective of selling to the *world market* (not the local market), was still not a pervasive phenomenon at the time (Rudra 1995). The "open regime," that would have been required for attracting such investment, would still have the effect of jeopardizing the country's food security.

For pure political reason the United States and the Western nations gave tremendous preferences for the countries like Japan, Korea, Taiwan, and later even China. In the multi-fiber arrangement, China had the share, which was four times as great as that of India. The share of the newly industrializing countries of South East Asia was eight times that of India.

The seriousness of the food security issue has to be seen in the historical context. At the beginning of the twentieth century, the annual per capita food grain availability in "British India" was around 200 kilograms. By 1945–1946, it had declined to 136.8 kilograms. Even if we take the quinquennial average for 1939–1944, it was 148.5 kilograms. The basic reason for the decline in food grain availability was that land under food grains was being diverted for commercial crop production, even though gross cropped area was not increasing, and little was being done to affect any yield increase (Rudra 1992).

It was essential in this situation to increase per capita food grain output and availability, both by undertaking measures of "land augmentation," such as expanding net sown area, providing irrigation, and bringing about yield increases, and also by preventing the diversion of land for commercial crop production, at least for exports. The Nehru-Mahalanobis strategy (J. L. Nehru, the first prime minister of India, gave the political support to Mahalanobis until 1960) did precisely that while attempting to boost land augmenting investment (such as irrigation). It eschewed any attempt at boosting agro-based exports, which is essentially what an "outward-looking" strategy, such as the one advocated by the World Bank and the neoliberal economists, would have entailed (Kaushal 2004).

There is, in fact, a basic problem with the "free trade" or the "more liberal trade" argument, which is being propounded to this day at fora such as the World Trade Organization (WTO), which has not received adequate attention. The argument assumes not only perpetual full employment (thus precluding any possibility of "de-industrialization," which, for countries such as India, has been a fact of life) but also that all countries have the same basic "factor" endowments (though in different proportions) and can, therefore, produce all goods. Trade simply ensures that among countries, all of which can produce all goods, which country produces what gets determined by their respective "comparative advantages." However, this assumption is obviously absurd, since tropical goods, which are producible only on the tropical landmass, cannot be produced in the temperate regions (where metropolitan capitalism is located) (Karmakar 2012; Kaushal 2004; Rudra 1992).

It may be thought that this should not matter much since food grains can always be imported with the foreign exchange earned through the export of commercial crops or of manufactures based on commercial crops. However, this is problematic for at least two reasons.

First, in the case of some of the food grains such as rice (which happens to be the most important grain demanded in the country), adequate surpluses were simply not available in the world market for import at that time so that India has little option but to produce the bulk of its own rice requirement (Rudra 1992).

Second, dependence on the Western economies for food imports was used by them for arm-twisting, as the India government realized before launching the "Green Revolution." India was forced to take IMF loan in 1966 and had to stop the planning for three years; otherwise, it could not get any grain from the United States.

Its so-called "inward-looking" nature, far from being a mistake caused by an erroneous assumption of export pessimism, was essential for improving food security and overcoming hunger. Indeed the average annual per capita net food grain availability, which had come down to 148.5 kilograms for "British India" during 1939–1944, had increased by the end of the Nehru government to 168.44 kilograms (between 1961 and 1965) (Rudra 1992). The Congress government succumbed to the pressure of landed interests to desist from radical land redistribution suggested by Mahalanobis. That arrested the development of the productive forces in agriculture, apart from keeping the old social structure intact in some crucial ways.

Domestic industries were protected from international competitions. Import controls and self-sufficiency were the goal. Foreign investments were discouraged due to the industrial policy act of 1956 due to many restrictions it had created. The industrial sector used to depend on domestic resources and generous aid from the Soviet Union only. Trade protections and industrial licensing system gave monopoly power to the politicians and bureaucrats, which encouraged corruptions and regional discrimination.

The causes of the lower growth rates of India compared with China were the regional jealousy supported by the politicians, which had destroyed industries in Eastern India, total corruption at all levels, bureaucratic control, inadequate infrastructure, lack of electricity, and bias against exports. While in China, since the death of Mao Tse Tung in 1974, politicians promoted regional economic autonomy and competitions, in India politicians promoted regional discriminations and favoritism.

Chapter 2

Chinese Economy until 1990

CHINA'S ECONOMIC DEVELOPMENT SINCE 1949—TIMELINE

1949: Period of strict political control and isolation from the most of the world (Russia gave support until 1961).
1953: "Five-Year Plan" aimed at boosting heavy industry started.
1958–1961: The Great Leap Forward. Economic disaster and famine.
1960s to 1970s: Third Front Policy, moving some strategically important manufacturing industries inland (especially to Sichuan), away from the east and vulnerability to invasion.
1966–1976: The Cultural Revolution. Economic stagnation.
1978: Deng Xiao Ping era of "opening up." Economic reforms included.
* Opening up to trade with the outside world.
* Encouraging inward investment.
* Increasing exports.
* De-collectivization of farmland-household responsibility system.
* Allowing private enterprises, township and village enterprises (TVEs), and joint ventures with foreign companies.
1978–1983: Household responsibility system spread, productivity and rural incomes increased.
1979: Primary and primary processed goods 75 percent of exports.
1980s: Growth of the TVEs, industries in the countryside.
1980: Onward China started opening up areas for foreign businesses, starting with the first four SEZs—all on southeast coast—Shenzhen; Zhuhai, Shantou, and Xiamen.
1997: Asian financial crisis.
2001: China joins WTO.

2009: 95 percent of exports were manufactured goods.
2011: China overtakes Japan to become the world's second largest economy.
2014: Outward investment will overtake inward investment soon.
2010: Per capita GDP RMB 29,992 (about $4,837), 79 times higher than 1978 when reforms began.
1978–2010: China's GDP grew 9.99 percent p.a on average.
2020: GDP rose 7.3 percent. Industrial production rose 8.6 percent. Unemployment 4.1 percent.

CHINA DURING 1949–1969

Communist Party of China came to power in 1949 with the aim to transform China from a feudalist country to a socialist country. The model was the Soviet Union but the economic policies of China had undergone dramatic changes since 1960, when China separated itself from the Soviet Union mainly due to the difference of opinion between Mao Tse Tung and Khrushchev regarding their international policies toward the capitalist world, which affected its domestic economic policy as well. Khrushchev wanted China to continue with its heavy industry-first policy but Mao had a novel idea to bring heavy industry to the villages by having rural steel plants and to give importance to agriculture by asking people to go to the villages to produce. Extensive land reform program was already implemented in early 1950s by nationalizing most of the lands (Abraha 2016).

Farmers were encouraged to cooperate in some phases of production through the formation of small "mutual aid teams" of six or seven households each. These units were later formed into large Soviet-style collective farms. In the first plan of 1951–1957 the Soviet engineers and agricultural experts helped China extensively.

By 1956 approximately 67.5 percent of all modern industrial firms were in the state sector, and 32.5 percent were under joint public-private ownership. The handicraft industries were organized into cooperatives. In 1957 about 93.5 percent of all farm households were in the collective farms. The first Five-Year Plan under the guidance of the Soviet Union was quite successful (Scarlett 2013). Heavy industry, iron and steel manufacturing, coal mining, cement production, electricity generation, and machine-building industries were developed with industrial production increased at an average annual rate of 19 percent between 1952 and 1957, and national income grew at a rate of 9 percent a year. Agricultural output increased substantially as well (Naughton 2007).

Naughton (2007) wrote about the Great Disaster of Great Leap Forward, 1958–1960:

> In 1958 the Second Five-Year Plan (1958–62), which was intended to continue the policies of the first plan, was curtailed and all Soviet Consulates in China

> were closed down in 1960. Mao wanted to follow an independent policy to demonstrate his leadership that brought economic and social disasters. The entire population was asked to produce a dramatic "great leap" in production for all sectors of the economy at once.

To overcome this problem of lack of capital, the leadership decided to employ huge number of farmers to build vast irrigation and water control works. Surplus rural labor was also employed in thousands of small-scale, low-technology, "backyard" industrial firms in farms. These would produce machinery required for agricultural development and components for urban industries. Mobilization of surplus rural labor and further improvements in agricultural efficiency were to be accomplished by the people's communes, which were created by combining some 20 or 30 advanced producers' cooperatives. Ninety-eight percent of the farm population was grouped into communes between April and September 1958. In 1959 and 1960, most governmental responsibilities were returned to county and township administrations. During the Great Leap Forward, in the industrial sector enterprising party branches took over the direction of many factories. In addition, central planning was replaced by production decisions from individual units (Li 1994; Naughton 2007; Abraha 2016).

The result of the Great Leap Forward was a severe economic crisis. In 1959, 1960, and 1961, adverse weather conditions, improperly constructed water control projects, and serious misallocations of resources resulted in disastrous declines in agricultural output. In 1959 and 1960, the gross value of agricultural output fell by 14 percent and 13 percent, respectively. Widespread famine occurred, especially in rural areas. From 1958 to 1961, over 14 million people apparently died of starvation, and the number of reported births was about 23 million fewer than under normal conditions.

The government used the country's foreign exchange reserves to import over 5 million tons of grain a year beginning in 1960. Mines and factories continued to expand output through 1960, because many new plants constructed during the first Five-Year Plan went into full production in these years. In the 1960s, the withdrawal of Soviet engineers caused industrial output to plummet by 38 percent in 1961 and by a further 16 percent in 1962.

Faced with total economic collapse in the early 1960s, the government devised a new set of economic policies to replace those of the Great Leap Forward. Importance was given to improving agricultural output to meet the needs of the growing population. Planning and economic coordination were revived to restore efficient allocation of resources to the economy. Investment priorities reversed, with agriculture receiving the prime consideration (Lin 1992).

The government had taken measures to bring about technological advancement in agriculture and the decentralization of production decision-making.

The role of the central commune administration was reduced. Production teams were empowered to make all decisions concerning production and the distribution of income to their members. Private plots were officially restored to farm families. Agricultural taxes were reduced, and the relative prices paid for agricultural products were raised. In industry, control over most firms remained in the hands of provincial-level and local governments. This decentralization was reaffirmed and strengthened in the 1961–1965 period (Li 1994; Fan 1992).

In place of Soviet machinery and technology, then Japan, France, and West Germany became the suppliers of imported technology and materials. France even supplied nuclear weapons-grade materials to China at that time so that without having any nuclear reactor China had managed to develop nuclear weapons in 1964.

Between 1961 and 1966, agricultural output grew at an average rate of 9.6 percent a year. Industrial output was increased in the same years at an average annual rate of 10.6 percent, largely by reviving plants with the help of imported technology for small-scale industries, coal mines, hydroelectric plants, chemical fertilizer plants, and agricultural machinery plants.

CULTURAL REVOLUTION, 1966–1976

The Cultural Revolution was set in motion by Mao Tse Tung in 1966. The Cultural Revolution, unlike the Great Leap Forward, was primarily a political upheaval and did not produce major changes in official economic policies or the basic economic model. Agricultural production stagnated, but in general the rural areas experienced less disruption than the cities. Production was reduced in the modern nonagricultural sectors in several ways. The most direct cause of production halts was the political activity of students and workers in the mines and factories. An extensive disruption of transportation took place during this time, resulting in great shortages of raw materials and other necessary inputs in many factories (Kroeber 2016).

Revolutionary committees, with party workers and members of the army, used to manage firms without any knowledge of either technology or management. Those who had this knowledge were criticized and sent away to remote rural areas to maintain animals. The result was a serious decline in the production. Foreign equipment was banned due to extreme nationalism. Universities were closed. Thus, China had suffered from the lack of talents and further development of technology (MacFarquhar 1974; MacFarquhar and Schoenhals 2006).

China in 1970–1974

Gradually stability was restored after the intervention of the army. Former managers got back their position. Universities started opening. Foreign companies were invited to supply equipment and provide training. Industrial production grew. In 1975, Chou En Lai emphasized the modernization of agriculture and industry in his "Four Modernization" plan. During the early and mid-1970s, the Gang of Four group including the wife of Mao attempted to steer China toward a pure socialist economy with no foreign companies, equal distribution of income, no private plot in agriculture but a decentralized economy without the Soviet-style central planning. They were arrested after the death of Mao in 1975 before they had managed to paralyze the economy (McMillan and Naughton 1992).

After the arrest of the Gang of Four, Hua Guofeng and Deng Xiaoping restarted the modernization program supported by Chau En Lai in 1975. The new policies included replacements of the party officials by managers and technocrats, increased wages for the workers, and increased role of foreign trade, foreign investments, and foreign companies. This new policy initiative was initiated at the Fifth National People's Congress in February and March 1978, with Hua Guofeng advocated a 10-year plan for the 1976–1985 period, where imports of foreign technology and much higher targets for agricultural and industrial growth rates were sought. That was the beginning of the reform period.

As a result of these incentives, industrial output jumped by 14 percent in 1977 and agricultural production also expanded. The reform program reduced the importance of central planning by promoting production by state-owned enterprises (SOEs) and collective and individual enterprises, out of any plans (Lau and Zheng 2015).

Role of Economic Planning

The economy was under a central planning system of the Soviet style under the guidance of the Soviet engineers and technologists. Central planners used to estimate, as they used to do in the Soviet Union, demands and supplies. That system was thrown out by the "Great Leap Forward," after the dispute between Mao and Khrushchev regarding the direction of the international communist movement. Economic management became decentralized, and industries were asked to move to the rural areas and in small-scale rural steel plants. The result was a disaster and death due to famine. Then since 1965 came the Cultural Revolution and resultant chaos. Long-range plans, as protracted as 10 and 12 years also, were announced at various times with little practical effects until the reform plan presented by Hua Guofeng in February 1978 (Perkins 1977; Oi 1999).

First Five-Year Plan (1953–1957), under the direction of the Soviet Union, was a blueprint for industrialization. The second (1958–1962), third (1966–1970), fourth (1971–1975), and fifth (1976–1980) Five-Year Plans were ineffective and promoted upheavals. The sixth Five-Year Plan (1981–1985) was a reflection of the reform program. Economic reforms in China, to reduce the role of central planning and to expand the power of the local administrative bodies, in the beginning were experimental in 1979 and 1980. By the mid-1980s, the contribution of central planning was greatly reduced.

Price and Monetary Policy

During the 1950s, inflation was a major problem. Chinese government used currency reform, nationalization of the banks, and control over money supply. As a result, China achieved a price stability for a long time and inflation rate during 1952 and 1978 was only 0.6 percent a year. However, due to the relaxation of government control on prices, after the introduction of economic reform, consumer prices rose by 7.5 percent in 1980 and 11.9 percent in 1985. Economic reform meant high rate of investment on the manufacture of producer goods and the shortage of consumer's goods. Money supply increased to allow the consumers to have material incentives with higher wages. By 1987, the Chinese economy had made major achievements toward improved living standards (Edith 2015; Bardhan 2010; Brandt, Hsieh, and Zhu 2008).

Five-Year Plans.

Strategies for the nation's economic and social development, begun in 1953.

Renamed "Guidelines" from the 11th plan (2006).

12th plan (Guideline) (2011–2015).

11th plan (Guideline) (2009–2010).

During the 1950s, all of China's individual household farms were consolidated into large communes as it was in the former USSR. To support rapid industrialization like in the USSR, the central government invested large scale in manufacturing and heavy industry and tried to develop the corresponding skills for the industrial workers. Supports from the USSR were very crucial during this period at least until 1960. As a result, by 1978, nearly three-fourths of industrial production was produced according to the central plans in the SOEs. Private sector and foreign companies were not allowed in those days in China, except in the areas like defense, where France had supplied the nuclear material to China to explode its first nuclear bomb and the U.S. companies through Israel and West Germany supplied defense technology to China. A central goal of the Chinese government, like in the USSR, was to make China's economy self-sufficient. The planning authority used to determine production goals and consumption targets, controlled prices, and allocated resources throughout the economy, as was in the USSR, although China has little relationship with the USSR since 1960. Foreign trade was generally restricted to importing those goods that could not be made in China. Its ability to import was restricted by limited export items mainly agricultural products and petroleum to its neighboring countries (Zhang 1995).

China's real GDP grew at an average annual rate of 6.7 percent from 1953 to 1978, although Chinese government officials (especially at the subnational levels) produced fake statistics for the fear of punishments. According to Angus Maddison (2007a), China's actual average annual real GDP growth during this period was about 4.4 percent. India with the average rate of growth of 3.5 percent per year achieved the same per-head GDP as China during that period.

China's economy suffered significant economic disaster during the leadership of Chairman Mao Tse Tung, including during the Great Leap Forward from 1958 to 1962. That caused a massive famine with the deaths of up to 45 million people. The Cultural Revolution from 1966 to 1976 caused widespread political chaos and disrupted the economy. From 1958 to 1962, Chinese living standards fell by 20.3 percent, and from 1966 to 1968, they dropped by 9.6 percent. In addition, the growth in Chinese living standards was very low compared with those in the West and Japan. In 1978, the Chinese government embarked upon the reform of the economy with liberalization of international trade and foreign investment, to increase living standards (Weber 2021; Wong 1987).

COMMENTS

The high growth rates of the reform period were caused by the shift of control of the national resources from central to regional ownership. Until 1990, China was one of the poorest countries in the world. The real per capita GDP in China was more or less the same as it was in India until 1989. Lack of investment and resources prohibited China from producing or importing foreign technology after 1960. Agriculture got lesser investment than industry. Although the Soviet Union provided a significant number of tractors, trucks, electric pumps, and mechanical threshers, most agricultural activities in China were performed by people.

The Chinese economy was never stagnant as production grew significantly between 1800 and 1949 and increased rapidly after 1949, but due to population growth very little surplus was there. Very few resources were available for the production of capital goods, such as machinery, factories, mines, railroads, and other productive assets, although during the period 1949 to 1960 the Soviet Union supplied those in significant amount. After 1960 and 1990, relatively small size of the capital stock was responsible for the low productivity per worker. That was the inability of the economy to generate a substantial surplus before 1990 when massive amount of foreign capital started arriving from Japan, Taiwan, Singapore, and Hong Kong (Borekov and Koloskov 1980; Zhang 1995; Xu 1995).

Chapter 3

China

New Economic Policy since 1990

Prior to the initiation of economic reforms and trade liberalization nearly 40 years ago, China maintained policies that kept the economy poor, stagnant, vastly inefficient, and relatively isolated from the global economy. Since opening up to foreign trade and investment and implementing free-market reforms in 1979, China has been among the world's fastest-growing economies, with real annual gross domestic product (GDP) growth averaging 9.5 percent through 2018, a pace described by the World Bank as "the fastest sustained expansion by a major economy in history." Such growth has enabled China, on average, to double its GDP every eight years and helped raise an estimated 800 million people out of poverty. In 1990, per capita income of China was $318; in 2019 it became $10,276. For India, the corresponding figures are $368 and $2,055. In 2020, when the GDP of China was $14.5 trillion, for India it was $3.0 trillion and for the United States it was $20 trillion (Naughton 2007; Gechev 2020).

Chinese economic reforms, which have been in flux for three decades, have more than doubled China's economic growth, from an average of 4.4 percent annually before 1978 to an average of 9.5 percent after 1978 (Brandt and Rawski 2008; Brandt et al. 2020). This process has transformed the world's largest developing country from a centrally controlled economy to a mixed economy, while simultaneously reducing poverty at a scale unparalleled in world history (World Bank 2002).

During the reform period the Chinese per capita GDP increased by almost eightfold, and China has transformed from one of the poorest countries in the world to a major economic power. Today's China is the world's largest producer and largest consumer of many conventional industrial staples and high-tech products, such as steel, cars, TV sets, personal computers, cell phones and internet usage, and so on, and has the world's largest foreign reserves.

The current size of the Chinese economy, in terms of GDP, is larger than the sum of 83 countries in Eastern Europe, the Commonwealth of Independent States or the former Soviet Union (CIS), and all of Africa (the author's calculation based on Maddison 2007b).

What are the sources of this Chinese economic growth? There are three main sources for growth of the economy of China: (a) export growth; (b) technological development by the imports of scientists and engineers from Russia since 1991; and (c) decentralized economic planning and competition between different regions.

China has become the world's largest economy (on a purchasing power parity (PPP) basis), manufacturer, merchandise trader, and holder of foreign exchange reserves. This in turn has made China a major commercial partner of the United States. China is the largest U.S. merchandise trading partner, biggest source of imports, and third largest U.S. export market. China is also the largest foreign holder of U.S. Treasury securities, which help fund the federal debt and keep U.S. interest rates low.

As China's economy has matured, its real GDP growth has slowed significantly, from 14.2 percent in 2007 to 6.6 percent in 2018, and that growth is projected by the International Monetary Fund (IMF) to fall to 5.5 percent by 2024. The Chinese government has embraced slower economic growth, referring to it as the "new normal" and acknowledging the need for China to embrace a new growth model that relies less on fixed investment and exporting and more on private consumption, services, and innovation to drive economic growth.

The Chinese government has made innovation a top priority in its economic planning through a number of high-profile initiatives, such as "Made in China 2025," a plan announced in 2015 to upgrade and modernize China's manufacturing in 10 key sectors through extensive government assistance in order to make China a major global player in these sectors. However, such measures have increasingly raised concerns that China intends to use industrial policies to decrease the country's reliance on foreign technology (including by locking out foreign firms in China) and eventually dominate global markets.

In 2017, the Trump administration launched a Section 301 investigation of China's innovation and intellectual property policies deemed harmful to U.S. economic interests. It subsequently raised tariffs by 25 percent on $250 billion worth of imports from China, while China increased tariffs (ranging from 5 percent to 25 percent) on $110 billion worth of imports from the United States. Such measures have sharply decreased bilateral trade in 2019. On May 10, 2019, President Trump announced he was considering raising tariffs on nearly all remaining products from China. A protracted and escalating trade conflict between the United States and China could have negative consequences for the Chinese economy (Kroeber 2016; Weber 2021; Zhu 2012).

However, the most important question is how China had managed to achieve so much when India staggered. A comparison of China and India in terms of human and industrial development in 1978 shows that the average Chinese person was one-fourth poorer than the average Indian, but China achieved higher levels of human and industrial development than India. Specifically, it is clear that China adopted a quite different approach from India to improve human capital. While India put more emphasis on higher education, China aimed at raising the educational level of ordinary citizens. As a result, China was able to achieve a much higher adult literacy rate than India, even though India produced more university graduates than China until 2002. China's approach paid off in its early stage of economic growth, when a large number of workers was needed. China began to expand its higher education after 1998, and this corresponded to China's entry into the middle-income stage (China became a middle-income country in 2002), when more skilled workers were needed. To be sure, China's initial approach to human capital improvement was not designed to push for economic growth but to improve equality for the population. Nevertheless, this approach contributed significantly to the country's economic takeoff. In 2018, the service exports of China were $233.6 billion; for India the corresponding figure was $205 billion. School education is compulsory in China; it is still not in India (Indurthy 2016; Altbach 2009; Edith 2015; Brandt et al. 2020).

China's performance has been praised for avoiding the major shocks and inflation that plagued the Eastern Bloc. The Eastern Bloc economies saw declines of 13 percent to 65 percent in GDP at the beginning of reforms, while Chinese growth has been very strong since the beginning of reform. China also managed to avoid the hyperinflation of 200 to 1,000 percent that Eastern Europe experienced. This success is attributed to the gradualist and decentralized approach of the Chinese government, which allowed market institutions to develop to the point where they could replace state planning.

This contrasts with the "big bang" approach of Eastern Europe, where the state-owned sector was rapidly privatized with employee buyouts but retained much of the earlier management. Other factors thought to account for the differences are the greater urbanization of the CIS economies and differences in social welfare and other institutions. Another argument is that, in the Eastern European economies, political change is sometimes seen to have made gradualist reforms impossible, so the shocks and inflation were unavoidable. China's economic growth has been compared with other developing countries, such as Brazil, Mexico, and India. GDP growth in China outstrips all other developing countries, with only India after 1990 coming close to China's experience. Scholars believe that high rates of investments, especially increases in capital invested per worker, have contributed to China's superior economic performance. China's relatively free economy, with less government intervention and regulation, is cited by scholars as an important factor in China's superior performance compared to other developing countries. India was constrained by the wrong advice of the IMF and World Bank that suggested instead privatization, like that was implemented in the former Soviet Union and East European countries with devastating effects (Weber 2021; Branstetter and Lardy 2008).

Such growth has enabled China, on average, to double its GDP every eight years and helped raise an estimated 800 million people out of poverty. China has become the world's largest economy (on a PPP basis), manufacturer, merchandise trader, and holder of foreign exchange reserves. This in turn has made China a major commercial partner of the United States. China is the largest U.S. merchandise trading partner, biggest source of imports, and third largest U.S. export market. China is also the largest foreign holder of U.S. Treasury securities, which help fund the federal debt and keep U.S. interest rates low.

REFORM OF THE ECONOMIC SYSTEM, 1978

At the milestone Third Plenum of the National Party Congress's 11th Central Committee, which opened on December 22, 1978, the party leaders decided to undertake a program of gradual but fundamental reform of the economic system. They concluded that the centrally planned economy had failed to produce efficient economic growth and had caused China to fall far behind not only the industrialized nations of the West but also the new industrial powers of Asia: Japan, South Korea, Singapore, Taiwan, and Hong Kong. In the late 1970s, while Japan and Hong Kong rivaled European countries in modern technology, China's citizens had to make do with barely sufficient food supplies, rationed clothing, inadequate housing, and a service sector that was inadequate and inefficient. All of these shortcomings embarrassed China internationally. The process of reform was incremental. New measures were first introduced experimentally in a few localities and then were popularized and disseminated nationally if they proved successful (Branstetter and Lardy 2008).

Period of Readjustment, 1979–1981

The major goals of the readjustment process were to expand exports rapidly; overcome key deficiencies in transportation, communications, coal, iron, steel, building materials, and electric power; and redress the imbalance between light and heavy industry by increasing the growth rate of light industry and reducing investment in heavy industry. Agricultural production was stimulated in 1979 by an increase of over 22 percent in the procurement prices paid for farm products (Gechev 2020; Cheremukhin et al. 2015).

The most successful reform policy, the contract household responsibility system of production in agriculture, was suggested by the government in 1979 as a way for poor rural units in mountainous or arid areas to increase their incomes. The responsibility system allowed individual farm families to work a piece of land for profit in return for delivering a set amount of produce to the collective at a given price. This arrangement created strong incentives for farmers to reduce production costs and increase productivity. Soon after its introduction the responsibility system was adopted by numerous farm units in all sorts of areas (Coase and Wang 2016; Nölke et al. 2019).

Agricultural production was also stimulated by official encouragement to establish free farmers' markets in urban areas, as well as in the countryside, and by allowing some families to operate as "specialized households," devoting their efforts to producing a scarce commodity or service on a profit-making basis. By the end of 1984, approximately 98 percent of all farm households were under the responsibility system, and all but a handful of communes had been dissolved. The communes' administrative responsibilities were turned over to township and town governments, and their economic roles were assigned to townships and villages. In industry, the main policy innovations increased the autonomy of enterprise managers, reduced emphasis on planned quotas, allowed enterprises to produce goods outside the plan for sale on the market, and permitted enterprises to experiment with the use of bonuses to reward higher productivity (Gechev 2020).

The government also tested a fundamental change in financial procedures with a limited number of state-owned units: rather than remitting all of their profits to the state, as was normally done, these enterprises were allowed to pay a tax on their profits and retain the balance for reinvestment and distribution to workers as bonuses.

The government also actively encouraged the establishment of collectively owned and operated industrial and service enterprises as a means of soaking up some of the unemployment among young people and at the same time helping to increase supplies of light industrial products. Individual enterprise also was allowed, after having virtually disappeared during the Cultural Revolution, and independent cobblers, tailors, tinkers, and vendors once again became common sights in the cities (Sondhi, Pang, and Chatterjee 2021; Bardhan 2010).

Foreign trade procedures were greatly eased, allowing individual enterprises and administrative departments outside the Ministry of Foreign Trade (which became the Ministry of Foreign Economic Relations and Trade in 1984) to engage in direct negotiations with foreign firms. A wide range of cooperation, trading, and credit arrangements with foreign firms were legalized so that China could enter the mainstream of international trade (Sondhi, Pang, and Chatterjee 2021).

REFORM AND OPENING, BEGINNING IN 1982

The practice of remitting taxes on profits and retaining the balance became universal by 1985, increasing the incentive for enterprises to maximize profits and substantially adding to their autonomy. The role of foreign trade under the economic reforms increased far beyond its importance in any previous period. Before the reform period, the combined value of imports and exports had seldom exceeded 10 percent of national income. In 1969 it was 15 percent, in 1984 it was 21 percent, and in 1986 it reached 35 percent. Under Deng Xiaoping foreign trade was regarded as an important source of investment funds and modern technology. As a result, restrictions on trade were loosened further in the mid-1960s, and foreign investment was legalized. The most common foreign investments were joint ventures between foreign firms and Chinese units (Ramesh 2017; Naughton 2007).

The most conspicuous symbols of the new status of foreign trade were the four coastal special economic zones that were created in 1979 as enclaves where foreign investment could receive special treatment. These zones were to create productive exchanges between foreign firms with advanced technology and major Chinese economic networks.

Private entrepreneurship and free-market activities were legalized and encouraged in the 1980s. By 1987 the state-owned system of commercial agencies and retail outlets coexisted with a rapidly growing private and collectively owned system that competed with it vigorously, providing a wider range of consumption choices for Chinese citizens than at any previous time.

There were problems in the society. The most fundamental tensions were those created by the widening income disparities between the people who were "getting rich" and those who were not and by the pervasive threat of inflation. These concerns played a role in the political struggle that culminated in party general secretary Hu Yaobang's forced resignation in 1987.

Industry

In 1985, industry employed about 17 percent of the labor force but produced more than 46 percent of gross national product (GNP). It was the fastest-growing sector with an average annual growth of 11 percent from 1952 to 1985. There was a wide range of technological levels. There were many small handicraft units and many enterprises using machinery installed or designed in the 1950s and 1960s. There was a significant number of big, up-to-date plants, including textile mills, steel mills, chemical fertilizer plants, and petrochemical facilities but there were also some burgeoning light industries producing consumer goods. China produced most kinds of products made by industrialized nations but limited quantities of high-technology items. Technology transfer was conducted by importing whole plants, equipment, and designs as an important means of progress. Major industrial centers were in Liaoning Province, Beijing-Tianjin-Tangshan area, Shanghai, and Wuhan. Mineral resources included huge reserves of iron ore, and there were adequate to abundant supplies of nearly all other industrial minerals. Outdated mining and ore processing technologies were gradually being replaced with modern processes, techniques, and equipment, imported from Taiwan, Singapore, Japan, and South Korea (Ramesh 2017; Naughton 2007).

Agriculture

In 1985, the agricultural sector employed about 63 percent of the labor force, and its proportion of GNP was about 33 percent. There was low worker productivity because of scant supplies of agricultural machinery and other modern inputs. Most agricultural processes were still performed by hand. There was very small arable land area (just above 10 percent of total area, as compared with 22 percent in United States) in relation to the size of the country and population. There was intensive use of land; all fields produced at least one crop a year, and wherever conditions permitted, two or even three crops were grown annually, especially in the south (Sondhi, Pang, and Chatterjee 2021).

Energy Resources

China was self-sufficient in nearly all energy forms. Coal and petroleum were exported since the early 1970s. Its coal reserves were among the world's largest, and mining technology was inadequately developed but steadily improved in the late 1960s. Petroleum reserves were very large at the time but of varying quality and in disparate locations. Suspected oil deposits in the northwest and offshore tracts were believed to be among the world's largest. Exploration and extraction was limited by scarcity of equipment and trained personnel until 1992 when the scientists and engineers from new Russia started arriving. Substantial natural gas reserves were in the north, northwest, and offshore. The hydroelectric potential of the country was the greatest in the world and sixth largest in capacity, and very large hydroelectric projects were under construction, with others were in the planning stage. Thermal power, mostly coal fired, produced approximately 68 percent of generating capacity in 1985 and was increased to 72 percent by 1990. Petroleum production growth continued in order to meet the needs of nationwide mechanization and provided important foreign exchange but domestic use was restricted as much as possible until the end of the decade (Sondhi, Pang, and Chatterjee 2021; Xu 2011).

Foreign Trade

Foreign trade was small by international standards but was growing rapidly in size and importance, as it represented 20 percent of GNP in 1985. Trade was controlled by the Ministry of Foreign Economic Relations and Trade and subordinate units and by the Bank of China, the foreign exchange arm of the central bank. Substantial decentralization and increased flexibility in foreign trade operations occurred since the late 1970s. Textiles were leading the export category. Other important exports included petroleum and foodstuffs.

Leading imports included machinery, transport equipment, manufactured goods, and chemicals. Japan was the dominant trading partner and accounted for 28.9 percent of imports and 15.2 percent of exports in 1986. Hong Kong was a leading market for exports (31.6 percent) but a source of only 13 percent of imports. In 1979 the United States became China's second largest source of imports and in 1986 was the third largest overall trade partner. Western Europe, particularly the Federal Republic of Germany, was also a major trading partner (Cheung 2014).

1990–2000

China's economy saw continuous real GDP growth of at least 5 percent since 1991. The 14th National Communist Party Congress later in the year backed up Deng's renewed push for market reforms, stating that China's key task in the 1990s was to create a "socialist market economy." In 1996, the Chinese economy continued to grow at a rapid pace, at about 9.5 percent, accompanied by low inflation. The economy slowed for the next three years, influenced in part by the Asian financial crisis, with official growth of 8.9 percent in 1997, 7.8 percent in 1998, and 7.1 percent in 1999. From 1995 to 1999, inflation dropped sharply, reflecting tighter monetary policies and stronger measures to control food prices. The year 2000 showed a modest reversal of this trend. GDP in 2000 grew officially at 8.0 percent that year and had quadrupled since 1978. In 1999, with its 1.25 billion people but a GDP of just $3,800 per capita (PPP), China became the second largest economy in the world after the United States (Edith 2015).

The Asian financial crisis affected China at the margin, mainly through decreased foreign direct investment and a sharp drop in the growth of its exports.

However, China had huge reserves, a currency that was not freely convertible, and capital inflows that consisted overwhelmingly of long-term investment. For these reasons it remained largely insulated from the regional crisis, and its commitment not to devalue had been a major stabilizing factor for the region.

During the 15th National Communist Party Congress that met in September 1997, General Secretary, President Jiang Zemin announced plans to sell, merge, or close the vast majority of SOEs in his call for increased "non-public ownership" (feigongyou or privatization in euphemistic terms). The 9th National People's Congress endorsed the plans at its March 1998 session. In 2000, China claimed success in its three-year effort to make the majority of large state-owned enterprises (SOEs) profitable (Ramesh 2017).

FROM 2000

Following the Chinese Communist Party's (CCP's) Third Plenum, held in October 2003, Chinese legislators proposed to provide protection for private property rights. Legislators also indicated there would be a new emphasis on certain aspects of overall government economic policy, including efforts to reduce unemployment (now in the 8–10 percent range in urban areas), rebalance income distribution between urban and rural regions, and maintain economic growth while protecting the environment and improving social equity. The National People's Congress approved the amendments when it met in March 2004.

The Fifth Plenum in October 2005 approved the 11th Five-Year Economic Program (2006–2010) aimed at building a "socialist harmonious society" through more balanced wealth distribution and improved education, medical care, and social security. On March 2006, the National People's Congress approved the 11th Five-Year Program. The plan called for a relatively conservative 45 percent increase in GDP and a 20 percent reduction in energy intensity (energy consumption per unit of GDP) by 2010. China's economy grew at an average rate of 10 percent per year during the period 1990–2004, the highest growth rate in the world. China's GDP grew 10.0 percent in 2003, 10.1 percent in 2004, and even faster 10.4 percent in 2005 despite attempts by the government to cool the economy (Nölke et al. 2019).

China's total trade in 2006 surpassed $1.76 trillion, making China the world's third largest trading nation after the United States and Germany. China's GDP stood at US$3.4 trillion while Germany's GDP was US$3.3 trillion for 2007. This made China the world's third largest economy by GDP (Kroeber 2016).

Social and economic indicators have improved since various recent reforms were launched, but rising inequality is evident between the more highly developed coastal provinces and the less developed, poorer inland regions. According to UN estimates in 2007, around 130 million people in China—mostly in rural areas of the lagging inland provinces—still lived in poverty, on subsistence wages of less than $1 a day. About 35 percent of the Chinese population lives under $2 a day (Nölke et al. 2019).

China launched its Economic Stimulus Plan to specifically deal with the global financial crisis of 2008–2009. It has primarily focused on increasing affordable housing, easing credit restrictions for mortgage and SMEs, lowering taxes such as those on real estate sales and commodities, and pumping more public investment into infrastructure development, such as the rail network, roads, and ports.

Major natural disasters of 2008, such as the 2008 Chinese winter storms, the 2008 Sichuan earthquake, and the 2008 South China floods mildly affected national economic growth but did do major damage to local and regional economies and infrastructure. The Chinese economy is significantly affected by the 2008–2009 global financial crisis due to the export-oriented nature of the economy, which depends heavily upon international trade. However, government economic stimulus has been hugely successful by nearly all accounts.

Determination of Prices

Until the reform period of the late 1970s and 1980s, the prices of most commodities were set by government agencies and changed infrequently. Prices of most goods produced by private and collectively owned enterprises in both rural and urban areas generally were free to float, as were the prices of many items that state-owned enterprises (SOEs) produced outside the plan. Prices of most major goods produced by SOEs, however, along with the grain purchased from farmers by state commercial departments for retail sales in the cities, still were set or restricted by government agencies. State commercial agencies paid farmers a higher price for grain than the state received from the urban residents to whom they sold it. The approach of the government was to encourage the growth of nonplanned economic activity and thereby expand the proportion of prices determined by market forces (Coase and Wang 2016).

HOW CHINA AVOIDED "SHOCK THERAPY" ECONOMICS

Deng Xiaoping suggested early on that there should be a great role for markets, but how markets should be introduced was vehemently contested. Some followed an idea grounded in mainstream economics that markets had to be universal and protected by the state. Others thought of markets as a tool that could be used by the state to further its policy goals. These two broad positions have continued to prevail over the years. As the market was becoming a more and more important tool in the hand of the state, there were repeated calls to complete reform and move toward universal marketization. Recent events around the tech sector and the private tutoring sector suggest that the state is reasserting its leading position over private business. China still has so many elements of a command economy, such as some state-set prices, fairly rigid and long-term economic plans, and goals and SOEs.

The elements of state planning and price steering in China as simple remnants of the past command economy. They are part of that legacy, but as the Chinese system has undergone a fundamental change over decades of gradualist experimentalism, their role has also changed. SOEs have turned from socialist production units that are meant to fulfil a central plan to market-oriented enterprises, often global players. The model of economic governance has changed from planning and command to state market participation. The state steers the market by participating in it and by structuring markets. This is very different from a traditional planned economy (Weber 2021).

If China Avoided Shock Therapy, Why Did the Soviet Union Succumb?

Of the three facets of shock therapy—sudden price liberalization, fiscal austerity, and privatization—Weber's focus is on the last. The Soviet disaster was the result of taking a wrong turn. "The Russians were easy prey for the messianic appeal of the zealous advocates of wholesale economic and political reform"(Weber 2021). Whereas the CCP had a robust and sophisticated policy argument, nothing similar was possible in the culture of the Soviet Communist Party.

Gorbachev was fascinated with the Pacific and Asia and saw it as the new frontier for economic development, a prospect that was far from unattractive from a Soviet point of view. Far from dismissing China's gradualist approach to reform, Soviet economic experts studied it in detail. Both subsidies and investment spending were raised. The result was to dramatically worsen the macroeconomic imbalances that lurked behind the fixed prices of the Soviet economy. Up to the mid-1980s, the inflationary pressures were manageable. By 1989, the entire Soviet economy was overshadowed by excess purchasing power (Sondhi, Pang, and Chatterjee 2021).

Too much purchasing power was chasing an inadequate supply of goods, whose prices were rigidly fixed. Inspired by Eastern European advice, Soviet package reformers began to think in terms of a 500-day program. Boris Yeltsin backed them in his bid to upgrade the power of Russia within the USSR. As he ripped Russia out of the Soviet Union, Yeltsin completely liberalized all prices on January 2, 1992, in a desperate effort to unblock markets and restart supply chains. The effort to impose fiscal and monetary austerity had only limited success. In the first instance, Russia slid toward hyperinflation. The hurried and inequitable privatizations created a kleptocratic oligarchy whose net contribution to innovation was close to zero but whose ability to extract surplus from political connection was infinite. The upheaval in Russia was dramatic. After 1992, the combination of the Big Bang price reform, escalating inflation, and the violent disposition of the spoils hurled Russian society into deep crisis, inflicting a shattering blow to the real incomes of working-class Russians above all. Yeltsin enjoyed the indulgence of the West even as he shelled the opposition in parliament into submission and rigged elections (Sondhi, Pang, and Chatterjee 2021).

After the crisis of 1998, the recovery in the oil and gas sector and the restoration of fiscal and monetary apparatus set the stage for Putin's revival of the Russian state. Putin had expressed his opposition to the hegemony of NATO and the Western advisers. In the period of rebuilding in the 2000s, Russia siphoned fossil fuel revenues into a sovereign wealth fund. Huge foreign exchange reserves, a reduced but nevertheless potent military, and gas and oil exports give Putin the platform he needs. In China, the crackdown of 1989 only temporarily slowed the reform process. China's economy grew out of the plan. Growth boomed on the back of a huge export surge. Inequality surged, as did corruption.

Economic and Market Reform Was Always Seen as a Long-Term Project

In the 1980s, when China's market reforms were first defined, a Big Bang in price liberalization was very much part of the discussion; and in fact, China came close to implementing it twice—once in 1986 and again in 1988. In 1988, attempts at price liberalization gave way to the first episode of very high inflation and a reversal in reform course.

The basic premise of shock therapy is that all institutions of direct state control over the economy must be destroyed to make space for the market. Instead, unlike India, China pursued a strategy of market creation that utilized the institutions of the planned economy. It kept the core of the planned industrial economy working, while transforming the old institutions into market players by first allowing for market activities on the margins. This strategy is manifested in the dual-track price system.

Under this system, SOEs and farmers had to deliver the state-set quotas at a state-set price, but if they managed to produce more, they could market their surplus at market prices. In this way, China's economy was gradually marketized under active bureaucratic guidance by reorienting its core economic institutions from the plan to the market. Nonessentials were liberalized first. Surpluses as well as sectors producing nonbasic goods were nonessentials. They could be completely marketized without immediately endangering the stability of the whole system. As a result of this strategy, China kept much closer control over core sectors of the economy, such as energy, steel, finance, and infrastructure.

A technocratic policy agenda became dominant, and China became amenable to what is called neoliberal governmentality (Zhang and Ong 2008). China is under constant attack for disobeying the rules of the game of neoliberal globalization. China has not implemented the quintessentially neoliberal policies of the Washington Consensus and unlike Russia escaped shock therapy (Weber 2021). China has not pursued the core policies of full-fledged price, trade, and financial liberalization and privatization (Lo 2016). In fact, some go so far as to claim that China has established an alternative development model to the Washington Consensus (Horesh and Lim 2017), a Beijing Consensus.

For three days in the middle of May 1989, the Soviet general secretary Mikhail Gorbachev visited Beijing. After Gorbachev went home, the two countries' paths divided. Over the next two and a half years, the Soviet Union and its alliance system were dismembered. As the apparatus of Soviet command was dismantled, the economies of the former Union and its allies imploded. People suffered a disastrous collapse in their standard of living. The life expectancy of Russian working-class men plunged. China, by contrast, was on the path to Communist Party-led rocket-ship growth.

Western economists superintended Russia's disaster. In Russia and Eastern Europe, shock therapy—comprehensive and sudden price liberalization otherwise known as the Big Bang; fiscal austerity to consolidate budgets and slash aggregate demand; and privatization—became synonymous with the callous insouciance of market economics. China, on the other hand, profited from globalization but retained a high degree of autonomy in economic policy (Weber 2021).

A common explanation of China's success is that it has had the good sense to ignore Western economics. In the Xi Jinping era, Chinese nationalists relish this interpretation. They are only too happy to claim that China's economic miracle was "grown out of the soil of China." It is neither Western nor Chinese economics per se but rather the act of opening the economy up to the world that is at the center of the success of China. The more pragmatic reformers favored a dual-track system, in which a certain portion of output was delivered to state agencies at fixed prices, while another portion was reserved for sale at market prices. This would enable a gradual process (Lo 2016; Horesh and Lim 2017).

The pragmatic group concentrated their attention not on inflation in general—as measured by aggregate price indices—but on the prices for key consumer and producer goods, as determined by specific supply and demand conditions in each case. They viewed investment not just as a source of demand but also as a factor determining what productive capacity might be available to meet demand. After years of experience in agriculture, they were well aware of the consequences of starving crucial sectors of public funds. In determining the risk of inflation, they refused to give priority, a priori, either to macroeconomics over microeconomic factors or to demand over supply conditions (Weber 2021).

In 1986, it was, above all, opposition from within the ranks of the experts that stopped Zhao Zemin's price liberalization push. On the basis of extensive enquiries in Hungary and Yugoslavia, the System Reform Institute that advised Zhao concluded that China was in no condition to attempt comprehensive and immediate liberalization.

The second great set piece came in 1988 when Zhao made his most fateful push for price reform. After a sustained campaign—including, among other stunts, a visit from Friedman—at a meeting held in August, the Politburo announced the imminent liberalization of all prices. The result was a wave of panic-buying and bank runs. Inflation accelerated ominously. Deng Xiaoping immediately slammed on the breaks. Chen Yun, the veteran inflation fighter of the 1950s, was summoned to the frontlines. Zhao was humiliated.

All further moves toward price liberalization were halted; in 1989, amid the repression of the protest movement, Beijing embarked on a fiscal and monetary consolidation. After surging to an annual rate of 28 percent in April 1989, by the middle of 1990 inflation was brought virtually to a halt. As a result, China suffered a major political shock and a fiscal and monetary contraction, but economic growth as a whole proceeded without dislocation.

Once the dust of the mass murder of the students had settled, it was the package reformers who, under Jiang Zemin and Zhu Rongji, came dramatically to the fore. Zhou Xiaochuan, one of the most brilliant exponents of package reform in the late 1980s, would serve as governor of the People's Bank of China from 2002 to 2018.

THE "THREE REFORMS" IN CHINA: PROGRESS AND OUTLOOK

Kobayashi, Baobo, and Sano (1999) gave a different explanation for China's growth. Inflows of foreign capital from Taiwan, Singapore, and Japan, technology from Russia, and management knowhow enabled China to turn its vast labor resources and space to rapid economic growth. The positive consequences of the reform of state-owned enterprises, banking reforms, and administrative reforms with open-door policy have contributed to economic development and rising national incomes.

With the shift to the open-door policy, however, Deng Xiaoping indicated that it was acceptable for some regions to become wealthy before others. The result was a huge wealth disparity between coastal and inland regions and between the cities and rural areas. It is historically unprecedented for an economy to grow at such a high rate over such a long period of time. However, the Chinese economy has begun to slow down, to an annual rate of growth of around 7 percent, in a process of transition to a "New Normal."

Why has China been able to grow at such a high rate and for such a long period of time? What are the sources of Chinese economic growth since 1978? The rate of growth of Chinese real GDP has been higher than that of the United States in every single year since 1978, but per capita GDP was the same as India. By comparison, the U.S. GDP of approximately US$17.4 trillion was approximately 1.7 times that of Chinese GDP in 2014.

What are the sources of this Chinese economic growth? Long-term economic growth of a country depends on the rates of growth of its primary inputs—tangible (or physical) capital and labor—and on technical progress (also known as the growth of total factor productivity (TFP))—that is, the ability to increase output without increasing inputs. The rate of growth of tangible or physical capital depends on the rates of investment on structure, equipment, and basic infrastructure, which in turn depends on the availability of national savings (Herd 2020). The rate of technical progress depends on investment in intangible capital, which includes human capital and research and development (R&D) capital. Chinese economic growth since 1978 has been underpinned by a consistently high domestic investment rate, enabled by a national saving rate of over 35 percent except for a brief start-up period in the early 1950s. The Chinese national saving rate rose to around 40 percent in the early 1990s and at times approached or even exceeded 50 percent in more recent years. The high Chinese saving rate means that the Chinese economy can finance all of its domestic investment needs from its own domestic savings alone, without having to depend on the more fickle foreign capital inflows (including foreign direct investment, foreign portfolio investment, foreign aid, or foreign loans). In particular, it does not need to borrow abroad and bear the potential risks of a large, short-term, and often interruptible foreign-currency-denominated debt. Thus, the Chinese economy is always assured of a high rate of growth of its tangible capital stock. It is therefore also more immune from external disturbances than most other economies (Young 2003; Jefferson, Rawski, and Zhang 2008, 1996; Jin et al. 2010).

China, like Japan, Taiwan, and South Korea in their respective early stages of economic development, has an unlimited supply of surplus labor—there is therefore no shortage of and no upward pressure on the real wage rate of unskilled, entry-level labor over an extended period of time. The agricultural sector employed 29.5 percent of the Chinese labor force but produced only 9.2 percent of the Chinese GDP in 2014. Thus, labor can be productively transferred to the other two sectors where labor productivities and wage rates are higher as long as complementary capital and demand are available (Kroeber 2016; Herd 2020).

The huge size of the domestic market with 1.37 billion consumers and their pent-up demands for housing and transportation and other consumer goods and services (e.g., education, health care, and, more recently, elderly care) enable the realization of significant economies of scale in production, based entirely on the domestic demand in China. The huge domestic market also greatly enhances the productivity of intangible capital (e.g., R&D capital and goodwill, including brand building) by allowing the fixed costs of the R&D for a new product or process or advertising and promotion in brand building to be more easily amortized and recovered.

In addition, the huge domestic market also enables significant "learning-by-doing" so that the unit costs of production decline with rising cumulative output. This is yet another form of manifestation of economies of scale. Another important implication of the huge size of the domestic economy is the relatively low external dependence.

Thus, while the rates of growth of Chinese exports and imports fluctuate like any other economy, the quarterly rates of growth of the Chinese real GDP can be clearly seen to be relatively much more stable than those of other economies. It never turned negative whereas many of the other Asian economies would experience absolute declines in their real GDPs. This is of course also due in part to the fact that China does not have to depend on the inflow of foreign savings for its investment.

The Monopsonistic Labor Market in China

China has an extraordinarily high national saving rate. This rate would be considered high even by the standards of East Asian economies. Why is this the case, especially considering that the Chinese GDP per capita is still significantly below those of other East Asian economies? One explanation is that the Chinese government was and still is the largest single employer of nonagricultural workers in China and therefore has both the ability and the incentive to keep wage rates low.

Before the economic reform of 1978, the Chinese government was the sole employer for all workers in the urban areas of China and set their wage rates. As the sole employer, the Chinese government could exercise its monopsonistic power and pursued a low (and egalitarian) wage policy, resulting in a low share of labor in GDP of less than 50 percent over the past several decades.

The low-wage policy reflected three considerations: First, it was designed to increase national savings through higher profits of the enterprises, most of which are state-owned, so that the needed domestic investments could be readily financed. This objective of the low-wage policy is similar to the "price scissors" policy of maintaining a large gap between industrial and agricultural prices, practiced in the former Soviet Union in the early twentieth century. Second, it helped to maximize employment and, in particular, the absorption of surplus labor from the agricultural sector into the industrial and service sectors.

Third, it was compatible with the ideological preference of the CCP for thrift and egalitarianism in the distribution of income. Note that if the government is the sole employer, the wage and individual income tax policies can be de facto integrated—no separate individual income tax is necessary (Herd 2020; ten Brink 2019).

In this context, a low-wage (and low- or no-tax) policy has a similar economic effect as a high-wage and high-tax policy but is politically easier to adopt, implement, and sustain. Even as recently as 2010, the share of Chinese public sector employment, which includes the employees of central and local governments and their affiliated units, SOEs, and publicly financed educational and health care institutions, was still over 50 percent of all urban employment. The government could therefore exercise a decisive influence on not only the wage rates of the public sector employees but also the level of wage rates in the economy as a whole. Today, a government job is still the preferred choice for many Chinese workers because of the job and income security and the significant fringe benefits that it offers.

This low-wage policy has had two major effects: first, it has kept the labor share (and the household share) of GDP low; and second, it has created large profits for state-owned (and other) enterprises. The disposable household income share of GDP in China may be estimated at around 50 percent in 2014, much lower than the corresponding share in a developed economy, where it would typically be around 60 percent, and also lower than those of other developing economies with a comparable real GDP per capita. The Chinese share of labor is likely to be lower than the share of household disposable income, as the latter includes, in addition to wages and salaries, also net proprietor's income, net asset income, and net transfers (which amounted to 43 percent of the total household disposable income) but excludes direct taxes and other mandatory charges such as social security contributions.

As Chinese households have less disposable income to spend relative to Chinese GDP, China also has a lower household consumption to GDP ratio than others. This ratio, as well as the total final consumption (which is the sum of government consumption and household consumption) to GDP ratio, has been declining over time. As of 2014, the total final consumption ratio was just over 50 percent and the household consumption ratio was approximately 38 percent, both significantly lower than most other economies with a comparable real GDP per capita. The Chinese household saving rate may be estimated at around 30 percent from survey data, comparable to those of ethnically Chinese households in Hong Kong and Taiwan ((ten Brink 2019; Weber 2021).

What all of this means is that the high Chinese saving rate is not due to a particularly high household saving rate but instead due to high enterprise profits and reinvestment rates. Thus, Chinese household consumption cannot be expected to be a major source of growth of Chinese aggregate demand in the short or medium term as long as household disposable income remains relatively low.

The high Chinese national saving rate of between 40 percent and 50 percent should therefore be attributed to the high propensity to save on the part of Chinese enterprises out of their profits, especially since they distribute very little in terms of cash dividends to their shareholders, which include the Chinese government (the majority shareholder of the SOEs) and the households.

Household income and government revenue can both be increased if the SOEs are required to distribute a greater proportion of their profits as cash dividends to their shareholders, which may in turn lead to higher household and government consumption.

Then in early 1992, Deng Xiaoping, the paramount Chinese leader at the time, undertook his famous southern inspection tour. Everywhere he went, he urged the people to seize the moment and grasp the opportunities. His words changed expectations in the entire country almost overnight. Enterprises began investing, and households began consuming once again. As a result, the rest of 1992 as well as 1993 and 1994 were boom years with double-digit rates of economic growth.

In mid-1997, the East Asian Currency Crisis broke out, first in Thailand and then in South Korea until it engulfed almost all of the East Asian economies, with the exception of Japan.

In 2000, the whole world was suffering from the burst of the internet bubble in the United States and China was no exception (the negative expectations then were reflected in the exceptionally low rates of growth of fixed asset investment). Then in December 2001, China became a member of the WTO. The Chinese accession to the WTO also changed expectations in a dramatic way, which also reflected the expected expiration of the Multi-Fiber Agreement that governed global trade in textiles in 2005.

In 2005, the Renminbi began to be allowed to appreciate relative to the U.S. dollar, which adversely affected the growth of exports, and the rate of growth of fixed asset investment fell back to more normal levels. In 2008, in the immediate aftermath of the collapse of Lehman Brothers in the United States, all credit dried up in the United States as well as the other developed economies. Overnight, importers in the United States and other developed economies could no longer place their import orders to China and other trading partner countries because their banks were not in a position to issue acceptable letters of credit. As a result, export orders received by Chinese enterprises declined by approximately 50 percent. There was real panic in the air. Fortunately, barely six weeks later, Chinese premier Wen Jiabao unveiled the 4 trillion yuan (approximately 6 percent of the then Chinese GDP) economic stimulus program, which once again managed to maintain the confidence of Chinese enterprises and households in their economy (Weber 2021). Actually, the economic stimulus program did not really take effect until at least a year later, but the announcement of the program itself alone managed to restore positive expectations among the Chinese public. In all of these cases, the Chinese government was able to turn around the very negative domestic expectations about the future of the Chinese economy into positive ones and in so doing greatly reduced the uncertainty pertaining to the future and increased general business as well as consumer confidence.

These changes in turn fueled investment booms that resulted in the subsequent economic growth. However, with the bursting of the Chinese stock market bubble in July 2015 and the slight but unexpected devaluation of the Renminbi of approximately 4 percent in August 2015, the confidence of the Chinese enterprises and households has been somewhat shaken. At the same time, reacting to these developments in China, the world markets have also panicked and doomsayers have been coming out in droves, predicting the imminent collapse of the Chinese economy (Weber 2021; ten Brink 2019).

Chinese economic growth during the past 36 years can be attributed to the growth of tangible inputs—tangible capital and labor and, in particular, tangible capital—rather than the growth in intangible capital or technical progress, just as the past economic growth of other East Asian economies at a similar stage of economic development. The successful Chinese experience strongly reaffirms the fundamental importance of having and maintaining a high investment rate, enabled by a high national savings rate and surplus labor. A low-wage policy was instrumental in a high national saving rate and a rapid rate of absorption of surplus labor. In addition, the size of the Chinese domestic economy is a favorable factor allowing the ready realization of economies of scale and reducing vulnerability to external disturbances. The prior economic slack, inherent in any previously centrally planned economy, has also been a significant source of economic growth upon Chinese transition to a market economy. Expectations will continue to play an important role in the Chinese economy. A strong Chinese central government with the unique power to mobilize domestic aggregate demand can credibly change expectations from negative to positive at critical junctures to keep the economy growing (ten Brink 2019; Ramesh 2017).

China's Foreign Investments

Many Chinese firms are now powerful foreign investors, particularly in important sectors like extractive industries, telecommunications, hydropower, and infrastructure development. In 2000, Chinese outbound foreign direct investment (COFDI) was just $2.3 billion. In 2018/2019, it was $129.8 billion, taking the total stock from $27.8 billion to $1.94 trillion.

China's largest companies—including those operating internationally—are predominantly state-controlled. The largest so-called private firm Huawei is with massive public investments. Measured by number or output, however, most Chinese companies are officially private. These so-called private firms generated about two-thirds of China's GDP and 80 percent of economic growth by 2000 and 44 percent of Chinese FDI in 2018 (Herd 2020)

Many firms, particularly smaller ones, are purely private, raising capital and selecting investments contributing for about 25 percent of Chinese FDI in 2016. Limited liability companies (LLCs), which contributed 43.2 percent of Chinese FDI, involve a mixture of private and public shareholders, with SOEs have important stakes. It is also unlikely that any private company could have become a giant like Huawei, Alibaba, or Xiaomi without party–state patronage. Huawei, is 99 percent employee-owned, through a trade union committee, and is ultimately under CCP control. All companies ultimately have a constitutional obligation to cooperate with the state. Chinese government now owns just 97 mega-conglomerates, largely in "strategic" sectors, but most of these privatized organizations are owned by town-municipal enterprises whose managers are recruited by the CCP. SOEs have also been "corporatized," with ownership with the State-owned Assets Supervision and Administration Commissions (SASAC), whose leaders are appointed by the CCP. SOE contributes about 25 percent of the GDP of China but it has 60 percent of corporate debt, $12.5 trillion by 2014, when China's total corporate debt was 163 percent of GDP. SOEs have privileged access to China Development Bank and the Export-Import Bank, which are the major instruments of the BRI initiative. In 2006, China's Ministry of Commerce (MOFCOM) reported that only half of China's foreign investments were profitable. Despite efforts to improve due diligence, by 2014, China's overseas assets, now totaling US$6.4 trillion, were still yielding a net loss but have become the instrument for expanding Chinese empire overseas.

Chinese firms are becoming major shareholders in foreign companies, with 61 percent of financing came from overseas, in 2018. The value of M&As in Europe ($60.8 billion) and North America ($8.4 billion) vastly exceeded the combined total for Latin America, Africa, Asia, and Oceania ($37.7 billion). Chinese firms are increasingly targeting high-tech American or European companies, to acquire foreign technologies (Herd 2020; Weber 2021).

After China enters the World Trade Organization in 2001, exports surge dramatically for China's firms. As a result, saving in China's corporate sector (i.e., retained earnings) increased rapidly. Imports have not increased as the people could not get the share of that increased profit. China's trade surpluses shot up to 10 percent of GDP in 2007. In the years after 2007, China's exports were growing more slowly than GDP. One main reason for China's high rate of household savings has been that China has a poorly financed system for pensions and health care for the elderly. China's one-child policy (only abandoned in 2015) is that the elderly cannot depend on the younger generation for support. Births in China have been falling; in fact, the 14.6 million babies born in 2019 was the lowest number since 1961 (Ramesh 2017; Stephen and Parízek 2019).

When President Trump first imposed tariffs on China in March 2018, the aim was to reduce U.S. trade deficits. The "Phase I" agreement, announced in January 2020, had two main aspects. China agreed to purchase an additional $200 billion from the United States in the next two years. Second, the agreement touched upon China's treatment of intellectual property, U.S. exports of agricultural products, and financial services. China's real GDP growth has declined, from 14.2 percent in 2007 to 6.6 percent in 2018, and that growth is projected by the IMF to fall to 5.5 percent by 2024 (Herd 2020; Weber 2021; Coase and Wang 2016).

MEASURING THE SIZE OF CHINA'S ECONOMY

There are two measures of national income for a country: PPP and nominal national income in U.S. dollars using nominal exchange rates. One U.S. dollar in China would purchase more goods and services there than it would in the United States, because prices for goods and services in China are generally half of that in the United States.

However, in the PPP measurement, China's 2018 nominal per capita GDP became $18,110, which was 28.9 percent of the U.S. level. China has become the largest manufacturer of the world according to the World Bank. Gross value-added data reflect the actual value of manufacturing that occurred in the country as they subtract the value of intermediate inputs and raw materials used in production. In 2016, China's gross valued-added manufacturing was equal to 28.7 percent of its GDP, compared to 11.6 percent for the United States (Coase and Wang 2016; Herd 2020).

Changes in China's Wage and Labor Cost Advantages

The decline in China's working age population may have contributed rising wages in China. "In Figure 9, China's average monthly wages (converted into U.S. dollars) in 1990 were $55, compared with $32 for Vietnam and $221 for Mexico. However, in 2018, China's average monthly wages (at $990) were 316% higher than Vietnam's wages ($238) and 158.5% higher than Mexico's ($383). From 2007 to 2018, China's average monthly wages rose by 263%" (American Chamber of Commerce in China, AmCham China).

Industrial Policies and SOEs

According to the World Bank,

> SOEs constituted 50% of the 500 largest manufacturing companies in China and 61% of the top 500 service sector enterprises. China has become a major global producer of steel. From 2001 to 2016, China's production of raw steel rose from 152 million metric tons to 805 million metric tons, an increase of 459.9%. During this period, China's share of global production rose from 17.9% to 50.3% and China accounted for 87.1% of the increase in global steel production. In 2015, China was the second-largest exporter of semifinished and steel products (after the EU) at 111.6 million metric tons, or 24.1% of global total.

China's steel industry is heavily financed by government at the central and local government level (Herd 2020; Weber 2021).

A State-Dominated Banking Sector, Excess Credit, and Growing Debt

China's banking system is largely controlled by the state-controlled banks with the top five largest banks in China were state-owned. Foreign participation in China's banking system is comparatively small. The Chinese central government uses the banking system to obtain its GDP growth objectives. From 2007 to 2016, China's domestic credit increased in dollar terms by 218 percent, and as a share of GDP, the level rose from 125 percent to 212 percent. From 2006 to 2016, China's total nonfinancial sector debt as a percentage of GDP increased from 143 percent to 254 percent. In dollar terms, China's corporate debt rose from $3 trillion to $17.8 trillion (up $14.8 trillion) and currently greatly exceeds U.S. corporate debt levels, thus taking China to a dangerous level regarding debts (Herd 2020; Weber 2021).

Debt of the industries belonging to local government is viewed as a big liability in China. Chinese subnational government enterprises normally borrow heavily to help stimulate local economies and to support local infrastructure projects.

Agriculture

After Deng Xioping implemented the household responsibility system, agricultural output increased by 8.2 percent a year, compared with 2.7 percent in the pre-reform period, despite a decrease in the area of land used. Food prices fell nearly 50 percent, while agricultural income rose.

Comparison to India

China's high growth was on resource-intensive manufacturing and exports, and it has largely reached its limits and has caused economic, social, and environmental imbalances. Following real GDP growth of 2.3 percent in 2020, China's economy was expected to grow by 8.5 percent in 2021. India has grown in 2021 by 9.2 percent after having a decline of 7 percent in 2020.

Curious about why China has done so well, an IMF research team recently examined the sources of that nation's growth and arrived at a surprising conclusion. Although capital accumulation—the growth in the country's stock of capital assets, such as new factories, manufacturing machinery, and communications systems—was important, as were the number of Chinese workers, a sharp, sustained increase in productivity (i.e., increased worker efficiency) was the driving force behind the economic boom. During 1979–1994 productivity gains accounted for more than 42 percent of China's growth and by the early 1990s had overtaken capital as the most significant source of that growth. This marks a departure from the traditional view of development in which capital investment takes the lead. This jump in productivity originated in the economic reforms begun in 1978. However, productivity growth is the consequence of economic growth due to institutional change; it cannot be the source of growth. Thus, the argument of the IMF is not correct (Edith 2015; Cheung 2014; Nölke et al. 2019; Ramesh 2017).

A considerable part of recent growth in China is due to capital investment that contributed to the growth of the economy; although the capital stock grew by nearly 7 percent a year over 1979–1994, the capital-output ratio was not changed and along with a huge expenditure of capital, production of goods and services per unit of capital remained about the same. Increase in productivity was the answer for this puzzle. Chinese productivity increased at an annual rate of 3.9 percent during 1979–1994, compared with 1.1 percent during 1953–1978 due to institutional changes in China. These changes include profit incentives to rural collective enterprises, family farms, small private businesses, and foreign investments.

The Future of China's Economic Growth

Demographic Challenges

The existence of a large and underemployed labor force was a significant factor to provide cheap workforce in China's rapid economic growth. China is beginning to lose this labor advantage. According to the Chinese government, the size of its working-age population (ages 16 to 59) peaked at 925 million in 2011 but then fell for seven consecutive years to 897 million in 2018. The one-child policy has also resulted in a rapidly aging society in China. The population share of people aged over 60 could reach 20 percent by 2020 and 27 percent by 2030. With a declining working population and a rising elderly population, the Chinese government will face problem related to rising labor costs (Herd 2020).

China's Belt and Road Initiative

China's Belt and Road Initiative (BRI) is an effort to increase exports of steel, glass, road-railways, and Chinese labor by providing loans to a number of countries. However, the BRI could pose financial burden for the recipient countries if they could not repay in time. The recipient countries got to convert the debt into equity and give up their ports, mines, and land.

In July 2014, China, along with Brazil, Russia, India, and South Africa, announced the creation of a $100 billion "New Development Bank," which is headquartered in Shanghai, China, which will finance infrastructure projects in developing countries. In October 2014, China launched the creation of a new $100 billion Asian Infrastructure Development Bank (AIIB), aimed at funding infrastructure projects in Asia (Ramesh 2017).

The "Made in China 2025" initiative aimed at turning China as the world's leading manufacturer of telecommunication, railway, electrical power equipment, robotics, high-end automation, and new energy vehicles industries. China's Made in China 2025 initiative was "a very, very serious challenge, not just to us, but to Europe, Japan and the global trading system" (USTR).

Inequality in China

Inequality as the "Gang of Four" was afraid took place after the reform program was introduced. Now according to the OECD report of 2022, 1 percent of the top earners in China have greater share of wealth of China than the bottom 50 percent of the people. The richest 20 percent have their average disposable income of $12,000 in 2021, which is 10.2 times of that of the poor 20 percent. The same ratio was 8.4 in the United States, 5 in Western Europe, but 10.4 in Mexico. Gini coefficient for China in 2021 was 38.5, which was 30.3 in the advanced economies but 45.5 in the emerging countries. Thus, China was better than other emerging countries but at a much lower level of equality than the advanced countries. India also suffers from the same disease of the reform era (Kanbur and Zhang 2005; Ravallion and Chen 2007).

APPENDIX 1

China GDP

In 1992, the State Council of China adopted the System of National Accounting (SNA) to measure the national economy in place of material product system, the Soviet system. China's economic reform process began in December 1978 when the Third Plenum of the 11th Central Committee of the Communist Party adopted Deng Xiaoping's economic proposals. Implementation of the reforms began in 1979. China's real GDP growth rate fell from 11.3 percent in 1988 to 4.2 percent in 1989 and declined to 3.9 percent in 1990. In 1991, economic reforms were restarted and foreign sanctions against China were reduced or removed, and real GDP grew by 9.2 percent. Chinese FDI to the United States was in 2017 at $24.5 billion (compared to $54.6 billion in 2016), making the United States the largest destination of Chinese outward FDI. China's largest U.S. acquisition in 2017 was HNA's purchase of CIT Group's aircraft leasing business for $10.4 billion (Brandt et al. 2020).

Chapter 4

China

Factor Productivity Growth

SECTORAL SHIFTS AND PRODUCTIVITY GROWTH SINCE 1978

Total factor productivity (TFP) grew rapidly in both the agricultural and the nonstate sectors. For the overall period from 1978 to 2007, the average annual growth rates of TFP in these two sectors were 4.01 and 3.91 percent, respectively. In contrast, the average growth rate of TFP in the state sector was only 1.68 percent per year. Prior to 1998, in particular, the state sector had very low productivity growth rates. After 1998, though, TFP in the state sector grew rapidly, averaging 5.5 percent annually, although there are disputes regarding the accuracy of these figures (Zhu 2012; Ramesh 2017; Nölke et al. 2019)

Prior to the 1978 reforms, nearly four in five Chinese worked in agriculture; by 1994, reforms expanded property rights in the countryside and touched off a race to form small nonagricultural businesses in rural areas. De-collectivization and higher prices for agricultural products also led to more productive (family) farms and more efficient use of labor. Together these forces induced many workers to move out of agriculture. The resulting rapid growth of village enterprises has drawn tens of millions of people from traditional agriculture into higher value-added manufacturing. However, data showed that there was hardly any movement of unskilled laborers from agriculture to highly skilled manufacturing but to the low-skilled service sector.

The post-1978 reforms in the industrial sector gave greater autonomy to enterprise managers, who "became more free to set their own production goals, sell some products in the private market at competitive prices, grant bonuses to good workers and fire bad ones, and retain some portion of the firm's earnings for future investment" (Lin 1992). China's open-door policy has stimulated the economic transformation. This foreign money has linked China to international markets and led to important transfers of technology. Strong export growth appears to have added productivity growth in domestic industries (Li 1994).

Productivity Growth in Agriculture and Structural Transformation

Since China had experienced recurring food crises before 1978, it is not surprising that its economic reform started in the agricultural sector. There were two important reforms. First, the government increased prices for agricultural goods. Second, the previous "collective farming system" was shifted to the "household responsibility system." Under the new system, each farm household was assigned a fixed quota of grains that the household had to sell to the government at official prices. However, any extra grain the household produced could be sold at market prices. The reforms were implemented gradually and completed in 1984.

Between 1978 and 1984, TFP in the agricultural sector grew 5.62 percent per year. Several studies argue that most of the productivity growth during this period can be attributed to the price and institutional reforms that generated strong positive incentive effects on farmers' efforts and input choices (McMillan, Whalley, and Zhu 1989; Lin 1992). As a result of the productivity growth, China's agricultural output increased by 47 percent during this period. The increase in food availability alleviated China's subsistence food constraint and started a structural transformation that reallocated a large amount of labor from agriculture to industry.

From 1978 to 1984, agriculture's share of total employment fell from 69 percent to 50 percent: that is, in just six years, 9 percent of China's labor force—more than 49 million workers—reallocated out of the agricultural sector. Most of the 49 million reallocated workers did not move to urban centers. Instead, they went to work in the rural industrial enterprises set up by township and village-level governments that are called "township and village enterprises" (TVEs). Both agricultural productivity and structural transformation stagnated in the second half of the 1980s. Starting around 1990, markets for agricultural inputs and outputs were gradually liberalized and government interventions were significantly reduced (Nölke et al. 2019).

The average annual growth rate of TFP in agriculture reached 5.10 percent between 1988 and 1998 and remained at 4.13 percent between 1998 and 2007. Most of agriculture's growth in TFP after 1990 came from technological progress (Jin et al. 2010). The standard argument is that productivity growth in agriculture not only contributes to aggregate productivity growth directly but also indirectly through structural transformation. Arguments provided by capitalist-minded Chinese economists like Cheung (2014) and several American economists like Coase and Wang (2016) support these types of institutional argument that capitalism itself was responsible for the recent economic development of China, although these arguments are not supported by statistical evidence.

Growth Outside Agriculture

Before economic reform started in 1978, resource allocation was centrally determined by the government's plan rather than by the market. The state sector dominated nonagricultural activity, accounting for 80 percent of the total urban employment and more than three-quarters of industrial output. The nonstate sector at that time mainly consisted of collective firms. Urban collectives were confined to producing a small number of consumer goods and providing neighborhood services. Rural collectives were only allowed to manufacture producer goods for the agricultural sector.

1978–1988: Rise of the Nonstate Sector

In the early 1980s, encouraged by the success of the rural reforms, the Chinese government started two market reforms in the nonagricultural sector. First, a dual-track system was introduced. State-owned enterprises were still given quotas on both production inputs and output that transacted at official prices, but they were also allowed to buy inputs and sell output beyond quotas at market prices.

Moreover, the non-state-owned enterprises, including collectives small-scale individual businesses, and foreign-invested firms in the special economic zones, were allowed to enter previously forbidden industries, buying and selling their inputs and outputs at market prices.

Second, the central government also devolved economic decision-making powers to lower-level governments and provided them with fiscal incentives. As a result, provincial-, city-, and county-level governments controlled most of the state-owned enterprises while the township- and village-level governments controlled the group of rural collective enterprises that became known as the "township and village enterprises."

The number of TVEs increased from 1,520,000 in 1978 to 18,880,000 in 1988 (National Bureau of Statistics of China 1999). The success of the agricultural reforms made available to these enterprises a large number of local workers, and the dual-track system allowed them to gain rises to capital and raw materials from the markets. Between 1978 and 1988, the share of total employment in nonstate enterprises increased from 15 percent to 39 percent. The expansion of employment in the nonstate sector was also accompanied by TFP growth averaging 5.87 percent a year during this period.

The reforms did less for state-owned enterprises. Local governments at county level and above sought to improve the economic performance of the state-owned enterprises under their control by implementing a "managerial responsibility system" that linked managers' and workers' income to financial outcomes of the enterprises. The reforms did have some positive effect on productivity. Using a panel data set of 272 industrial state-owned enterprises collected by the Chinese Academy of Social Sciences, Li (1994) estimates that their TFP on average grew at 4.68 percent per year between 1980 and 1989, and that most of the productivity growth could be attributed to stronger incentives, increased market competition, and better allocation of production inputs. Using the same data set, Groves et al. (1994) also report positive incentive effects of the managerial responsibility system on productivity.

Jefferson, Rawski, and Zhang (1996) estimate that between 1980 and 1988, the average annual growth rate of TFP was 2.96 percent for state-owned enterprises and 3.66 percent for the nonstate collective enterprises. However, these estimated rates of productivity growth are based on a production function that uses gross output rather than value-added output. Until 1988 India and China were at the same level regarding per head national output.

1988–1998: From Reform without Losers to Inevitable Trade-Offs

Lau, Qian, and Roland (2000) call it "reform without losers,"; when to avoid laying off workers or shutting down factories, the government usually asked the state-owned banks to bail out loss-making state-owned enterprises.

In contrast, the central government had no commitment to support employment in the TVEs. These local governments had only weak influence on banks. For example, millions of TVEs went bankrupt when there was a general tightening of credit in 1989 (Qian and Xu 1993). Thus, TVEs faced a much tighter budget constraint and stronger market discipline than did the state-owned enterprises.

Between 1988 and 1998, the average annual growth rate of TFP was only 0.27 percent, while the comparable growth rate of the nonstate sector was 2.17 percent. Nonperforming loans in the state banking system increased rapidly, and the creation of money to make these loans was leading to chronic high inflation (Brandt and Zhu 2000). By 1994, it had become clear that the strategy of "reform without losers" could no longer be sustained. In 1995, the Chinese government reduced its commitment to stable employment in the state sector. Many small-scale state-owned enterprises were allowed to go bankrupt or be privatized through management buyouts. Between 1995 and 2001, the state sector's share of total employment declined from 17 percent in 1995 and to 12 percent in 2001. More diversified ownership forms were also introduced within the state sector. Some of the large-scale state-owned enterprises were converted into shareholding companies, with a majority of shares controlled by the state.

1998–2007: Privatization and Trade Liberalization

The 15th Congress of the Chinese Communist Party held in 1997 was a milestone in China's economic policies. The Congress formally sanctioned ownership reforms of the state-owned firms and also legalized the development of private enterprises. With the reduction of legal barriers, private enterprises grew rapidly.

Collective enterprises such as TVEs lost their edge; some were closed and many of them were privatized. As part of the lead-up to China's joining the World Trade Organization in 2001, China's government also started to cut tariffs, broadened trade rights, and liberalized its regime for foreign direct investment (Branstetter and Lardy 2008). Between 1998 and 2007, the share of total urban employment in domestic private enterprises and foreign-invested enterprises increased from 8 to 24 percent.

The increase in the manufacturing sector was even more pronounced. By 2007, domestic private enterprises alone accounted for 51 percent of total urban employment in the manufacturing sector (National Bureau of Statistics of China 2009).

The combination of privatization and trade liberalization had strong effects on productivity growth in both the state and nonstate sectors. Between 1998 and 2007, the average annual TFP growth rates of the state and nonstate sectors were 5.50 percent and 3.67 percent, respectively.

In the manufacturing sector, productivity growth during this period is higher. Brandt, Van Brandt, Van Biesebroeck, and Zhang (2012) estimate that, for the manufacturing sector, the TFP growth rate is 13.4 percent a year, which is certainly absurd.

In 2007, the state sector still accounted for 77 percent of total urban employment in services, in contrast to 15 percent in manufacturing.

Sources of Aggregate Productivity Growth in China

From 1978 to 2007, China's annual growth rate of TFP was 3.61 percent per year. We can summarize the sources of aggregate productivity growth in China during the reform period as follows. In the agricultural sector, productivity growth contributed 1.5 percentage points a year to aggregate productivity growth over the 1978–2007 period, both directly and indirectly through structural transformation. However, this source of growth diminished over time as agriculture's share of GDP diminished, and its contribution to China's future growth will be small. In the nonstate sector, productivity growth contributed 2.27 percentage points per year to aggregate productivity growth over the 1978–2007 period.

When agricultural productivity increases, food demand can be met with a smaller number of workers in the agricultural sector than before. As a result, some workers can be reallocated to the nonagricultural sector. Because average labor productivity is generally higher in the nonagricultural sector than in the agricultural sector, the reallocation of workers from agriculture contributes positively to aggregate productivity. However, studies showed that most of these workers from agricultural sector went to the nonfarm, nonmanufacturing services with stagnant or negligible productivity changes (Brandt et al. 2020). Thus, one can suspect the conclusion of Zhu (2012) seriously.

Again, according to Herd (2020), considering the contributions to the average annual change in real output per worker, percentage change in the period 1979 to 2018, TFP, was about 2 percent, during 1979 to 1988, it was 2.5 percent, but during 2009 to 2018, it declined to 1 percent.

In a comparative study of China and India until 2008, Prat, Yu, and Fan (2009) concluded that TFP increased due to efficiency gain in China as a result of institutional changes whereas in India it increased due to technical change. Institutional change cannot be continuous and sustainable forever, admitted by even Solow (1957). TFP is considered as a measure of our ignorance. It cannot explain anything (Shaikh 1974).

Solow measured TFP indices using the existence of separable aggregator functions for inputs and outputs g(x) and h(y) to obtain $\text{TFP} = \frac{h(y)}{g(x)}$, this presupposes independence between input and output substitution possibilities. It is a restrictive and unrealistic requirement; it also needs price data for each inputs and outputs, which make this estimate subjective. An economist's (Western) idea of technical progress or technical efficiency is very different from a technologist's idea of technical progress or efficiency. According to the economists, technical progress is expected to reduce costs; as a result the economists may disregard scientific inventions or product quality improvements, which may not necessarily reduce costs. In India, there were a number of studies on TFP of the Indian economy and manufacturing industry in particular (Bosworth and Maertens 2010; Deb and Ray 2014; Saha 2014). These studies give conflicting results as shown in table 4.1.

These conflicting results are due to the different methods of calculation of net national income, net domestic product and gross domestic products, price indices, and cost structure assumed in the calculations. However, in all studies, TFP declines over time.

Sudden upsurge of growth after institutional change from a repressive system to a comparatively relaxed system can improve productivity, but that is the result or the consequences of institutional change but not the cause. Thus,

Table 4.1. Total Factor Productivity of the Indian Economy, 1992–2004

	TFP in Deb and Ray (2014)	*TFP in Saha (2014)*	*TFP in Bosworth and Maerten*
1992–1996	1.77	3.09	
1997–2004	0.76	2.33	
1995–2003	0.81	2.54	
1990–2000	0.90	2.06	1.80
2000–2004	0.60	2.10	2.40

Source: Economic Survey, Govt of India.

Zhu was confused and accepted the results of institutional changes as causes for growth.

However, when China joined the World Trade Organization in 2001, the walls, which had been limiting China's trade, were removed. Exports of goods and services spiked from 20 percent of GDP in 2001 to 36 percent in 2007. China's imports climbed from 18 percent of GDP in 2001 to 28 percent in the same period. In other words, China's economy became thoroughly intertwined with the global economy in just a few years.

This was textbook "export-led" growth that paralleled the earlier successes of Japan and South Korea. China's exports had grown faster than its economy from 1980, rising from 6 percent of GDP in 1980 to 20 percent of GDP in 2001. Up to 2001, the rise in China's imports had mostly kept pace. But after 2001, the current account surplus ballooned to an astonishing 10 percent of GDP in 2007.

APPENDIX

Let the relationship between production inputs (physical capital, human capital, and labor) and GDP be represented by a standard Cobb–Douglas production function: ion function:

$Y = AK\ \alpha\ (h\ L)1 - \alpha.$

Here Y is GDP, K is physical capital stock, L is labor (number of workers), h is the average level of human capital, A is TFP, and α is the output elasticity of physical capital, which is usually measured by capital's share of national income. The growth rate of per capita GDP can be decomposed as the sum of four terms:

Growth rate of per capita GDP = growth rate of labor participation rate
+ $\alpha/(1 - \alpha)$ growth rate of the capital/output ratio
+ growth rate of average human capital
+ $1/(1 - \alpha)$ growth rate of TFP.

Note that in this decomposition the contribution of TFP growth is weighted by $1/(1 - \alpha)$, taking into account both the direct contribution of TFP and the indirect contribution through its impact on capital accumulation.

This decomposition reveals very different patterns of growth in the two periods.

Chapter 5

China

Decentralized Economic System

Chinese reform policies are often against the so-called IMF-World Bank-U.S. Treasury standard policy recommendations. Up until 1988, China's per capita GDP was about the same as that of India (Maddison 2007b). According to usual Washington Consensus, the government should honor private property rights, have legal system to honor contracts, and promote private enterprises (North 1981; Acemoglu and Johnson 2005; Rodrik 2006). In China, the government has large public sector companies and is in full control of the private sector. There is no legal protection for the Chinese private sector enterprises or foreign companies, until 2004 constitutional amendment (Allen et al. 2005). Thus, Chinese institutions are not qualified, according to the IMF-World bank, for any development aid. With high levels of trade protection, lack of privatization, extensive industrial policies, and lax fiscal and financial policies, China has avoided the Washington Consensus. Indeed, had it been dismal failure instead of the successes it turned out to be, it would have presented evidence in support of Washington Consensus policies. China has a "Corruption Perception Index" level of 5, which is similar to Indonesia, Iraq, Myanmar, Nigeria, Sudan, and Somalia (Svensson 2005).

Regionally decentralized authoritarian (RDA) system is the most important new institution, which has caused the impressive growth of the economy of China. In this system, subnational governments administer most part of the economy. They innovate new proposals, create administrative system, policies, rules, and laws to implement these proposals (Coase and Wang 2016; Xu 1995).

The RDA system has the characteristics of centralization on the political level and decentralization on the economic level. It is not federalism as the central government appoints the officials, promote them, and transfer them. The officials follow the main instructions of the central government but at the same time, they have considerable independence regarding new initiatives and how to implement these. Regional administrative units (provinces, municipalities, and counties) have overall responsibility for initiating and coordinating reforms. That makes China very different from a centrally planned economy of Soviet type.

"In effect, it is the sub-national levels of Government that implement China's national development agenda. Nearly 70 percent of total public expenditure in China takes place at the sub-national level (i.e. provincial, prefecture, county, and township), of which more than 55 percent takes place at sub-provincial levels" (The World Bank 2002).

In the RDA system, subnational governments have control over land, firms, financial resources, energy, raw materials, and others resources within their area. They are responsible for the development of foreign and nonstate firms, the township and village enterprises, and state-owned and collectively owned companies (Granick 1990). They are responsible for law making and law enforcements. They can do regional reform experiments. Most reforms since mid-1980s were initiated and executed through their experiments.

MUNICIPAL LEVEL (OR PREFECTURE LEVEL), COUNTY LEVEL, AND TOWNSHIP LEVEL

"The total expenditure of Chinese sub-national governments accounted for about 70% of the national total, which was far larger than that of the world's largest federal countries such as the U.S. (46%), Germany (40%) and Russia (38%)" (Wong 2013). The reason is that most of the functions of the governments are executed by these subnational governments. These are within a new institutional form, MFORM or multi-regional governance form (Qian and Xu 1993). In it, regional governments are self-contained and control major functions of the government within its area of operation.

Centralized Political Governance

However, China's RDA system does not promote the system of federal states. Chinese regional leaders, governor, and other senior administrators are appointed by the Chinese Communist Party (CCP). The CCP determines the promotions and transfer of the officers of these regional governments (Huang 1996). While CCP decides on appointment and removal of provincial governors, most municipal leaders, for example, mayors, are directly appointed by corresponding provincial governments. This system expands the central control on officials of all levels of regions, from provincial to municipal and township government (Burns 1994). From 1978 to 2005, 80 percent of provincial governors were transferred by the central government (Xu et al. 2007; Huang 1996).

RDA system may have stabilized the reform policies of post-Mao period (Deng 1980; Zhao 2009; Li 2008). On political aspects, Hu Jin Tao and Zhao Zemin pushed for political pluralism within the one-party system as a part of the reform. Capitalist entrepreneurs are considered as "advanced social productive forces" and are recruited into the party (the CPC Constitution, the 16th CPC Congress, 2002) (Dickson 2003). The Chinese constitution has also been amended to protect private property rights according to the Constitutional Amendment of 2004.

Personnel Control

By controlling the appointment of senior officers of the RDA regimes the central government controls and coordinates subnational officials. With this instrument, the Chinese RDA system implements a decentralized economic institution, in which subnational governments perform most tasks of reforms and economic development. Although regional officials have control over resources their future career is determined by the central government. Regional officials at subordinate levels have specified responsibility (Tsui and Wang 2004).

Economic development plan and tax revenue targets are often political. Fulfillments of these targets are important for political rewards (Edin 2003).

The process of selection for the future leaders at the subnational levels includes nominations and approvals by top leaders of the country regarding their commitments regarding the core values and their capability to perform. That keeps a balance between national and regional interests. This structure plays important roles in national macroeconomic policies and encourages regional initiatives.

These subnational governments played a decisive role in the reform process of China. "Governors Zhao Ziyang of Sichuan and Wan Li of Anhui initiated land reform experiments in a few localities within their jurisdictions in the late 1970s when the national policy, including the Party's 'reform' manifesto, did not allow any ownership change to collective farming. Similarly, governor Xi Zhongxun of Guangdong proposed the special economic zone reform while some top central leaders were hostile to this reform plan" (Tsui and Wang 2004). During the period of the HRS reform between 1978 and 1984, output in the Chinese agricultural sector increased by over 61 percent. Seventy-eight percent of the increase in productivity in Chinese agriculture in this period of time was due to the changes brought about by the HRS reform (McMillan 1989). When these reforms were successful, Zhao and

Wan became the premier and executive deputy premier of the state council, respectively, responsible for national reform; Xi became a vice chairman of the National People's Congress (Tian 2008).

Thus, regional experimentation is an essential part of the central decision-making process in China. Starting from 1978, almost every major step on the path of reform was tried out by a few regions first before being launched nationwide (Bardhan 2002). Subnational governments play a critical role in attempting reforms due to the uncertainty of political opinions of the top leaders of the CCP.

In the late 1970s, "prototypes" of the household responsibility system (HRS), in which responsibility of supplying grain crops was vested on individual household rather than the commune, with household having land ownership contract, were tried by a handful of local officials in a few provinces like Anhui, Sichuan, and Guangdong. After this, the nationwide land reform experiment expanded, and in 1981 about 45 percent of rural households participated in the reform. Subsequently participation increased to 80 percent in the next year and finally reached 99 percent in 1984 (Lin 1992). Thereafter, in agricultural reforms most of those are based on successful regional experiments.

The Township and Village Enterprises

Large-scale and rapid development of the nonstate and private sector are special features of China's reforms. The most important nonstate sector was the TVEs. The market share of China's state sector in the national economy declined from 78 percent in 1978 to 53 percent in 1991. A standard TVE is a communal-owned enterprise located in a township/village (Byrd and Lin 1990). Regional competition is the reason for the rapid development of these TVEs. Local state-owned enterprises (SOEs) provide technology including managerial techniques (Xu and Zhang 2009). Gradually TVEs gave rise to small private companies in China. Many Chinese townships have specialized in certain products.

"Datang township makes one-third of the world's socks; 40% of the world's neckties are made in Shengzhou township; more than 70% of the buttons for clothes made in China come from Qiaotou township; Songxia township produces 350 million umbrellas every year; and Puyuan township produced 60% of China's cashmere sweaters, of which China is the world's largest producer. There were six thousand family-owned highly specialized workshops and three thousand private trading shops in the cluster coordinated strategically by the township government" (Xu and Zhang 2009).

Special Economic Zone (SEZ) Development and the Foreign Direct Investment (FDI)

Due to these TVEs, China today is the destination of largest FDIs in the world. China also has the largest foreign exchange reserve. SEZs are the main responsible factor in the FDI recipient in China and the export development of China. In 1985, 37 percent of FDI was located in SEZs, and 89 percent of the exports came from the SEZs. In 2005, 93 percent of FDI was located in SEZs, and 93 percent of China's exports came from the SEZs (Cai 2008).

The idea of regional experimentation played a vital role in setting up the SEZs in four remote cities in 1979. In August 1980, four SEZs in Guangdong and Fujian were approved. In 1992, SEZs were in all the capital cities of inland provinces and autonomous regions, 15 free trade zones, 32 state-level economic and technological development zones, and 53 new and high-tech industrial development zones (Cai 2008).

Reform of the State Sector

Subnational governments are the real owners of the state industries. China's state sector reforms means regional competition and regional experiments. A region's state sector is a state-run regional conglomerate in which subnational governments of municipalities and townships are like the headquarters of regional conglomerates (Oi 1999). An important experiment was the utilization of competitive auctions in the selection of management teams.

2002 and 2004 versions of the bankruptcy law gave local governments the responsibility to compensate the affected workers of insolvent companies. SOE productivity in the corresponding period improved significantly.

Privatization: Locally Initiated Experiments

In China, municipal governments decide the time and magnitude of privatization and the aim is to achieve success in regional growth. As a result, China has avoided the shock therapy and never suffered from a depressed economy which was normal in most transition economies during their privatizations (Estrin et al. 2009). Privatization was not encouraged by the central government until the late 1990s. Even in the late 1990s, it was still a city government's decision whether or not to privatize and how to privatize within their jurisdictions (Garnaut 2001; Gan, Guo and Xu 2010). One of the methods of reforms was the leasing of SOEs, by paying the subnational government a fixed proportion of the firms' profits. Another method was incorporation, where employees of some SOEs bought substantial amount of shares of the firms where they worked, that is, to sell the ownership of SOEs to their employees. Other methods are share issue privatization (SIP), joint ventures with foreign firms, management buyouts (MBO), and sales to outsiders (Gan, Guo, and Xu 2010).

Influence of the Soviet Union and Czarist Russia

In Czarist Russia there was an interesting organization called "artel," which was very similar to the township organization in China. Artel was for a specific profession like artists or soldiers or for a specific region. These are cooperative organization, as Vorontsov specified that "our capitalistic manufacturing must be transformed into a state or artel production; our further industrial progress will rest on truly people's principles represented by communes and artels" (Vorontsov 1895; Drozdova 2016).

According to Pinkus the artel forced into existence in the first instance by economic pressure, that is, inefficiency of individual efforts due to peculiar geographical features of Russia (inclement and uncertain climate, vast and monotonous surface, lack of fertile soil, inadequate for effective intercommunication river systems, paralyzing influence of the long distances, etc. (Pinkus 1902; Imai 1990). The artel definition was specified in the 1823 Statute, which declared that "artel means that each worker is responsible for everybody in artel and the whole artel is responsible for each worker, they are paid from a common fund (duvan) and work is done collectively"; "associations of workers set up voluntarily to carry out work or production which is beyond one worker's capabilities" (Ustav Torgoviy 1903).

Another interesting example is in the USSR, in Khrushchev's "Sovnarkhoz" reform (decentralization reform) launched in 1957 and 1958 through a trial-and-error process. Initially, there were 105 "Sovnarkhozes" in the USSR. The regional party secretaries had the power to appoint SOE directors in their areas. They were encouraged to initiate reform measures. But this "Sovnarkhoz" reform failed after the removal of Khrushchev in 1964 (Markevich and Zhuravskaya 2009).

In the USSR, all Soviet farming operations were administered by specialized ministries like Ministries of Agriculture, Trade, Cereal and Grain Production, Tractors and Farm Machinery, Food Industry, Rural Construction, Fertilizer, Land Reclamation and Water Resources, Fruit and Vegetable Farming, and so on. In 1989, Gorbachev launched a comprehensive agriculture reform where all relevant ministries were included. In that reform, peasants could lease land with long-term contracts, similar to the HRS in China. The tasks of providing inputs to the farmers, of managing their operations, storage, processing, transport and road infrastructure were all allocated to the collective farms (Wädekin 1992). However, removal of Gorbachev in

1991 removed that reform and collective farms were privatized with terrible consequences.

In India, under the control of the IMF, privatization was accepted by the central government from the beginning without any role of the local governments to raise finance for the central government. As a result, the economy was privatized without any corresponding success stories as it was in China and gradually India lost the game to China. Privatization in India meant, so far, some corrupt politicians and businessmen with political contact with the central politicians gained a fortune by taking over the vast resources of the public sector, like in Russia since 1992. There was no massive FDIs or massive export growth as it was in China, but gradually since 2001 Chinese companies have taken over the domestic market in India, making Indian companies bankrupt and creating unemployment in the manufacturing sector in India.

Chapter 6

China

Foreign Trade and Foreign Investments

EXPORTS AND ECONOMIC GROWTH IN CHINA

China began its export-led growth in the mid-1980s, much inspired by the successes of its East Asian neighbors. A version of the flying geese theory (Akamatsu 1935, 1937, 1956, 1961), this theory divides China into three regions, eastern, central, and western, that are assigned different levels of priority of development. According to the theory, the eastern (coastal) region should start economic development first and then the central region and the western region. This theory was written into the government's seventh Five-Year Plan for the period 1986–1990 (State Council 1986).

The share of the central government's investment in the coastal region increased from 39.5 percent in the period 1953–1978 to 53.5 percent in the period 1979–1991. Another characteristic was processing trade became the long-term strategy of China, which was started in Guangdong province by mid-1980s (Wang 1988). At the end of the 1990s processing trade accounted for 60 percent of China's total trade. In the period between 2001 and 2005 processing trade surplus exceeded the total trade surplus.

China joined the World Trade Organization (WTO) in 2001, which was the landmark for China. The contribution of export to China's economic growth is significant. Net export alone has accounted for 6 to 12 percent of China's GDP between 2002 and 2008. The overall contribution of export to GDP ranges from 11 percent to 19 percent (Lin and Li 2003; Shen and Wu 2003; Li 2003; Lu and Xu 2005; Fan, Mao, and Wang 2005). The contribution of export to China's GDP growth was 41 percent. Export grew by 42 percent in the first half of 2010 and still continuing despite of the COVID-19 epidemic.

The proportion of China's exports in global trade increased from less than 2 percent in 1978 to about 13 percent in 2015. Joining the WTO allowed

China to fully capitalize its large labor supply by offering the opportunities to the foreign companies to produce cheaply. That has created persistent current account surplus and a faster growth of corporate income and government revenue, as wage rates are suppressed. Enterprises have reinvested their profits. The government has spent a large proportion of its revenue on capital formation both in China and abroad and to sustain its public sector enterprises.

Foreign firms became more significant forces in China. Apple's suppliers (most noticeably the Taiwanese company Faxconn) alone created 1.9 billion dollars surplus for China in 2007 (Xing 2010). Labor is the most important input in processing trade production; foreign companies engage in processing trade in China to use the low wages due to China's abundant labor supply.

During the initial period of the reform, industrialization was mainly conducted by the township and village enterprises (TVEs). In recent years, industrialization has been mostly due to exports. About 90 percent of China's export comes from the nine coastal provinces. The countryside still has a labor force of 468 million, 45 percent of the national total. That creates a depressive situation for the wage rates of rural workers. Because wage rates do not increase the share of labor income in GDP declines. As a result, the share of consumption in GDP declines (Bai and Qian 2009). Between 1991 and 2009, labor productivity in the manufacturing sector grew by 12.3 percent per annum (Lu 2010), but the wage rate grew only by 7.1 percent per annum.

China became the assembly center, and the surrounding countries became suppliers of materials and intermediate goods. The changes brought by the Asian financial crisis have helped this process. The massive devaluation of China in 1994 caused the Asian financial crisis of 1998 by converting the East Asian countries from exporters of final goods to exporters of natural resources and semi-finished products.

CHINA'S 40 YEARS OF REFORM AND DEVELOPMENT: 1978–2018

The Initial Stage (1978–1991)

Reforms in the first period included administrative decentralization of trade planning, foreign exchange retention for exporters, the foreign trade contract responsibility system for foreign companies, exchange rate devaluation, and other measures that reduced the obstacle toward exports. The fundamental objective of these reforms was to support China's drive toward export growth.

Each province was permitted to create its own trade agencies and corporations to promote its products in the foreign markets. In July 1979, foreign-funded enterprises were allowed to import raw materials and capital goods for their production of products, which they had to export. A number of special economic zones, 29 provinces, autonomous regions and municipalities, and the cities of Guangzhou, Dalian, Wuhan, Xian, Shenyang, Harbin, Chongqing, Qingdao, and Hainan Island were also allowed to have ports to promote foreign trade.

The number of export trade-oriented companies increased from 12 in 1978 to about 1,200 in 1986, reaching a peak of 5,075 in 1988. From 1985 to 1989, reform reduced administrative controls and gradually removed the government from trade management (Koves and Marer 1991). It simultaneously sought to promote exports via incentives, while keeping significant protection for domestic products; this was similar to that of South Korea's export-led strategy.

The Second Stage (1992–2000)

Since 1992, China has taken some important steps to gradually reduce its tariff and nontariff barriers like import quotas. In January 1993, it was officially announced that all import substitution lists would be abolished.

The third stage: Post-WTO accession in 2001

After joining the WTO, China has implemented its commitments in various ways.

Regulations and Laws

All enterprises in China have rights to trade, except those covering a small number of products in which state monopolies remain: grain, cotton and other agricultural products, coal, metal minerals, crude oil, and refined oil.

Tariffs

Tariff rates for all taxable items have been reduced. The average tariff rate for most favored nations (MFNs) dropped from 15.6 percent in 2001 to 9.7 percent in 2005 and from 14.3 percent to 8.9 percent for manufactured goods. Tariff rates for automobiles and spare parts and textiles and clothing were reduced by almost half, while those for agricultural products fell from 23.2 percent to 14.6 percent. In January 2005, the tariff rates for all information and technology products were reduced to zero from the pre-WTO accession level of 13.3 percent.

Nontariff Barriers

After WTO accession, China began to phase out import licenses and quotas and specific bidding requirements, all of which had been removed by January 1, 2005.

Trade-Related Investment Measures

For consistency with the Agreement on Trade-Related Investment Measures (TRIMs), trade and foreign exchange balances and local content and export performance requirements in foreign capital laws and regulations have been cancelled.

Trade-Related Intellectual Property Rights

For consistency with the WTO Agreement on Trade-Related Aspects of Intellectual Property Rights (TRIPS), China's copyright, trademark, and patent laws were amended in 2001 to ensure national and MFN treatment for foreigners was consistent with the TRIPS agreement.

Trade in Services

China has opened more than 100 of the 160-plus sectors and 9 of the 12 main categories in the General Agreement on Trade in Services (GATS) list. China has abolished the requirements relating to local content, export performance, technology transfer, and research and development for those sectors in which it had made liberalization commitments.

Trade disputes and friction between China and its main trading partners have become increasingly disruptive. By the end of 2016, China was the subject of 866 antidumping measures—the highest number in the world. India has initiated the most antidumping measures against China, followed by the United States and the European Union. In China, SOEs still receive

Table 6.1. Structural Change of Exports by Technology: China and the World (Percent)

	1985	*1990*	*1995*	*2000*	*2005*	*2010*	*2016*
Low Tech							
China	17.0	40.2	46.4	41.2	15.9	29.3	30.9
World	14.1	16.6	16.7	14.7	9.7	13.0	14.5
Medium Tech							
China	4.9	20.8	18.9	19.6	23.0	24.0	24.5
World	32.4	33.5	32.6	29.6	26.8	27.6	29.7
High Tech							
China	2.1	5.3	13.0	22.4	41.0	34.9	32.6
World	13.3	15.6	19.6	23.0	18.6	19.6	21.3
Others							
China	76.1	31.6	21.1	16.1	19.9	11.4	11.3
World	37.5	31.1	27.3	27.6	44.6	33.9	27.7

Source: Calculated from UN Comtrade database.

various central and local government financial subsidies, investment and tax subsidies, which can discriminate against imported goods and foreign enterprises. Industrial policies for some sectors, particularly automobiles and steel, created trade and investment barriers. The antitrust law is used to implement industrial policies.

The Performance of China's Trade

Before 1998, SOEs dominated China's export growth. After 1998, private enterprises and foreign companies in the SEZ have gained more importance. Most of China's exports are of low-quality goods, and these became obvious after China's accession to the WTO.

China rapidly secured a huge market share in processing trade, which is dominated by mechanical and electrical products and medical supplies. Due to the aggressive policy of Xi administration, external market environment continues to deteriorate, with increasing trade friction between China and its major trading partners and emerging markets.

Foreign Direct Investment (FDI) in China

China's trade and investment reforms and incentives led to a surge in FDI since the early 1990s, which had stimulated China's productivity gains and rapid economic and trade growth. Foreign-invested enterprises (FIEs) now contribute an important share of China's industrial output and China's foreign trade. FIEs contributed 58.3 percent of Chinese exports in 2005 and 59.7 percent of imports; these were declined to 41.7 percent and 43.7 percent, respectively, in 2018.

China's FDI inflows in 2018 were $139 billion, making it the world's second largest recipient of FDI after the United States, to enhance China's efforts to obtain advanced technology and other strategic assets. However, at the same time, China was the world's second largest source of FDI outflows, after Japan. Chinese government uses FDI to gain access to IPR, technology, know-how, famous brands, and so on, in order to move Chinese firms up the value-added chain in manufacturing and services and help Chinese firms to become major global competitors. Chinese overseas FDI expands business opportunities beyond the China market. In 2018, Chinese nonfinancial FDI in BRI countries totaled $15.6 billion. The largest foreign investors in China (based on FDI stock through 2017) were Hong Kong (52.6 percent of total), the British Virgin Islands (10.6 percent), Japan (6.1 percent), Singapore (4.0 percent), and Germany (3.2 percent).

Problems with Chinese investment are the same as any other capitalist enterprises: these are in profit, not human needs or the environment

Table 6.2. Sources of China's FDI Inflows to China: 1979–2017

	($ billions and percentage of total)	
	Estimated Cumulative Utilized FDI: 1979–2017	
Country	*Amount*	*% of Total*
Total	2,688	100
Hong Kong	1,241	46.2
British Virgin Islands	286	10.6
Japan	165	6.1
Singapore	108	4.0
Germany	87	3.2
South Korea	73	2.7
United States	72	2.7
Cayman Islands	49	1.8
The Netherlands	37	1.4
Taiwan	33	1.2

Source: IMF Coordinated Direct Investment Survey.

Table 6.3. U.S.–China Goods Trade and Job Displacement, 2001–2017

	2001	*2008*	*2017*
U.S. goods trade with China ($ billions, nominal)			
U.S. total exports*	$19.2	$71.5	$130.4
U.S. general imports	$102.3	$337.8	$505.6
U.S. trade balance	–$83.0	–$266.3	–$375.2
U.S. trade-related jobs supported and displaced (thousands of jobs)			
U.S. total exports—jobs supported	179.2	564.2	959.1
U.S. general imports—jobs displaced	1,170.7	3,616.9	5,311.3
U.S. trade deficit—net jobs displaced	991.5	3,052.7	4,352.2

Source: U.S. Census Bureau 2013, U.S. International Trade Commission 2018, Bureau of Labor Statistics.

(see Table 6.2). Regulatory laws in China are to protect corporate interests. China is now an imperial power, deliberately pursuing "debt-trap diplomacy."

A significant factor behind China's drive for more outward FDI flows is to obtain technology and natural resources, such as oil and minerals, necessary to support China's rapid economic growth. For example, in April 2005, Lenovo Group Limited, a Chinese computer company, purchased IBM Corporation's personal computer division for $1.75 billion. The largest destinations of cumulative Chinese FDI outflows through 2017 were Hong Kong (54.2 percent of total), the Cayman Islands (13.9 percent), the British Virgin Islands (6.7 percent), and the United States (3.7 percent).

A significant level of Chinese FDI that goes to Hong Kong, the British Virgin Islands, and the Cayman Islands likely is for redirection elsewhere.

According to the China Global Investment Tracker (CGIT) total Chinese outward nonbond outward investment from 2005 to 2017 included the United States ($172.7 billion), Australia ($103.7 billion), the United Kingdom ($75 billion), Brazil ($61.2 billion), and Russia ($53.8).

WTO and China

The WTO was created out of General Agreements on Tariffs and Trade (GATT), which was created in turn with the spirit of International Trade Organization (ITO) but far away from its original objectives. The ITO was designed after the Second World War with the objectives of creating conditions for full employment by reducing tariffs, with workers' rights, promoting competition, helping the developing countries with capital and technology, and promoting trade. The WTO has other objectives: to implements the trade negotiations of the Uruguay Round (1986–1994) among the member countries and further negotiations on trade, agricultural, manufactured goods, the services sector, and investment to implement "Washington Consensus" of the IMF, World Bank, and the U.S. Treasury. The WTO works for a global economic policy of total free trade and free market system all over the world (Stichele 1997).

Since the end of the Uruguay Round, developed countries and China have refused consistently to deliver on their reciprocal response to the developing countries. As a result, the multilateral trading system is full of double standards that favor the business interests of the developed countries and China undermining the economic and social development requirements of the developing countries. Doha declaration in 2001 provided an opportunity for the WTO and the developed countries to demonstrate that they are serious about poverty reduction. The developed countries should have addressed the incomplete agendas of the Uruguay Round rather than expanding the WTO agenda to include new issues on investment, patent laws, and competition policy. However, the Doha declaration failed because the developed countries have not changed their attitude. Bali declaration of 2014 was a total victory for the developed countries. Although the declaration was opposed by some of the developing countries but their objections were ignored. Hypocrisy and double standards in the WTO have prevailed over the concern for poorer countries. This has undermined the efforts of poorer countries to apply trade for development. It threatens the credibility of the multilateral trading system as designed by the WTO, where privatization and market system dominate.

The agreements on trade in goods are as follows:

- Reductions of tariff and removal of restrictions on imports of industrial products;

- Reductions of restrictions on imports of textile and clothing in the industrialized countries;
- Reforms of marketing and subsidies in agriculture and government export subsidies;
- Removals of restriction on investment measures (TRIMs);
- Removals of subsidies safeguard measures, by which a country can restrict imports saying a related industry is in danger of unemployment, and anti-dumping measures.

The agreements on trade in services (GATS) are as follows:

- Transparency or making information on laws that concern services easily comprehensible and freely available;
- Foreign companies can have equal access in the service sectors.

The agreement on TRIPs is as follows:

- Copyrights, trademarks, industrial designs, patents and trade secrets of a member country must be respected in all WTO member countries.

WTO Protocol

Section 9 of WTO Protocol of Accession made it clear that the member countries "shall allow prices for traded goods and services in every sector to be determined by market forces, and multi-tier pricing practices for such goods and services shall be eliminated."

Prices in every sector must be determined by market forces. All subsidies to be notified to the WTO and prohibited subsidies to be eliminated. Under Section 15 of WTO Accession Protocol, member countries have the obligation to notify to the WTO any subsidy granted or maintained.

State-owned enterprises (SOEs) will operate free of state influence. Under Section 6 of WTO Accession Protocol, and Article XVII GATT 1994, member countries agreed that these SOEs enterprises would make purchase and sales involving imports or exports based solely on commercial considerations such as price, quality, marketability, and availability.

WTO rules suggest that except as otherwise provided for in the protocol, foreign individuals and enterprises shall be accorded equal treatment that accorded to domestic individuals and enterprises in respect of the procurement of inputs and goods and services necessary. All member countries agreed to join the *Government Procurement Agreement (GPA)* following accession to the WTO.

Member countries of the WTO agreed to repeal or revise all laws, regulations, and other measures inconsistent with the GATT MFN and National Treatment rules, with regard to all other WTO members. According to the WTO rules, all member countries should harmonize in conformity with the Technical Barriers to Trade (TBT) agreement and all technical regulations, standards, and conformity assessment procedures. All member countries of the WTO had agreed to remove all trade barriers to open the domestic market to foreign or private companies.

China and the United States: Effects of China's Entry to the WTO

China entered the WTO in 2001. Conservatives all over the world supported that expecting that they can control China and China will be a democratic country. However, the results are totally opposite. The reports of Scott and his associates of the Economic Policy Institute explained the effects of massive trade deficits of the United States with respect to China and its contribution on the unemployment situation in the United States (Scott 2013; Scott and Wething 2012; Kimball and Scott 2014).

Because imports from China have increased while exports to China have not increased much less, the United States is both losing jobs in manufacturing (in particular electronics and high tech, apparel, textiles, and a range of heavier durable goods industries) and missing opportunities to add jobs in manufacturing productions (in export-oriented industries such as transportation equipment, agricultural products, computer and electronic parts, chemicals, machinery, and food and beverages) (Scott 2017a; Scott and Glass 2016; Bivens 2008a, 2008b, 2013).

The growth of the U.S. trade deficit with China between 2001 and 2017 was responsible for the loss of 3.4 million U.S. jobs, including 1.3 million jobs lost since 2008 (the first full year of the Great Recession, which technically began at the end of 2007). Nearly three-fourths (74.4 percent) of the jobs lost between 2001 and 2017 were in manufacturing (2.5 million manufacturing jobs lost). The trade deficit in the computer and electronic parts industry grew the most: 1,209,000 jobs were lost in that industry, accounting for 36 percent of the 2001–2017 total jobs lost. Surging imports of steel, aluminum, and other capital-intensive products threaten hundreds of thousands of jobs in key industries such as primary metals, machinery, and fabricated metal products as well (Scott 2017b) (see Table 6.3).

Global trade in advanced technology products, often discussed as a source of comparative advantage for the United States, is instead dominated by China. In 2017, the United States had a $135.4 billion trade deficit in advanced technology products with China, and this deficit was responsible for 36.1 percent of the total U.S.–China goods trade deficit that year. In contrast, the United States had a $24.5 billion trade surplus in advanced technology products with the rest of the world in 2017. Between 2001 and 2011 alone, growing trade deficits with China reduced the incomes of directly impacted workers by $37 billion per year, and in 2011 alone, growing competition with imports from China and other low-wage countries reduced the wages of all U.S. noncollege graduates by a total of $180 billion (Nölke et al. 2019).

China has aggressively sought to obtain technology from American companies and undermine American innovation and creativity. China's intellectual property theft costs U.S. innovators billions of dollars a year, and China accounts for 87 percent of counterfeit goods seized coming into the United States. China's counterfeit fashion goods undermine seriously famous brand names of Italy and France.

United States Trade Representative's (USTR's) Section 301 investigation identified four of China's aggressive technology policies that put 44 million American technology jobs at risk. The examples are: forced technology transfer; requirements of licensing at less than economic value; Chinese state-directed acquisition of sensitive U.S. technology for strategic purposes; and outright cyber theft. China uses foreign ownership restrictions, administrative review, and licensing processes to force or pressure technology transfers from American companies. China requires foreign companies that access their *new energy vehicles* market to transfer core technologies and disclose development and manufacturing technology (Bivens 2013; Nölke et al. 2019).

The Conflict over Chinese Steel Exports

The Dispute Settlement Body (DSB) confirmed violations of the WTO's anti-dumping and anti-subsidy rules on the part of Chinese producers and the Chinese government. Chinese industrial policy suggests a rejection of not only the ways in which existing WTO rules are applied but also the validity of the underlying idea that fair competition is primarily based on market principles.

China joined with the status of a so-called *non-market economy* (NME). This status lowered the threshold for determining illegitimate state support and hence will allow the application of antidumping and anti-subsidy measures against Chinese steel exports. China's accession protocol mandated the expiration of its NME status on December 11, 2016 (Article 15); however any country, which still consider China as a NME country, can impose measures to control Chinese exports as India did recently (USTR 2016a).

Chinese trade officials dispute the existence of illegal subsidization and defend the continuation of state support in the steel sector and elsewhere in the economy as WTO compatible (Ministry of Commerce of China,

MOFCOM 2016a). They denounce the decision of trading partners in India, Europe and the Americas to allow antidumping proceedings against imports from China. However, India, Europe, and the United States argue that domestic prices in China are artificially low because of widespread subsidies and preferential treatment.

From the 1980s onward, the Chinese steel industry served as an important object of state intervention (ten Brink 2019). Assistance came in the form of direct monetary supports and low-interest loans from banks or the supply of goods and services like water, electricity, land, transportation, and other production factors at nominal prices from other state-affiliated units. China does not respect the relevant WTO rules on antidumping and anti-subsidies, since doing so would make the steel industry unviable. "Belt and Road Initiative" was created to support the steel industry in a substantial way.

Chinese Subsidies in Agriculture

Agriculture was the core issue in the Doha Development Round, and there are many conflicting issues. Traditionally, developing countries have put pressure on Western nations to liberalize their agricultural sector and to revise existing rules on agricultural subsidies accordingly (Narlikar 2019). China introduced its own subsidy schemes (Hopewell 2019). Chinese subsidies, including seed subsidies, direct payments, and agricultural input subsidies, increased from RMB 14.5 billion in 2004 to RMB 167.5 billion in 2014 (Li 2017). In response, the United States objected to the WTO against China in September 2016, claiming that in 2015 Chinese subsidies were nearly US$ 100 billion above WTO-permissible levels (USTR 2016a).

The conflict over agricultural subsidies potentially undermines fair competition among trading partners. However, when the GATT, the WTO's predecessor, was created in 1947, the United States, Australia, Canada, and their European partners put in place a protectionist regime that was according to their domestic requirement and included the provision of subsidies to protect their small-scale farmers.

The level of domestic support that China is allowed in its WTO treaty allows for subsidies of up to 8.5 percent of the value of production for China's farmers. This level of subsidies falls in between the suggested subsidies for developed country members (5 percent) and developing country members (10 percent). Chinese policy makers claim that China should be granted subsidy levels higher than the current threshold, because the existing rules on subsidies are biased toward developed countries. China is not entitled to use the special agriculture safeguard to protect domestic producers. Legitimacy of domestic support measures should correspond to the country's stage of economic development (Zhong 2016). This differs from subsidies to large farms and agribusinesses provided in the United States and EU and should thus be considered a legitimate exemption (MOFCOM 2016a,b). The United States and other developed countries argued that China being "the world's second largest economy" (USTR 2016b) cannot claim "developing country" status.

Chinese policy makers have relied on agricultural subsidies to achieve social goals, a practice that is common in Western nations as well. China remains a net food importer, and its competitiveness remains rather low regarding most agricultural products. The agricultural support is seen as necessary for employment, poverty alleviation, and development. Arable land is scarce in China and farms are often in hilly, mountainous areas. This is reflected in the small average size of farms.

Liberalization is risky given the fear of unemployment in rural areas (Wang 2013). In fact, large parts of China's population continue to depend on subsistence farming. Agriculture remains highly protected in Western nations (Scott 2017a). In contrast to the highly commercialized forms of agricultural production in the EU and United States, the setup of the Chinese agricultural sector requires different requirements regarding subsidies.

CHINA'S IT SECTOR: SELECTIVE SUPPORT FOR THE WTO'S LIBERAL TRADE ORDER

The IT industry includes both companies involved in the production of IT-related goods, such as semiconductors, computer hardware, or communications equipment, and those providing consulting and IT services. Chinese policy makers advanced an argument similar to the one they used with respect to agriculture: China is a developing country. Chinese IT industry has long been dominated by foreign (East Asian and Western) companies and is thus characterized by a profound integration into global production and supply chains. Export-oriented domestic firms already benefitted significantly from the original ITA agreement, which China joined in 2003. In 2004, China turned into the world's largest exporter of ITA products. The prospects for China to benefit from the extended ITA agreement are very high, and consequently, the state has a strong interest in liberalization. More than 60 percent of IT products are produced by export-oriented enterprises in zones that attract foreign R&D centers. The overall success of export-oriented firms, in turn, led Chinese officials to prefer tariff cuts (USTR 2018).

The United States has objected to Chinese regulation, 2017 Cyber Security Law, as incompatible with WTO commitments (USTR 2017). It is difficult for foreign firms to enter the Chinese e-commerce market. In addition, the

CCP retains direct influence over key firms. China bends existing WTO rules to justify alleged cases of rule breaking and is questioning the validity of the prevailing liberal compromise. China does not support the WTO's liberal trade order but wants to use WTO for its benefit (Hopewell 2019; Narlikar 2019; Nölke et al. 2019; Stephen and Parízek 2019; Wu 2016).

The U.S. Trade Deficit with China since China Entered the WTO

Imports from China increased dramatically in this period, rising from $102.3 billion in 2001 to $505.6 billion in 2017. U.S. exports to China rose at a rapid rate from 2001 to 2017 but from $19.2 billion in 2001 to $130.4 billion in 2017. As a result, China's exports to the United States in 2017 ("U.S. general imports") were nearly four times greater than U.S. exports to China (USTR 2018, 2019).

Overall, the U.S. goods trade deficit with China grew from $83 billion in 2001 to $375.2 billion in 2017, an increase of $292.2 billion. Since China entered the WTO in 2001, the U.S. trade deficit with China has increased annually by $18.3 billion, or 9.9 percent, on average. The data reveal that the cumulative U.S. trade deficit with China over the 2002–2017 era was $4.2 trillion (USTR 2018, 2019).

Between 2008 and 2017, the U.S. goods trade deficit with China increased $108.9 billion. This 40.9 percent increase occurred despite the Great Recession-induced collapse in world trade between 2008 and 2009 and the 23.4 percent decline in the U.S. trade deficit with the rest of the world between 2008 and 2017. As a result, China's share of the overall U.S. goods trade deficit increased from 32.2 percent in 2008 to 46.5 percent in 2017 (USITC 2018 and U.S. Census Bureau 2018).

China and the U.S. Job Losses

Each $1 billion in exports to another country from the United States supports some American jobs. However, each $1 billion in imports from another country leads to job loss—by eliminating existing jobs and preventing new job creation—as imports displace goods that otherwise would have been made in the United States by domestic workers. The net employment effect of trade depends on the changes in the trade balance. An improving trade balance can support job creation, but a growing trade deficit usually results in growing net U.S. job displacement.

The employment impacts of the growing U.S. trade deficit with China are estimated by the Economic Policy Institute, using an input-output model that estimates the direct and indirect labor requirements of producing output in a given domestic industry. The model includes 205 U.S. industries, 76 of which are in the manufacturing sector (Scott 2017a, 2017b; Scott and Glas 2016).

The Economic Policy Institute has examined the job impacts of trade in recent years by subtracting the job opportunities lost to imports from those gained through exports through a model that estimates the amount of labor (number of jobs) required to produce a given volume of exports and the labor displaced when a given volume of imports is substituted for domestic output. The difference between these two numbers is essentially the jobs displaced by the growing trade deficit, holding all else equal (Scott 2017a).

Therefore, the $83 billion trade deficit in 2001 displaced 991,500 jobs in that year. Net job displacement rose to 3,052,700 jobs in 2008 and 4,352,200 jobs in 2017. As a result, since China's entry into the WTO in 2001 and through 2017, the increase in the U.S.–China trade deficit eliminated or displaced 3,360,600 U.S. jobs. Also shown in table 6.1, the U.S. trade deficit with China increased by $108.9 billion (or 40.9 percent) between 2008 and 2017. During that period, the number of jobs displaced increased by 1,299,400 (or 42.6 percent). For comparative purposes, the growth of the U.S.–China trade deficit between 2001 and 2017 represents a direct loss of 1.5 percent of U.S. GDP in 2017. Total jobs lost or displaced between 2008 and 2017 alone amounted to 1,299,400, either by the elimination of existing jobs or by the prevention of new job creation through the displacement of domestic production by imports (Scott 2017a, 2017b; Scott and Glass 2016).

The growth in manufactured goods imports explained virtually all (99.4 percent) of total growth in imports from China between 2001 and 2017 and included a wide array of products. Computer and electronic parts were responsible for 39.7 percent of the growth in imports in this period, including computer equipment ($50.4 billion, or 12.5 percent of the overall growth in imports) and communications, audio, and video equipment ($81.3 billion, or 20.2 percent). Other major importing sectors included electrical equipment ($34.2 billion, or 8.5 percent), machinery ($30.5 billion, or 7.6 percent), apparel ($20.7 billion, or 5.1 percent), and miscellaneous manufactured commodities ($29.3 billion, or 7.3 percent) (Scott 2017a, 2017b; Scott and Glass 2016)

Other hard-hit industries include apparel (169,000 jobs displaced, equal to 5 percent of the total), electrical equipment, appliances, and components (145,300 jobs, or 4.3 percent), fabricated metal products (144,100 jobs, or 4.3 percent), furniture and related products (135,200 jobs, or 4 percent), miscellaneous manufactured commodities (126,600 jobs, or 3.8 percent), textile mills and textile product mills (119,100 jobs, or 3.5 percent), plastics and rubber products (78,700 jobs, or 2.3 percent), and motor vehicles and motor vehicle parts (44,700 jobs, or 1.3 percent). In addition, surging imports of steel, aluminum, and other capital-intensive products threaten hundreds of thousands of jobs in key metal-using industries such as primary metals, machinery, and fabricated metal products (Scott 2017a, 2017b; Scott and Glass 2016).

Between December 2001 and December 2017, 3.2 million U.S. manufacturing jobs were lost. The growth of the U.S. trade deficit with China was responsible for the displacement of 2.5 million manufacturing jobs in this period, or about 78.1 percent of manufacturing jobs lost (USTR 2016b, 2018, 2019).

Thus, manufacturing job loss due to the growing trade deficit with China accounts for roughly four out of five U.S. manufacturing jobs lost or displaced in this period. Even if macroeconomic policy is adjusted to offset the negative impact of the growing trade deficit with China on total employment, the structure of production and employment in the United States has been negatively affected (Scott 2017a, 2017b; Scott and Glass 2016).

The growing U.S. goods trade deficit with China has displaced millions of jobs in the United States and has contributed heavily to the crisis in U.S. manufacturing employment, which has heightened over the last decade largely due to trade with China. Moreover, the United States is piling up foreign debt, losing export capacity, and facing a more fragile macroeconomic environment (USTR 2016b, 2018, 2019).

The growing U.S. trade deficit with China has eliminated 3.4 million U.S. jobs between 2001 and 2017, including 1.3 million jobs lost since 2008 (the first full year of the Great Recession). Nearly three-fourths of the jobs lost were in manufacturing. These losses were responsible for a substantial share of the 3.2 million U.S. manufacturing jobs lost between December 2001 and December 2017. The growing trade deficit with China has reduced wages of those directly displaced by $37 billion through 2011 alone, and it is largely responsible for the loss of nearly $2,000 per worker per year, due to wage suppression, for all non-college-educated workers in the United States (USTR 2016b, 2018, 2019; Scott 2017a, 2017b; Scott and Glass 2016).

Currency Manipulation

A major cause of the rapidly growing U.S. trade deficit with China is currency manipulation. Unlike other currencies, the Chinese yuan does not fluctuate freely against the dollar. While the value of its currency should have increased as China exported more and more goods, it has instead remained artificially low, and China has aggressively acquired dollars to further depress the value of its own currency. China has tightly pegged its currency to the U.S. dollar at a rate that encourages a large bilateral surplus with the United States. China had to purchase $453 billion in U.S. treasury bills and other securities between December 2008 and December 2009, alone, to maintain this peg.

China has acquired a total of $2.4 trillion in foreign exchange reserves as of December 2009. About 70 percent of these reserves are held in U.S. dollars (Hopewell 2019; Nölke et al. 2019).

This intervention makes the yuan artificially cheap relative to the dollar, effectively subsidizing Chinese exports. The best estimates place this effective subsidy at roughly 40 percent of the U.S. dollar, even after recent appreciation in the yuan. Currency intervention also artificially raises the cost of U.S. exports to China by a similar amount, making U.S. goods less competitive in China (Davies 2018). It is not new as China caused the Asian financial crisis in 1998 through a massive devaluation in 1994, but IMF-World Bank refused to blame China but blamed "crony capitalism" in East Asian countries. IMF-World Bank in 1998 behaved like the WHO today, which also shielded China from any criticism regarding the spread of COVID-19.

Other policies by the Chinese government also encourage exports. China extensively suppresses labor rights, which lowers production costs within China. An AFL-CIO study estimated that repression of labor rights by the Chinese government has lowered manufacturing wages of Chinese workers by 47 percent to 86 percent (AFL-CIO 2006).

China has provided massive direct subsidization of export production in many key industries. Finally, it maintains strict, nontariff barriers to imports. As a result, China's exports to the United States of $337.5 billion in 2008 were more than five times greater than U.S. exports to China, which totaled only $67.2 billion. China's trade surplus was responsible for 68.5 percent of the U.S. total nonoil trade deficit in 2008, making the China trade relationship this country's most imbalanced and disastrous by far (Nölke, et al 2019; Stephen and Parízek 2019).

The main point of conflict between the United States and China is over China's state-subsidized efforts to conquer new market and new technologies. According to Rodrik (2012, 2016), the Trump administration does not have a coherent trade policy or a systematic approach to reforming the international trade regime; its approach is purely unilateralist and mercantilist.

The Doha Round launched in 2001 was ignored in 2015 due to serious disagreements among the United States, Europe, and the rising developing countries like India and China. China's entry into the WTO in 2001 had a surge of exports that contributed to the loss of well-paid manufacturing jobs in the United States, Europe, and elsewhere in the world that has fueled a backlash against globalization. President Trump taken out his country out of the Trans-Pacific Partnership (TPP) trade deal and launched a series of tariff protection measures particularly against China.

It is an acceptable practice in the WTO rules on agriculture where the practice of dumping, or the sale of items at prices below the cost of production, is allowed. Developed countries are also allowed to use export subsidies.

WTO Protocol

Section 9 of WTO Protocol of Accession made it clear that the member countries "shall allow prices for traded goods and services in every sector to be determined by market forces, and multi-tier pricing practices for such goods and services shall be eliminated."

Prices in every sector must be determined by market forces. All subsidies to be notified to the WTO and prohibited subsidies to be eliminated. Under Section 15 of WTO Accession Protocol, member countries have the obligation to notify to the WTO any subsidy granted or maintained.

SOEs will operate free of state influence. Under Section 6 of WTO Accession Protocol, and Article XVII GATT 1994, member countries agreed that these SOEs would make purchase and sales involving imports or exports based solely on commercial considerations such as price, quality, marketability, and availability.

WTO rules suggest that except as otherwise provided for in the protocol, foreign individuals and enterprises shall be accorded equal treatment that accorded to domestic individuals and enterprises in respect of the procurement of inputs and goods and services necessary. All member countries agreed to join the GPA following accession to the WTO.

Member countries of the WTO agreed to repeal or revise all laws, regulations, and other measures inconsistent with the GATT MFN and National Treatment rules, with regard to all other WTO members.

According to the WTO rules, all member countries should harmonize in conformity with the TBT agreement, all technical regulations, standards, and conformity assessment procedures.

All member countries of the WTO had agreed to remove all trade barriers to open the domestic market to foreign or private companies.

A Membership That Pays Off

The United States, China, and Germany are the countries that benefit the most worldwide from their accession to the WTO. For the United States, income gains amount to about 87 billion U.S. dollars (measured in gross domestic product, GDP). The Chinese generate income gains of about 86 billion U.S. dollars and the Germans about 66 billion U.S. dollars. These are the results of a recent study commissioned by the Bertelsmann Stiftung, which calculated the wealth effects of WTO membership for 180 countries worldwide, including all 164 member states.

The whole of the WTO membership achieved a total increase in prosperity of around 855 billion U.S. dollars. EU members benefit together with 232 billion and OECD countries with a total of 480 billion U.S. dollars. But the success story also has its downsides: Countries that are not members of the WTO are losing out due to the greater economic integration of WTO members. According to the analysis, nations with strong exports and production are the main beneficiaries of membership. This is true not only for Germany and South Korea (around US$31 billion in GDP growths), as industrial and innovation locations, but also for Mexico (around US$58 billion in GDP growths) and China.

China and the WTO

China became a member of the WTO in the middle of this process, in December 2001. With its WTO entry, textile exports of China were subject to immediate quota removals on product groups that would have been liberalized between 1995 and 2002 (the first three phases of quota removals), while the remaining product groups would be liberalized in 2005. Therefore, in 2002 and 2005, India was faced with the removal of import quota not only on their own exports but also on Chinese exports. Thus, India lost its import quota and it has to face competition on its export markets from China. Due to the dismantling of the MFA, increased Chinese export competition was particularly significant in the textiles sector. Between 2000 and 2005, China's share of U.S. and EU textiles imports doubled (increased by 5123 percent in the United States and by 98 percent in the EU). In 2013, China accounted for 29 percent of global textile exports. Confidence on the WTO is undermined due to its failure to control trade practices of China. WTO is complicit on China. That caused suspicions on the effectiveness of the WTO.

According to the World Bank, global wealth increased by nearly two-thirds from 1995 to 2014, to more than $1.1 trillion. The share going to middle-income countries such as China and India grew from 19 percent to 28 percent, while the advanced economies of the West saw their share fall from 75 percent to 65 percent. The global great convergence, however, coincided with a great divergence within the wealthy countries and many developing countries as well. American companies have enormous choice—workers who demand more wages can be replaced, either by cheaper workers in some developing countries or by robots at home. In the two advanced economies, the United States and the United Kingdom, inequalities are the gravest and public backlash against globalization is also greatest.

Since it has joined the WTO, China has gained maximum economic advantage but it has no respects for the rules and obligations of WTO membership.

It has heavily subsidized industry after industry, used discriminatory regulations to disadvantage foreign companies and favor its own national champions, and engaged in a broad campaign of technology acquisition by forcing foreign investors to share technology with Chinese competitors. For many years it devalued and kept the exchange rate of yuan low, to gain competitive advantage. These are the issues that have caused trade dispute between the United States and China. China is spending more on its state industries, trying to control foreign multinational companies, and using debt as a control mechanism for smaller countries that took loans from China. The tariffs against China are far more popular in the United States. There is little confidence that that U.S. sanctions and bilateral pressure will produce changes in Chinese behavior.

China: A "Rule Shaker" or a "Rule Maker"?

The West's open invitation for China to join the WTO in 2001 paved the way for its rise to a global economic power. Since then, the balance of power at the WTO has changed dramatically. Chinese outward investment in the global economy has increased thirtyfold, from $7 billion (making up only 1 percent of the global FDI) to almost $200 billion (13 percent of the global FDI).

China entered the WTO as a "rule taker," evolved into a "rule shaker," and now aims to become a "rule maker." In fact, economic relations between China, the United States, and the EU define many of the agreements and disputes at the WTO. Xi Jinping's "China Dream" of national rejuvenation could be seen as a way to reshape the international economic system, putting China at the center. Initial optimism that China would turn toward a free market economy has yet to be fulfilled. With the existing WTO rulebook, it is difficult to hold China accountable. Due to high trade deficits, the United States is pushing for WTO reforms, increasing tariffs, and blocking the nominations of seats on the WTO's appellate body (where the United States is a major player in the dispute resolution process) as leverage. Desired reforms aim to regulate market distortions caused by government interventions, simplifying the process of gathering information on unfair trade and investment practices, broadening the scope of banned subsidies, and setting boundaries to proportionate retaliations.

According to Wallach (2019), "The World Trade Organization is not mainly about *trade*. Rather the organization has the primary task of carrying out what the Harvard economist Dani Rodrik calls hyperglobalization—the worldwide imposition of one-size-fits-all rules, favored by global financial markets and three important institutions in Washington, the US Treasury, IMF and the World Bank, which restricts sovereignty of the national governments' ability to control the economy to satisfy their societies' needs."

If countries do not comply, they are subject to millions of dollars in trade penalties. Of the 242 completed WTO cases, in only 22 did the domestic policies, many unrelated to trade, survive challenged. Thus, the country-of-origin labels on meat that we relied on in American grocery stores were eliminated after the WTO classified them as "illegal trade barriers" and authorized $1 billion in sanctions. The United States was also forced to weaken regulations under the Clean Air Act, dolphin protection laws, and Endangered Species Act rules.

The United States has filed 49 challenges against other countries, with rulings against Indian policies promoting access to seeds for poor farmers and European limits on genetically modified foods and a ban on artificial growth hormones in meat. The United States has used threats to pressure Thailand, Brazil, and South Africa to reverse policies on access to AIDS medication and other lifesaving drugs. The United States won a case against a solar power program in India.

Trade negotiations have been dominated by corporate interests, while labor, consumer, and environmental groups are ignored. The WTO does not care about labor or environmental requirements, limit pollution, or about consumer safety standards. It also does not care about monopolistic megacorporations distorting global markets or China doing currency manipulations and creates unfair trade advantages. It does not care that China is not a market economy but a fascist dictatorship controlling every business organizations in the way it wants. American workers and workers in most countries do not believe in great gains from free "trade" agreements. During the WTO era, developed and developing countries have lost millions of manufacturing jobs, since China joined in 2001. Income inequality between rich and poor countries, and within countries, went up greatly (Wallach 2019).

In September 2018, the United States together with the EU and Japan expressed doubt about the future of the WTO, questioning its validity as the forum for multilateral trade. China would not accept any reforms at the WTO, or any level, as that would affect its own economic plan. China wants to preserve the existing global trade order. It is the rule that state-led economic systems are incompatible with membership in the WTO but there are pressures from China that changes in the WTO rules are necessary to accommodate countries like China.

The shift of manufacturing from both advanced and developing nations to China was very painful. Under Article 24 of the WTO, regional trade agreements are allowed and in 2019, 291 regional trade agreements were initiated. The EU, NAFTA, and ASEAN free trade agreements have been especially successful in supporting regional production. China's surplus went up significantly when China entered the WTO in 2001 because its imports increased much less faster than its exports as its domestic demands were suppressed.

Dependency of American Businesses on China

Here we have data up to 2017–2018. Contrary to the popular perception, Apple (AAPL) generates only about 17 percent of its revenue from China. Boeing (BA), Caterpillar (CAT), General Motors (GM), Starbucks (SBUX), Nike (NKE), and Ford (F) are some other U.S. companies with a strong presence in the country. However, none of them get more than 25 percent of their revenue from China (ten Brink 2019).

Topping the list is Wynn Resorts (WYNN), which operates three casinos in Macau. It also has two casinos in Las Vegas and another in Everett, Massachusetts. Wynn Resorts' Macau casinos account for 75.2 percent of its revenue. According to Tijori Finance, the Macau operations generate about 77.1 percent of its operating profits (USTR 2018)

Semiconductor giant Qualcomm (QCOM) is close behind with 66.6 percent revenue exposure. A large chunk of Qualcomm's shipments go to factories that assemble smartphones and other products. China is home to some of the world's largest smartphone vendors including Xiaomi, OnePlus, Oppo, Vivo, Lenovo, and others, most of which use Qualcomm chips in their products.

Micron Technology (MU) occupies the third spot with 57.1 percent revenue exposure to China. By comparison, the United States accounts for merely 11.9 percent of its revenue. It is one of the world's leading makers of computer data storage solutions such as USB flash drives and NAND flash memory.

Qualcomm is not the only semiconductor company in the top 10. Qorvo (QRVO) has 52 percent revenue exposure to China. It makes radio frequency systems that are used in wireless and broadband communications. Qorvo was created following the merger of TriQuint Semiconductor and RF Micro Devices (USTR 2018).

Broadcom gets close to 50 percent of its revenue from China, according to Tijori Finance. Broadcom is involved in designing, developing, and marketing semiconductor and infrastructure software products. Dallas-based technology giant Texas Instruments (TXN) is a leading manufacturer of semiconductors and a wide range of integrated circuits. It sells its products directly to electronics manufacturers, most of which are concentrated in China. About 44.3 percent of Texas Instruments' revenue comes from China alone. Oxford, Massachusetts-based IPG Photonics (IPGP) is a leading maker of fiber lasers. It doesn't have a manufacturing facility in China, but the dragon is a huge market for the company. IPG Photonics has 43.1 percent revenue exposure to China.

AMD is another chipmaker heavily exposed to the country. About 39 percent of its revenue comes from China. The Santa Clara-based company manufactures motherboard chipsets, graphics processors, and microprocessors for both consumer and enterprise markets (USTR 2018).

Veeco Instruments (VECO) makes processing systems that are used to build semiconductors, photonics, and display technologies. Its revenue exposure to China is 35.8 percent. Maxim Integrated Products (MXIM) rounds up the top 10 with 35.7 percent revenue exposure. It designs and manufactures analog and mixed-signal integrated circuits. Intel gets 26.5 percent of its revenue from China while Nvidia relies on the country for 23.9 percent of its revenue (USTR 2018).

Wall Street is the main financier of China. Companies from China and Hong Kong have raised $6.6 billion through Initial Public Offerings (IPO) in the U.S. financial market through Wall Street Banks in 2021, which is eightfold increases from the same period in 2020. The largest IPO is the $1.6 billion listing of e-cigarette maker RLX Technology Inc., followed by the $947 million offerings of the software company Tuya Inc. This is despite of the warning given by the U.S Securities and Exchange Commission that it will do financial audits of Chinese companies, which China opposes. Non-compliance could result in a delisting from the New York Stock Exchange or NASDAQ. Even then, Chinese companies raised about $15 billion through IPOs in the U.S financial market in 2020. Alibaba, the e-commerce giant, raised $25 billion in 2014.

Didi Chuxing has filed application for U.S. IPO of $100 billion in 2021. Uber-like trucking start-up Full Truck Alliance is trying on an IPO of $2 billion in 2021. Many Chinese companies do their listings in both New York and Hong Kong. Thus, Chinese financial strength is the result of the collaboration from the Wall Street Banks. It was not a surprise that they supported *CNN*, *MSNBC*, and *New York Times* to go against Trump (Vittori 2021).

WTO accession promoted the U.S. corporate investment in China. It went up and up in the first decade of the twenty-first century. For example, in 2012 Hospital Corp. of America, a company used to made walking boots, air casts, slings, and other low-end medical equipment. After China joined the WTO, this firm moved production mostly from the southeastern part of the United States to the province of Guangdong in southeastern China. The same experience was shared by many other companies of the United States. By 2015, the share of China's exports to the United States that came from foreign-owned companies was at least 60 percent.

This Chinese development strategy actually dates back to the early 1980s (Nölke et al. 2019). Its evolution over four decades is now reaching its zenith. The current China "Manufacturing 2025" policies, for example, target 10 specific industries including new advanced information technology, automated machine tools and robotics, aerospace and aeronautical equipment, maritime equipment and high-tech shipping, modern rail transport equipment, new energy vehicles and equipment, power equipment, agricultural equipment, new materials, and biopharmacy and advanced medical products. In areas such as new electric vehicles and battery technology, semiconductors, solar panels/modules, and wind power, interventions have been extensive, ongoing, and highly prominent (Autor, Dorn and Hanson 2012; Autor and Hanson 2014).

However, some companies are objecting. Honeywell in 2015 said that it was tried with China's demands for technology transfer. Executives at CISCO and Microsoft said the same. The complaints about companies like Huawei stealing intellectual property also increased. Ongoing trade negotiations in early 2019, for example, centered on Chinese state subsidies, government-directed credit (via thc state-controlled banking system), and public procurement, as well as forced technology transfer. In short, China appears to be using domestic legal, regulatory, and government interventions to favor its domestic firms. Policy makers, moreover, appear strongly committed to this type of state-controlled capitalism (Bernstein 2016).

In the European Union, like the United States, sentiment has also swung strongly against Chinese interventions. Greater reciprocity from China (i.e., market access, fewer institutional and regulatory blocks on foreign MNEs) has become a key issue, as has a strategic response from Europe. Recent EU attempts led by France and Germany, for example, to create a European champion in train-making (and engage with China using similar strategic approaches) have been launched. In early 2019 efforts were made by France and Germany to merge the train manufacturing operations of Alstom (France) and Siemens (Germany). This was a direct response to Chinese industrial support for CRRC (the biggest train maker in the world). The merger was blocked, however, by the EU's very own competition commission; thus there are enemies within (Pierceand Schott 2016; ten Brink 2019).

The Chinese legislative system, moreover, lacks transparency and favors domestic firms, particularly in some high-tech related industries such as renewable energies and robotics (Gao 2019). Many current geopolitical conflicts between China and the Unites States/EU are related to such asymmetrical industrial policies (Shi 2010.)

Chapter 7

India

Structural Adjustment Trap

The major argument of the proponents of "Economic Reform" was that the earlier planned development in India from 1951 to 1990 has restricted the growth of the Indian economy (Ahluwalia 2002; Bhagwati 1978; Dollar 1992; Dollar and Kraay 2004; Edwards 1992; Srinivasan and Bhagwati 1999). International financial institutions have long argued that a market economy will release the tiger of India caged by the restrictions of the planned regime (Balakrishnan 2000; Sen 1996). The so-called "Economic Reform Program" has started in 1991 with a lot of expectations, but after 20 years of reforms, Indian economy in 2012 was in a sorry state with declining growth rate, high inflation, and capital flights. The recent behavior of the Indian economy with rising balance of trade deficits brought back the fear of a repetition of the bankruptcy of 1992.

The Economic Survey of 2012 presented a dismal picture of the economy of India. Slowdown in growth, particularly in industry and agriculture, persisting inflation, and a volatile external environment reflected in a widening current account deficit and fluctuating rupee. India's GDP growth in 2011–2012 has been the lowest in nine years. The Indian economy was estimated to grow by 6.9 percent in 2011–2012, after having grown at the rate of 8.4 percent in each of the two preceding years.

For the purpose of analysis, we divide the whole period into two parts: (a) period of structural adjustments from 1991 to 2001 and (b) period of the reformed economy since 2001.

The period from 1991 to 2000 can be broadly defined as the period of structural adjustment, where the old structure of planned mixed economy was dismantled gradually and public sector enterprises were privatized in many extents. The period from 2000 to present can be broadly defined as a reformed economy when the balance of payments is yet not fully liberalized and there are still some public sector enterprises left to be privatized.

ECONOMIC GROWTH DURING THE STRUCTURAL ADJUSTMENTS

Economic reforms started in 1991–1992. The argument of the proponents was that the previous regime of the planned economic development in India has the result of a very slow growth of the economy, the so-called "Hindu" rate of growth. The "Reform process" was expected to bring in a new phase of rapid economic development by removing the distortions caused by restrictive government policies under the "planned" regime of 1951–1990. Let us examine what are the consequences of the "Reform Process" on economic growth. Table 7.1 gives us the comparative figures.

The overall growth rate of the gross domestic product (GDP) in the "planned regime" has not done that badly during 1980–1990 compared with the "reformed" regime during the 1990s. In fact, in the later part of the "reformed" regime from 1997 the growth rate of the economy was much worse than during the "planned" regime.

This is true in almost every area, per-head income, fixed capital formation, government consumptions, and growth rates for industry, agriculture, and the efficiency of capital. Only in service, sector and private investments did better during the "reformed" regime. In agriculture, the most important part of the economy, the performance of the "reformed" regime is the worst.

The most important argument of the supporters of the "reformed" regime that planned economy was inefficient is not supported by the facts. The incremental capital-to-output ratio (ICOR) signifies the inefficiency of capital; if it is growing the economy is getting increasingly inefficient to utilize capital.

This is what had happed in the "reformed" regime of the 1990s, where the ICOR had gone up from 3.65 during the 1980s to 4.35 during the 1990s and

Table 7.1. Comparative Economic Growths under "Planned" and "Structural Adjustment Regime" in India (Growth Rates)

	1980–1981	*1990–1991*	*1992–1993*	*1997–1998*
GDP	5.81	5.61	6.68	5.35
Per-head GDP	3.67	3.68	4.75	3.42
Investments	6.48	6.93	9.63	6.68
Fixed capital formation	6.72	6.88	8.49	6.48
Public investment	6.91	3.24	2.28	7.75
Private investment	7.60	9.01	11.68	10.98
Public consumption	6.92	9.38	4.66	12.58
Industry	6.83	5.91	7.61	4.86
Agriculture	4.61	2.83	4.64	1.23
Services	6.62	7.61	7.55	8.82
ICOR				

Source: Economic Survey (2001–2002).

Notes: ICOR = Incremental capital-to-output ratio, an index of inefficiency of capital.

to 4.47 during 1997–2000, proving exactly the opposite of what the World Bank-IMF economists and their Indian supporters have suggested.

The saving rate during the "reformed regime" was stagnant for a long time. In 1990–1991, the national saving as a percentage of the national income was 23.1; in 2000–2001, it was 23.4 percent (Government of India, Ministry of Finance, Economic Survey 2001–2007). Recently, it has gone up mainly due to the massive flows of portfolio investments, which is the most volatile element in the financial status of the country and causes high level of debt.

How India is going to pay these debt back when India's balance of payments is in chronic deficits is unknown to the government. At the same time, India has a very high level of foreign exchange reserve, signifying the inability of the Indian economy to absorb foreign capital. That is preventing rupee to go down in order to maintain India's competitiveness in the world economy. A country must devalue when it receives foreign investments; if it is unable to do that, its balance of payments will sooner or later collapse and there would be sudden outflow of money, which can destroy the economy. A situation similar to that already took place in Southeast Asia in 1998; however, India has not learned any lesson from it.

Liberalization measures have benefited a minuscule section of the society. They have encouraged growth of monopoly houses, which reflected in rapid growth of their assets. For example, assets of Tatas increased from Rs. 85,310 million in 1991 to Rs. 474,460 million in 1998–1999, that is, in just eight years. Over the same period, assets of Reliance rose from Rs. 36,000 million to Rs. 337,570 million and that of Essar rose from Rs. 7,560 million to Rs. 171,450 million. Likewise, other industrial houses also registered phenomenal growth in their assets (Standard & Poor 2001–2007).

Economic "reforms," particularly the liberalization measures, have enabled private companies to earn huge profits even during the latter half of the 1990s when industrial growth was sluggish. In the year 2000, net profits of Reliance industries, the largest private sector company, increased by 41.3 percent. Net profits of Tata Steel rose by 49.7 percent, of Grashim industries by 43.3 percent, and of Hindustan Lever by 27.8 percent. Among the top 10 private sector companies, Telco and Larsen and Toubro were the only companies that failed to register an increase in their profits in the year 2000 (Standard & Poor 2001–2007).

AGRICULTURE AND THE PUBLIC DISTRIBUTION SYSTEM

The government in a way has rendered the public distribution system (PDS) irrelevant. People are divided into two categories—those below the poverty line (BPL) and those above the poverty line (APL).

A large number of people above the poverty line are poor but the issue prices of food grains, which were fixed for them under the PDS, are either equal to the prices prevailing in the market or even higher.

For the people below the poverty line, the issue price of wheat was raised from Rs. 250 per quintal in 1997–1998 to Rs. 450 per quintal in 2000–2001. Likewise, the issue price of rice has been raised from Rs. 350 per quintal to Rs. 565 per quintal. At these increased issue prices of food grains, most of the rural poor now find it difficult to purchase their monthly quota of ration. The food subsidy has been drastically reduced, and the results are there for everyone to see. Recently, 63 million tons of food grains are lying in the warehouses of the Food Corporation of India (FCI) and yet the people are dying of starvation in the rural areas. Table 7.2 indicates that due to slow growth of agriculture along with rapid rise of population, per capita availability of cereals is nearly stagnant and the availability of pulses declined seriously since 1961.

Two major factors are responsible for the present ruination of agriculture in this country. First, in its eagerness to reduce fiscal deficit, the government has substantially reduced the development expenditure in agriculture (Chand 2002; Chand and Jha 2001). Second, import liberalization has contributed in a big way in reduction in the prices of agricultural products. Having failed in getting remunerative prices for their products, many farmers have curtailed their farm operations, which in turn have increased unemployment among the agricultural workers. Import liberalization is thus a major cause of the existing plight of the peasantry. Suicides by many farmers in the recent past reflect the consequences of the liberalization measures.

Effects of the reformed trade policy are being felt in agriculture in India. Rice farmers are getting bankrupt because their cost of production is more than the market price as rice is being imported from Thailand and Southeast Asia. Wheat price is falling. However, because of the electoral importance

Table 7.2. Difference between MSP and Market Price

Crop	*MSP*	*Average (Modal) Price*	*Average MSP*
Bajra	2,150	1,460	–690
Chana	5,100	4,182	–918
Jowar	2,620	1,728	–829
Maize	1,850	1,459	–391
Tur/Arhar	6,000	4,943	–1057
Safflower	5,327	4,010	–1317
Moong/Green Gram	7,196	7,116	–80
Urad/Black Gram	6,000	6,166	+166

Source: APMC, Ballari.

Notes: All prices are rupees per quintal.

of the wheat-growing regions, the farmers are receiving price supports and subsidies from the governments. Wheat is being imported from Australia. In future, it will be imported from the EU.

Poverty and Inequality

The economic reforms have contributed to increased poverty and economic inequality. First, we need to examine as to what has happened to incidence of poverty.

According to the National Sample Survey (NSS) in 1983, while 45.6 percent of the rural population was below the poverty line, the incidence of poverty in urban areas was around 40.8 percent. Hence, the overall incidence of poverty for the country as a whole was 44.5 percent. By 1990–1991, the incidence of poverty had declined to 35 percent in the rural areas and to 35.3 percent in the urban areas. Taking the two sectors together, the incidence of poverty was 35.1 percent. This implies that during the 1980s the increase in growth rate, coupled with the poverty alleviation program, led to a significant decline in the spread of poverty. This trend was however reversed during the 1990s, and the liberalization decade witnessed a steep rise in the incidence of poverty particularly in the rural sector.

In 1998, 45.2 percent of the population in rural areas was below the poverty line. Even overall situation was not distinctly better as at the country level, rural and urban sectors considered together 43 percent of the population was below the poverty line. The rise in the overall poverty ratio during the post-reform period in spite of the higher GDP growth is to be attributed to the growing rural-urban divide. The 53rd round of the NSS data for 1997 (January to December) reveals that India's rural poverty ratio has gone up by 3.42 percent between 1991 and 1997 even as urban poverty ratio declined marginally by 1.32 percent (National Sample Survey).

Measured in terms of monthly per capita expenditure, the poverty ratio was estimated at 33.97 percent in the urban areas in 1997 against 35.29 percent at the beginning of 1991 (46th round of NSS data). On the other hand, the proportion of rural population in the poverty bracket had risen over the same period to 38.6 percent from 35.04 percent (National Sample Survey). The 54th round of NSS for 1998 conducted between January and June 1998 shows a widening of disparity between rural and urban expenditure at both current and constant prices. In absolute terms, the average per capita expenditure at current prices rose from Rs. 244 in 1991 to Rs. 382 in 1998 in rural areas and from Rs. 370 to Rs. 648 in urban areas. At constant prices, the expenditure has actually declined from Rs. 164 in 1991 to Rs. 153 in 1998 in rural areas and rose from Rs. 257 to Rs. 269 in urban areas (National Sample Survey).

Supported by the World Bank, India government has introduced a new method to calculate the poverty rate so as to hide the facts and propagate a massive reduction of the poverty rate, which, given the increasing rate of unemployment, cannot be supported by the facts.

The methodology for collecting data on consumption expenditure was changed by the NSS for the 55th round and the government got the estimates of the poverty, which were not comparable with the earlier estimates. One of the major flaws is to assume that the rate of poverty in the villages around an urban center is the same as the city itself. The minimum level of calorie intake for the poverty line is now reduced from 2,400 to 1,800; the minimum level of income for the poverty line is now reduced to Rs. 4,000 per year from Rs. 5,000 previously. If we keep the earlier criteria, the poverty level can very well reach 77.5 percent. However, these were not taken into account by the economists of the World Bank (Dollar and Kray 2004), which still cite the official figure of 26 percent.

The NSS data for 1999–2000 revealed that the rate of growth of total employment fell sharply from 2.04 percent per year during 1983–1994 to 1993–1994 to only 0.80 percent per year in the 1993–1994 to 1999–2000 periods. On the other hand, labor force has grown at a rate of 2 percent per annum during the same period. How can poverty go down when unemployment is increasing, which only the World Bank and the India government can answer.

However, since these biased estimates of poverty based on the data obtained from the 55th round of the NSS showed lower incidence of poverty, the government adopted some tactics to show by any means that the incidence of poverty declined during the decade of economic reforms. This approach of the government of manipulating the methodology to obtain convenient results is both unethical and contradictory to its own finding. An overwhelming 79 percent of workers in the unorganized sector, or 394.9 million workers or 86 percent of the working population, live on an income of less than Rs. 20 a day, according to the National Commission for Enterprises in the Unorganized Sector (Sengupta 2008). Based on the 66th round of the NSS for 2009–2010, if the average monthly consumption expenditure is taken as the benchmark of what an individual needs to survive, the poverty line would be Rs. 66.10 for urban areas and Rs. 35.10 for rural regions while about 65 percent of the population will be below the poverty line.

As a result, of the reform measures of the 1990s, income inequalities have increased. In 1992, the lowest 40 percent households had accounted for 20.6 percent of the national household expenditure. Their share however declined to 19.7 percent in 1997. In contrast, share of the top 10 percent households in the national household expenditure rose from 28.4 percent to 33.5 percent over the same period. This accentuation of income inequalities may be attributed to the reform measures of the 1990s, which on the one hand denied employment opportunities to the common people but enriched business community (National Sample Survey, National Commission for Enterprises in the Unorganized Sector, Sengupta 2008).

Employments during the "Structural Adjustment Period"

The most important indicator of success of an economic regime is in the employment generations. In this matter, the "reformed" regime has little to demonstrate. There is no reliable statistics regarding unemployment in India, so we do not know how far the fear of the ordinary people about the "Reform Process" as job destroyer is justified. The only statistics, the government produces on employment, are on the organized sector of the economy, which is a very small part of the economy.

Increase in employments in the public sector was much higher during the "planned" regime of the 1980s than during the "reformed" regime of the 1990s. This is true for both the manufacturing and the construction sector. In the private sector, although the total generations of employment are higher during the "reformed" regime, in the construction sector it has failed.

In manufacturing if we look at the detail, we can see that the employment actually went down from 6.85 million in 1998 to 66.2 million in 2000; in agriculture employment went down from 1.49 million in 1992 to 1.42 million in 2000; in mining it went down from 1.12 million in 1994 to 1.01 million in 2000.

The only sector that has showed improvement is the service sector of finance, real estate, and so on, where employment went up continuously from 1991. A revised estimate presented in table 7.3 gives a similar picture.

From the data obtained from the 55th round of the NSS, it is obvious that the usual status unemployment rose by 2.3 percent in the liberalization period. Unemployment increased far more, that is, 5.7 percent in terms of daily status over this period. The main factors, which have contributed to persistently increasing unemployment, are drastic reduction in development expenditure by the government, indirect layoff of workers in public sector

Table 7.3. Subsidies for farmers, 2019, in US$ Million

China	185.9
India	11.0
EU	101.3
United States	48.9
Japan	37.6
Indonesia	29.4

Source: Trade vistas, Economic Survey.

undertakings, massive retrenchment of workers in the private manufacturing sector, and closure of a large number of small-scale factories in different parts of the country (Government of India, Ministry of Finance, Economic Survey 2008; Report on Conditions of Work and Promotion of Livelihoods in the Unorganized Sector, 2008).

The daily status of unemployment had risen from 6.03 percent in 1993–1994 to 7.32 percent in 1999–2000. There is no official statistics on how many jobs were destroyed during the period of "Economic Reform" (National Accounts Statistics 2000–2007). From various fragmented information we can compile a list, which is certainly not exhaustive.

Coal mines: 20,000 already lost, another 95,000 are waiting to be unemployed. Coal is being imported from Australia and China.

Mica mines: 8,000 lost their jobs.

Fertilizer: 12,000 lost their jobs, now fertilizer is being imported.

Mining machinery: 4,000 people have lost their jobs; machineries are imported from Britain.

Steel: 20,000 workers have lost their jobs, another 23,000 in (IISCO) were waiting to be unemployed. Steel is being imported from Korea and China.

Rubber: Rubber farmers are committing suicides in South India; rubber is being imported from Malaysia; 8,000 workers of Dunlop are unemployed. There is increasing volume of imports of tires from abroad.

Railway wagon industry: 12,000 were unemployed, while wagons are imported from a number of countries. Burn Standard and Jessop were closed down.

Aluminum foils: 6,000 already lost their jobs; these are imported from the United States.

Medicines: In 1995, India made it compulsory for the drug industries to have foreign partners and to pay royalty. India government had closed down public sector medicine manufacturing plants; job losses were about 1,000. Medicine price since then went up by about 400 percent. In 2001 all price controls of medicines are abolished; very soon medicine price will sharply increase.

Electricity: The World Bank had made it a rule that India has to import electrical machineries from China if it wants loans from the World Bank in the reformed electricity sector in India. Indian public sector electrical machinery manufacturing companies are not in the list of approved contractors of the World Bank. Major job losses are expected in this sector very soon.

Railway engines: 6,000 people will lose their jobs when this sector will be privatized soon.

Aluminum: Already 4,000 have lost their jobs; others are waiting to be unemployed. Aluminum products are being imported from the United States (*Source*: Standard & Poor).

Most of the job losses are the result of the trade policy imposed upon India by the World Trade Organization (WTO) as part of the "Economic Reform" process. World Bank has anticipated that even in 1992 when it gave about US$10 billion loan to India to pay compensations to the future unemployed workers in the industrial sector of India. Now EU is offering similar kind of loan to India. It is essential to understand that the purpose is to scale down Indian industry in particular to open the economy for imports as part of the liberalized trade policy, the essential ingredient of the "Economic Reform" process.

India is not alone in this matter. In Thailand, after the devastating economic crisis of 1998, the World Bank-IMF has advised Thailand to close down as many industries as possible (Aoki, Murdock, and Okuno-Fujiwara 1996).

This is not a great success for the "reformed" regime. However, what the statistics could not tell us is the growing fear of job losses and replacements of permanent jobs by temporary jobs. Areas where jobs are being created are not the areas where jobs are being destroyed. Given the immobility of Indian labor and linguistic racism that exist in India, the result will be increasing unemployment.

The economy was nearly reformed by 2000. The analysis provided below gives the picture of that "reformed economy."

REFORMED ECONOMY: DEVELOPMENTS SINCE 2000

Bubble is an economic condition created by sudden influx of funds to an economy either by the short-sighted policy of the government to stimulate the economy by increased public expenditures and borrowings from foreign sources or by external factors like sudden inflows of funds from abroad. When a country is in bubble it forgets that there can be some unknown dangers lurking round the corner; but it is intoxicated in thinking that the flow of funds will last forever. The warning that uncontrolled inflows of foreign funds can make the adjustments in the balance of payments difficult is well known (Domar 1950; Lary 1946).

The adjustment normally happens like a storm, which may ruin the country's finances. The questions can be raised whether the economy of India since 2004 is in such a bubble or it has experienced self-sustained growth suddenly. A number of economies of the world have experienced these bubbles and the end result is always misery. Japan has experienced it from 1985 to 1993, and then it went into a long depression from which it is yet to recover. Britain has gone through it from 1988 to 1991, and then it had severe depression until 1997. Southeast Asia and East Asian countries, Thailand, Indonesia, and South Korea, went through this bubble from 1992 to 1998 and then collapsed completely. India itself has seen a bubble from 1985 to 1990 and it went bankrupt in 1991.

The newspapers from India are giving a very optimistic picture for India. The economy, which has been on a high growth path of 8–9 percent for the three years from 2004, was expanding faster in 2007 at 9.2 percent. Significantly, the 9.2 percent GDP growth in 2007 reduced from about despite the slowdown in farm sector growth to just 2.7 percent in 2007 came 6 per cent in 2006 (National Accounts Statistics 2000–2007; National Sample Survey 2001–2006; Standard & Poor 2001–2007). This picture mesmerizes the analysts. "Reforms are driving growth," Finance Minister P. Chidambaram said recently, "Reforms have brought in investment, fostered competition, and enhanced productivity and efficiency." The opinions of prominent Indian economists are the same. However, question should be raised, what is behind this temporary glamorous picture? Is it truly a success story of the reform process or just a bubble about to be burst if the situation that created this bubble will disappear suddenly?

Growth Picture of the Reformed Economy

The annual average growth rate, in constant price, during the Seventh Plan (1985 to 1990) was 3.6 percent; during the Ninth Plan of 1997 to 2002 it became 3.5 percent. India's high rate of growth started in 2003, when the gross domestic product (GDP) grew, in constant price, at the rate of 8.6 percent per year followed by 7.6 percent in 2004. However, the annual average for the period from 2000 to 2004 was 6 percent, which is not very different for the annual average of 5.8 percent, for the period of the earlier bubble of 1985 to 1989 (Government of India, Ministry of Finance, Economic Survey 2007).

In 1988 the rate of growth was already 10.1 percent. That period 1985 to 1990 was during the plan period, where "Reforms" were not introduced. Thus, the source of the current high rate of growth must lie elsewhere, not on the "Reforms." If we look at the source of the bubble of 1985–1989, we may get the clue.

A comparison of two bubbles can help us to understand the picture and its perspectives. The average growth rate for the period 1985 to 1989 was 5.8 percent; for the period 2000 to 2004, it became 6 percent, not a great advertisement for the "Reform" process.

The Cause of the Last Bubble of 1985–1989

The bubble of 1985–1989 was caused by unprecedented increase in borrowings from abroad and in domestic creation of money. Balance-of-payment deficits, along with budget deficit of the government, went on increasing due to increased expenditures of the government for mainly noninvestment purposes. That has forced India to borrow from abroad to pay for these deficits. Foreign borrowings went up and up. From 1985 to 1989, within five years, foreign borrowings per year increased by more than 100 percent. The total foreign borrowing for that period was a massive Rs. 120.8 billion. Increased domestic borrowings were the results of increased budget deficits, which had the results of increased money supply and the resultant inflation (Basu 1995; IMF-International Financial Statistics).

By 1990–1991, when the Soviet Union, which used to absorb 20 percent of India's exports, has collapsed and the remittances from the Indian workers in the Middle East suddenly vanished due to the invasion of Kuwait by Iraq, India found it impossible to pay back what it had borrowed and went bankrupt. As a result, the "Reform" process to dismantle the planning process was imposed upon India in 1991. The person in charge of Indian finance, as during the bubble of 1985 to 1989, is the same person who became the finance minister in charge of the "Reforms" since 1991 and now the prime minister of India in 2007 presiding over another bubble.

Financial Picture Behind the "Reformed Economy"

The upsurge of growth rate since 2004 to 2012 is the result of injections of huge funds to the economy either increased by increasing budget deficits or by foreign borrowings. A new picture is added, which was absent during the earlier bubble of 1985–1989 (Basu 1995). That is the short-term borrowings from abroad and allowances for foreigners to participate in the country's stock market and real estate developments.

In 1990 nondevelopment expenditure of the government was Rs. 69.2 billion. In 2000 it became Rs. 1,298.9 billion and Rs. 461.9 billion in 2004. The rate of growth of nondevelopment expenditure was 332 percent for the period 1990 to 2000 and 567.4 percent for the period 1990 to 2004. The rate of growth of development expenditure was 219 percent for the period 1990 to 2000 and 382.7 per cent for the period 1990 to 2004. Nondevelopment expenditure fuels both increased money supply and inflation. India has experienced both.

The budget deficits that were created by these massive increases in expenditures went up from Rs. 57.2 billion in 1990 to Rs. 256.3 billion in 2004 with a rate of growth of 348.6 percent during that period. The tax rate did not go up to cover the expanding expenditure of the government; instead, the government went on borrowing from both home and abroad. The tax to GDP ratio was 15.43 percent in 1990; it was 16.30 percent in 2004. Foreign capital inflows were Rs. 4.3 billion in 1990, which became Rs. 8.3 billion in 2000 and Rs. 11.7 billion in 2004 (Economic Survey 2008; Reports of the Task Force on Direct Taxes, 2002–2006).

The alarming factor is that short-term debt is increasing at a very fast rate. The ratio of short-term debt to total debt went up from 2.8 percent in 2002 to 6.7 percent in 2006. Foreign investments of short-term nature or portfolio investments went up from US$9.3 billion in 2002 to US$12.2 billion in 2005.

Investments by foreign institutional investors in India went up from US$377 million in 2002 to US$9.9 billion in 2005. However, at the same time foreign direct investment (FDI) of long-term nature was increased by a much slower rate from US$3.7 billion in 2002 to US$4.7 billion in 2005 (Government of India, Ministry of Finance, Economic Survey 2008).

At the same time, India's deficits in the trade balance went up from US$33.70 billion in 2002 to US$51.84 billion. Total deficits in the balance of payments of India went up from US$2.47 billion in 2002 to 9.19 billion in 2005. Financing of these deficits requires more borrowings. Total foreign borrowings went up from Rs. 163 billion in 1991 to Rs. 548.1 billion in 2005 or an increase by 3.36 times.

Commercial borrowings went up from Rs. 197.3 billion in 1991 to Rs. 1,242.99 billion in 2005 or by 6.36 times. In the meantime, foreigner's purchased shares of Indian companies went up from Rs. 6.5 billion in 1991 to Rs. 61.9 billion in 2005 or by 9.5 times. In fact, that type of purchases went up within a year from Rs. 42.8 billion in 2000 to Rs. 67.7 billion in 2001 because of certain changes in the legal restrictions on such purchases that were there before (Economic Survey 2009).

Foreign Funds in the Stock Market in the Reformed Economy

India has witnessed over a decade of portfolio flows and with each passing year, portfolio flows have gained in their significance and have played a key role in the overall Indian economy. Although investments by foreign institutional investors are typically synonymous with portfolio investments in India, investments in Global Depository Reserve and offshore funds should be included in any analysis relating to portfolio flows.

The year 2002–2003 was highlighted by significant events; both locally and internationally, that had a bearing on the Indian economy. By end of March 2003, cumulative portfolio investments totaled nearly US$16 billion, which constituted nearly 11 percent of the country's stock market capitalization.

The Union Budget, 2003, announced that dividends would be exempt from tax in the hands of a shareholder. Henceforth, dividends declared by an Indian company would not be liable to Indian taxes. However, the Indian company will be liable to pay 12.81 percent (including surcharge) dividend distribution tax. Further, long-term capital gains arising on transfer of equity shares (held at least for one year) in a listed company, acquired between March 1, 2003, and February 28, 2004, would be exempt from tax.

These initiatives were specifically targeted at attracting portfolio investments into India. India has emerged as the most favored private equity (PE) destination attracting $2.21 billion of PE investment in 2006 as against just $1,992 million in 2005. India was followed by China with $1.72 billion. Singapore came third with $1.53 billion (Standard & Poor). Foreign institutional investors increased their total investment in the domestic stock market in 2009–2010 to over Rs. 47,690 crore (or $10.4 billion at the prevailing exchange rate in those years).

Foreign Funds in Real Estate

India's FDI inflows have doubled to $2.9 billion during April-July 2006 as compared to the $1.5 billion during the same period in 2005. Sensing the demand of foreign investors, the Indian government has liberalized the laws relating to FDI in February 2005. Now nonresident Indians (NRIs) and overseas corporate bodies (OCBs) can invest up to 100 percent in the real estate sector (Government of India, Ministry of Finance, Economic Survey 2009). FDI in real estate is now possible without the need for permission by the Foreign Investment Promotion Board. Currently, FDI in India is targeting township, housing, construction development projects, built-up infrastructure, and so on. The Indian government repealed the Urban Land Ceiling Act in 2001, and a large quantum of land is now free for construction. Investment is now allowed for smaller projects of just 25 acres.

Impact of Reforms on the Real Economy since 2000

The sudden upsurge of growth rate of the national income in India has very different effects on the real economy. The two most important aspects of people's life are employment and food. From these points, the "Reform" program has little to offer during the entire period from 1991 to 2005.

Production of rice has improved from 1991 to 1999 but since then it has declined; it is true also about wheat and all food grains. As a result, the net availability of pulses per head went down from 41.6 gram in 1991 to 35.9 gram in 2004. Availability of cereals per head also went down from 468.5 gram in 1991 to 427.4 gram in 2004. Inflation has also taken its toll. Cost of living index of industrial workers went up from 201 in 1990 to 538 in 2005. For agricultural laborers, it went up from 145 in 1990 to 360 in 2005. For the urban nonmanual persons, it went up from 169 in 1990 to 463 in 2005. Thus, all sections of the population are affected very badly from the inflation and reductions in the availability of food (Government of India, Ministry of Finance, Economic Survey 2009).

The average rate of increase of the cost of living during the period of 1986 to 1989 was 6.38 percent for the industrial workers but the average annual increase during the "Reform" period since 1991 is now 11.17 percent.

For the agricultural laborers, it went up from 7.6 percent during the planned economy to 9.88 percent in the "Reformed" economy and for the urban non-manual people it went from 6.52 percent to 11.59 percent. Thus, the living conditions of the people in the "Reformed" economy do not paint a rosy picture (Government of India, Ministry of Finance, Economic Survey 2009).

Employment during the "Reformed Economy" since 2000

Data for employment are available only up to 2003; thus, we can compare the situation between 1991 and 2003 regarding employments in different sectors of the economy for the both private and the public sector. Employment increase only marginally during this first period of 12 years of the "Reformed" economy; it has declined in the public sector in both mining and manufacturing. In the private sector, too, employment declined in the mining and constructions; in agriculture it increased only marginally. In other sectors, it increased mainly in the finance sector. The improvements in the private sector could not compensate for the decline in employment in the public sector. The ratio of employment to gross national income declined significantly during the "Reformed" period. Thus, it proved the inefficiency of the "Reformed" economy regarding the generation of employment prospects for the country. It is a myth that the global financial crisis left India virtually unscathed. In fact, India is the biggest victim of financial crisis-induced poverty, according to data obtained from the United Nations Department of Economic and Social Affairs (UNDESA). The UNDESA data estimate that the number of India's poor was 33.6 million higher in 2009 than would have been the case if the growth rates of the years from 2004 to 2007 had been maintained. In 2009 alone, an estimated 13.6 million more people in India became poor or remained in poverty than would have been the case at 2008 growth rates.

In other words, while a dip from the 8.8 percent growth in GDP averaged from 2004–2005 to 2006–2007 to the 6.7 percent estimated for 2008–2009 may be nothing like the recession faced by the West, its human consequences for India were probably worse. The 2.1 percent decline in India's GDP growth rate has effectively translated into a 2.8 percent increase in the incidence of poverty. According to the UNDESA's World Economic Situation and Prospects, 2010, 47 million more people globally became poor or remained in poverty in 2009 than would have been the case at 2008 growth rates, and 84 million more than would have been poor at 2004–2007 growth rates. Of these, 19 and 40 million, respectively, are in South Asia.

The UNDESA report attributes this increase in poverty to a combination of reduced household incomes, rising unemployment, and pressure on public services. Job losses in India were primarily in export-oriented industries like textiles, while employment levels in Indian firms catering to the domestic market were largely unaffected, the report says. Monetary and fiscal policy intervention gave Indian growth some resilience, while safety nets like India's National Rural Employment Guarantee Act (NREGA) helped to mitigate the effects of the slowdown.

Problems in Balance of Payments after the Reforms

India's external debt climbed 6.6 percent to $326.6 billion by September 2011. The ratio of short-term external debt to foreign exchange reserves stood at 22.9 percent. The ratio of short-term debt to foreign exchange reserves rose to an 11-year high at the end of September 2011, raising concerns about the sustainability of the external obligations. The rise in external commercial borrowings has also raised concerns about corporate balance sheets, as rapid rupee depreciation has pushed up the debt service burden.

India was the fifth most externally indebted country in 2009 in terms of external debt stock, said World Bank in its report on Global Development Finance, 2011. However, there are other structural reasons for the fall of rupee over the last year. Since 1992 when the reform process, imposed on India by the IMF and World Bank, had started, rupee has depreciated by about 70 percent against U.S. dollar. However, considering the trade pattern of India, rupee has appreciated in recent years since 2007 against the basket of currencies of six major trading partners of India.

That made the Chinese products cheaper in India than in China itself, and India has lost already 36 percent of the employments of its manufacturing industries to China. Thus, a fall of the exchange value of rupee is beneficial to protect Indian economy against these Chinese invasions. Most of India's import costs, about 80 percent, are due to petroleum. India has deficits in trade. Value of India's exports in 2011 was of $303 billion, but the cost of imports in 2011 was about $488 billion, thus creating a huge gap, which normally gets filled up by remittances of the Indians working abroad and foreign investments. Short-term foreign investments are attracted by the prospect of the Indian economy, which used to have a very high growth rate, but it has gone down since 2011. That has discouraged flows of investments. Increasing price of crude petroleum has increased the cost of India's imports, too.

Foreign investors are worried that due to the deficits in India's balance of payments, India's foreign debt, which is now $327 billion in 2012, will go up. With the obligation of current debt service of $85 billion a year, India may have difficulties to repay the debt, particularly when the short-term debt of

India is about 22 percent of the total debt. Short-term debts can be recalled anytime, thus creating a situation of default for India if the reserve of India's foreign currencies and gold will go down due to continuous deficits in the balance of payments. Large current account deficits, which resulted from an overvalued currency after a difficult inflation process as well as the abnormal debt management policy, have caused the accumulation of sizable short-term dollar- or euro- or yen-denominated debt. The rapid expansion in the private financial sector had created a situation of poor-quality loan portfolios and a possible banking crisis because the captains of Indian industry avoid paying back their loans. These are factors that have exposed India to the risk of exchange rate devaluation and defaults. If India could keep the current account balance within moderate bounds, with deficits not exceeding 5 percent of GDP, it would reduce vulnerability to speculative attacks on rupee by international foreign currency dealers.

Speculative attacks are more intense when the deficits are financed by short-term debt or other easily reversible financial instruments like derivatives (bets on financial futures) or shares of Indian companies, which were invited by Chidambaram in 2007 by allowing foreigners to invest in the stock market and the real estate sector.

The experience of the Asian crisis of 1997–1998 put privatized financial markets as the main culprit. In the affected Asian countries, traditional sources of fundamental imbalances were absent. With the exception of Thailand, real exchange rates had not displayed any significant appreciation in the years leading to the crises, and although a slowdown in export growth had been recorded in some of the economies of the region since 1996, it had come after several years of very strong expansion. The loan portfolios of financial institutions, on the other hand by contrast, had deteriorated significantly with massive amount of nonperforming loans as the private sectors were unable to pay back, and the corporate sector was excessively indebted and financially fragile, which resulted from years of poor management and wrong investment decisions.

Weaknesses in the financial and corporate sectors seem to be the only common factor in all affected countries in the region. The crisis then was intensified by the herd behavior of the private foreign investors, not only in terms of joining in the stampede out of a currency but also in their propensity to flee from other countries in the same region. The situation is the same in India today.

The vulnerability of an economy to a balance of payments crisis increases significantly when the level of international reserves is inadequate, which was the case during the 1980s in India but not today. The level of liquid monetary assets in the country is a natural measure of potential demand for foreign currency from the domestic private commercial sector. Even if the currency is not fully convertible or purchases of foreign exchange are severely restricted, the money supply could fuel the demand for foreign currency through parallel markets of the black money holders or through the "Hawala" traders (illegal unofficial money traders).

Rapid decline of the exchange value of rupee in 2012 can imply a number of aspects. It can mean that rupee is adjusting for the growing inflation in India and the resultant falling export volumes; or it can mean that there is a fear for the greater deficits in balance of payment due to rapidly rising cost of imports of petroleum. It can also mean fear among the so-called short-run institutional investors, which have invested through Mauritius, that the government may clamp down on them soon through General Anti-Avoidance Rules (GAAR). It can also mean India is heading for a disaster after having a reckless party financed by foreign borrowing as it had happened in 1991.

In 2004 India has allowed India's black money, which was taken out of India through Hawala (private money traders) channels, to come back to India through Mauritius, where there is no capital gains tax, as new foreign investments, thus avoiding taxes in India but instead receiving subsidies. In 2007, India has allowed freedom for the foreigners to invest in the stock market and the real estate sector of India. Due to these measures, growth rate of India shot up suddenly since 2007 because of the massive inflows of short-term investments, the most volatile component of a country's balance of payments.

The "Reformed" economy has produced two India; one very tiny part of the economy, including the IT sector, the financial services, and trading sector, has prospered. However, there is a general decline in agriculture, construction, and mining. The growth of the economy is fueled by increasing flows of short-term foreign investments both in the share market and in the real estate business, which have suddenly raised the growth rate since 2004. The balance of payments still has deficits along with the balance of trade. The only positive factors in India's external account are the growth of exports of IT-related services and remittances from the Indians living abroad. The real economy and employment have not responded positively yet to the so-called "Reforms." In the case of India's earlier bubble of 1985–1989, the cause was the sudden increase of government consumptions for nondevelopment purposes financed by foreign borrowings and short-term foreign funds parked in India. In the bubble of 2004–2012, the cause is the sudden inflows of foreign funds to satisfy the appetite of speculative demands in the share market and real estate business. Borrowings by Indian companies from foreign sources are a major factor in this scene. The danger is that these speculative inflows of funds from abroad can dry up suddenly if there is any indication that due to increasing balance-of-payment deficits the exchange rate of rupee may fall (Domar 1950; Kregel 2008; Lary 1946). That would provoke a speculative drive against the rupee and there would be a general exodus of foreign funds from the share market, thus, to bring down the economy and invite serious depression in the economy destroying millions of jobs in India. A crisis of that nature has already erupted in the East Asian countries and Russia in 1998. India was protected at that time because its capital market was closed from the foreign speculators. That is not true anymore. The process of withdrawal of foreign funds has started already as the world economy is about to enter the phase of depression.

For the long-run solution, it is essential to look at the composition of India's balance of payments. Military and nonmilitary spending should be from non-Western sources to reduce the costs. New transport policy away from road transport and private transport should be implemented to reduce the level of petroleum consumption. Increased and better public transport, redesign of the cities, reduced freight rates of railways, and increased emphasis on both nuclear and solar energy also can help India greatly. Automobile running on electricity and hybrid vehicles also can reduce India's petroleum consumption, which is the most important cost of imports.

As in 1984–1989 India government had the emphasis only on the growth rate of the economy and forgot about the danger of borrowing from abroad to enhance these growth rates. During 1984–1989, India had achieved a very high growth rate of more than 10 percent per year, but as soon as the foreign exchange facility provided by the Soviet Union disappeared in 1991, India was unable to repay its debt. The same situation may develop soon for India if the foreign investors suddenly go away along with their investment and there will be a rapid fall of the India's foreign exchange reserve. It is essential to accept that the financial liberalization introduced by Chidambaram in 2007 has created a bubble in the Indian economy with the resultant very high inflation, which is eroding India's competitiveness in the international market by making India's exports very expensive with rising cost of production and increasing debt of India's corporate sector. The only way out is to reintroduce sanity and put emphasis on job creation rather than just growth rates.

Difference between China and India is very obvious. China had put emphasis on the manufacturing industries by inviting FDIs in plants and machinery. India has put emphasis on short-term borrowings to stimulate the economy artificially. China has devalued the exchange rate of yuan in 1994 by 40 percent and kept it almost fixed since then. India has revalued rupee and has a flexible exchange rate knowing fully well that inflows of foreign funds will increase the exchange rate of rupee, thus making India's exports increasingly uncompetitive in the world economy. China does not allow foreign institutional investors to invest in the Chinese share market or in the real estate sector, but India does. China has not relaxed its control on the capital market, but India is going steadily toward an open economy, thus inviting the danger of a sudden collapse when the speculative bubble would burst.

To protect the economy from the speculative bubbles, India should have devalued rupee much earlier, should have closed the foreign exchange market for rupee, banned participations of foreign funds in the share market and in the real estate business, could have very tight control on the capital flows, have control over the foreign borrowings by Indian private companies, and should have rejuvenated public investment program in agriculture and manufacturing to promote employment.

Without a vigorous public investment that feeds the private investments, the country could not be developed for the satisfaction of the people at large. Success or failure of any economic program is measured by the welfare it generates for the people. Economic and administrative reforms are needed in India but these reforms should be aimed at reduction of corruptions, increased efficiency, increased employments, and reduction of inequality and poverty. Given the rapidly declining prospect, it is high time to change tracks from a totally free enterprise economy to a regulated economy for the benefit of the people.

Domestic Policy Reforms: Comparison with China

Two important related facts emerge from our review of trade flows and growth from the viewpoint of domestic policy reform: the overall response of trade to India's opening up has been weaker than in countries such as China, and the economy has failed to move rapidly into the manufacturing of labor-intensive products. Both facts point to the need for some key domestic policy reforms.

The response of trade to liberalization has been an order of magnitude weaker in India than in China. In China, exports of goods and services grew at annual rates of 12.9 and 15.2 percent during the 1980s and the 1990s, respectively. Imports performed similarly. Consequently, China's ratio of total trade to GDP rose from 18.9 percent in 1980 to 34 percent in 1990 and to 49.3 percent in 2000.

FDIs into China rose from $60 million in 1980 to $3.5 billion in 1990, and then rose to $42.1 billion in 2000. China was slower to open its market to portfolio investment, but once it did, inflows quickly surpassed those into India, reaching $7.8 billion in 2000. Even if one allows for an upward bias in these figures, as some China specialists suggest, and a downward bias in the figures for India, there is little doubt that foreign investment flows into China are several times those into India. Part of the difference in performance between India and China can be attributed to the presence of Chinese entrepreneurs in Hong Kong and Taiwan, who have been eager to escape rising wages in their home economies by moving to China. However, a more central explanation lies in differences in the composition of GDP in the two countries and the asymmetric responses of their industries to opening up. Among developing countries, India is unique in having a very large share of its GDP in the mostly informal part of the services sector. Whereas in other countries a decline in the share of agriculture in GDP has been accompanied by a substantial expansion of industry in the early stages of development, in India this has not happened.

For example, in 1980 the proportion of GDP originating in industry was already 48.5 percent in China, whereas in India it was only 24.2 percent. Services, on the other hand, contributed only 21.4 percent to GDP in China but as much as 37.2 percent in India. In the following 20 years, despite considerable growth, the share of industry did not rise in India. Instead, the entire decline in the share of agriculture was absorbed by services. In China, in contrast, the share of industry started out very high in 1980, fell to 41.6 percent in 1990, but went back up to 50.9 percent in 2000. Correspondingly, services rose from its low 1980 level of 21.4 percent to 31.3 percent in 1990 and just 33.2 percent in 2000. The key point is that industry already accounted for a large share of GDP in China in 1980, and what it lost during the 1980s it more than recovered in the 1990s.

Under liberal trade policies, developing countries are much more likely to be able to expand exports and imports if a large proportion of their output originates in industry. Not only is the scope for expanding labor-intensive manufactures greater in a labor-abundant country, but a larger industrial sector also requires more imported inputs, thereby offering greater scope for the expansion of imports. In India, not only have exports failed to grow rapidly, but the response of imports has been just as muted. Consequently, in recent years the Reserve Bank of India has had to purchase large volumes of foreign exchange to keep the rupee from appreciating. Even then it was unsuccessful and had to let the currency appreciate by 5 to 7 percent against the dollar during 2003. Given the poor performance of industry, imports have simply failed to absorb the foreign exchange generated by remittances and relatively modest foreign investment flows.

Liberalization has failed to stimulate India's labor-intensive industries to any great degree. The industries that have shown the fastest export growth are typically capital- or skilled labor-intensive industries.

Absurd Agricultural Policy of India

Indian farmers were at war with the government of Narendra Modi, who otherwise is the most popular prime minister of India. All noneconomic policies of Modi administration are highly popular and just. However, all economic policies of the Modi government are wrong and unpopular. Demonetization, Goods and Services Tax (GST), abolition of the Planning Commission, and

New Agricultural Policy are all unpopular and unjust. When due to economic reform policy implemented by Rao, Manmohan Singh, and Vajpayee, massive amount of money, calculated up to 2016, $4,600 dollars, went away from India to various offshore banks, it is absurd to cancel all existing bank notes in India causing widespread difficulties and even deaths in India to catch the black money. GST has so far caused chaos and loss of revenue for the government and has done nothing good for the people, particularly for the owners of small business. We have no idea where the country is going and what would be plans for the country without the Planning Commission. Lastly, the New Agricultural Policy was rejected by the farmers for whose benefits the government is supposed to implement these.

However, repeal of these new laws regarding agriculture cannot solve the problem when these laws are there to implement the rules of the WTO. If the Modi government withdraws these new laws, a number of countries, our allies and friends, like Myanmar, Thailand, Brazil, the United States, and Australia, will take India to the WTO for nonimplementation of agreed rules of trade negotiations since 1995. As India is one of the developing countries, it got some exemptions for few years not to abolish subsidies and public distribution system but the time has come for India to implement these now without any delay, according to the WTO system.

Muchkund Dubey, India's representative to the GATT in 1995 (GATT treaty that led to the creation of WTO), expressed his objection that the abolition of subsidies and the public distribution system would not benefit India but would take away the long-term protection for both the consumers and producers in India. However, Monmohan Singh had ignored this good advice of Dubey and went ahead to sign the GATT treaty and joined the WTO in 1995. Since the beginning of the plan period of India, subsidies for fertilizers and the minimum support prices (MSPs) for two main crops, rice and wheat, were introduced in India to promote investments in agriculture and to protect the farmers from the dangers of the market system, which during the British Rule used to cause famine after famine.

British rulers, faithful followers of the directors of the East India Company, Adam Smith, Malthus, David Ricardo, Bentham, James, and John Stuart Mill, used not to interfere to the market and allowed the natives of the "rude" country, India, to die in millions, as a result. In 1951, when Five-Year Plans were introduced in India, the most important task of the planners was to make the people secure in life by providing sufficient supply of food and to provide incentives to the farmers to have fertilizers in affordable price and to cover their cost of production through the MSP.

These are considered as "market distortions" by the staunch supporters of the market system in the WTO, World Bank, and the International Monetary Fund, who wanted to abolish these protections for the consumers and producers in the developing countries, although they want to keep these market distortions for the developed countries and China. China has joined the WTO as a market economy in 2001, certified by the United States, although in China all companies foreign or Chinese are under government controls, regarding production, investments, and pricing.

These facts about China are ignored by the Western elites, who through the WTO have allowed China to dominate the world trade and destroy jobs in most countries of the world.

Subsidies are the rules in the Western countries and China for both agricultural and nonagricultural companies, even the social media companies like Facebook, Google, and Baidu. Agricultural price support is the foundation of the Common Agricultural Policy of the European Common Market, Japan, and China. However, for India, both agricultural subsidies and MSPs are distortionary and must be removed as soon as possible. Modi government is doing just that.

Supports for public companies and opposition to the private companies whether foreign or domestic also create market distortions, according to the WTO. That is the reason for the opposition to the FCI and its policy to procure products directly from the farmers and to provide products at affordable price to the consumers. Abolition of the FCI was the basic recommendation of the WTO and the World Bank. Thus, the FCI would not be allowed to procure food crops from the farmers at a MSP and subsidize the consumers by making food available at affordable prices.

Contract farming is designed to eliminate any discrimination that may exist between private and public companies and between foreign and domestic companies. Thus, State Farming that used to exist in Suratgarh in Rajasthan was disallowed, public fertilizer companies were closed down, but multinational foreign companies are invited to invest in Indian agriculture. Contract farming was introduced in 1834 in India during the days of East India Company, to promote the plantations for opium and indigo. That had ruined Indian agriculture and made Indian farmers paupers. The same will be repeated in India again, to produce cash crops instead of food, as recommended by the World Bank.

Minimum Support Price in India

The average monthly incomes of the farmers in Punjab and Haryana are Rs. 18,000 and Rs. 16,000, respectively, because they have MSP. In Bihar and West Bengal, these are Rs. 3,600 and Rs. 3,800 as they have no MSP (NITI Aayog 2021). Eight of the 11 commodities traded on March 6, 2021, were from the list of 23 crops that enjoy MSP. The seven crops were sold below what the government of India officially assures the farmers to be the minimum price that the farmers must get and the government will support the farmers to secure. This included all the five major crops of that area: tur, makka, jowar, chana, and bajra.

More or less the same prices were found all over Karnataka markets for most crops. The average February price for bajra and maize was actually lower in the rest of the state than in Ballari. Only tur fetched a better price elsewhere. An average of the last three years (2017–2018 to 2019–2020) by the Karnataka Agricultural Price Commission shows that as much as 72 percent of the agricultural produce in the state sells below the MSP. Farmers of Karnataka lost Rs. 3,119 crores last year due to distress sale below MSP.

None of the major kharif (summer) crops, except paddy, fetched anything close to the assured minimum. Paddy did better; it was solely due to the government procurement in many states. Fine varieties of long-grain paddy, which are not covered by MSP, suffered badly and were sold at less than the MSP for ordinary variety. No state other than Haryana, not even Gujarat, procured bajra at the MSP. As a result, bajra sold around Rs. 1,300 against the official MSP of Rs. 2,150. During the peak arrivals in the month of November, moong was sold for an average price of Rs. 5,556, about Rs. 1,600 below the official MSP.

In Ballari, urad was the only exception that fetched a price above MSP. But that was not so in the rest of the country at the time of peak arrivals in November 2021. In that month, it sold for an average price of Rs. 4,789 against the MSP of Rs. 6,000. Similarly, tur or arhar sold at around Rs. 4,500 to 5,000 against the MSP of Rs. 6,000. The average price for maize was Rs. 1,354 against the MSP of Rs. 1,850. Wheat, the biggest crop of the season, may get a decent price wherever the state procurement takes place. In other areas, farmers could suffer a loss of Rs. 300 to 500 below the official MSP of Rs. 1,975. For all other crops, the MSP is the "maximum aspirational price." Maize, for example, could get between Rs. 1,300 and Rs. 1400, much below the MSP of Rs. 1,850. Barley can get Rs. 1,300 against the MSP of Rs. 1,600. Jowar can get about Rs. 1,000 lower than the MSP of Rs. 2,620. Chana or Bengal gram can get between Rs. 4,400 and 4,800. That indicates a loss of Rs. 300 to 700 per quintal, since the MSP is Rs. 5,100.

MSP is a fraud imposed on farmers; what is called "minimum" price is for all practical purposes a dream price, and that the "support" promised in the support price never arrives. Small farmers are particularly vulnerable to three new laws, which deregulated the agricultural market and weakened the government-established minimum sale price for crops in ways that could put small farmers against big agribusiness firms. India's agriculture problems are severe indeed. Farmers face declining plot sizes, degraded soils, scarce water, and rising debt. In the past 25 years, over 300,000 farmers in the country have committed suicide. However imperfect, India's past agricultural regulations at least ensured that crop sale prices nationwide in India remained close to the price floor set by the government. The group fears the new "era of fragmented and unregulated markets" will be even less "farmer-friendly" than the old system.

Under the new laws, problems among the farmers and traders or agribusiness firms would be settled by a new agricultural board, not the local courts as is done now. Poor farmer's access to the legal system in India is already limited. If agribusiness firms file a claim in a far-off jurisdiction, poor farmers who lack access to transport and money to travel would be at an even greater disadvantage.

WTO Protocol

Section 9 of WTO Protocol of Accession made it clear that the member countries "shall allow prices for traded goods and services in every sector to be determined by market forces, and multi-tier pricing practices for such goods and services shall be eliminated."

Prices in every sector must be determined by market forces. All subsidies to be notified to the WTO and prohibited subsidies to be eliminated. Under Section 15 of WTO Accession Protocol, member countries have the obligation to notify to the WTO any subsidy granted or maintained.

State-owned enterprises (SOEs) will operate free of state influence. Under Section 6 of WTO Accession Protocol, and Article XVII GATT 1994, member countries agreed that these SOEs would make purchase and sales involving imports or exports based solely on commercial considerations such as price, quality, marketability, and availability.

WTO rules suggest that except as otherwise provided for in the protocol, foreign individuals and enterprises shall be accorded equal treatment that accorded to domestic individuals and enterprises in respect of the procurement of inputs and goods and services necessary. All member countries agreed to join the *Government Procurement Agreement* (GPA) following accession to the WTO.

Member countries of the WTO agreed to repeal or revise all laws, regulations, and other measures inconsistent with the GATT "*Most Favored Nation*" ("MFN") and National Treatment rules, with regard to all other WTO members.

According to the WTO rules, all member countries should harmonize in conformity with the Technical Barriers to Trade (TBT) agreement, all technical regulations, standards, and conformity assessment procedures. All member countries of the WTO had agreed to remove all trade barriers to open the domestic market to foreign or private companies.

Reduced Agricultural Protectionism under WTO

The Uruguay Round Agreement on Agriculture (AoA) was propagated by the media as the start of a new era in which the withdrawal of subsidies in rich countries would open up new opportunities for poor countries, but the opposite has happened. Agricultural trade has a major influence on efforts to reduce poverty. Approximately three-quarters of the poorest people in developing countries live in rural areas. Subsidies in rich countries diminish export opportunities of poor countries. Smallholder farmers of poor countries cannot compete with imports from the developed countries subsidized by their governments.

In Mexico, maize farmers have been ruined by cheap subsidized imports from the United States. Women rice farmers in Haiti are facing similar problems. EU export subsidies are having similar effects in sub-Saharan Africa. The AoA asked the developed countries to reduce subsidies by 36 percent on agricultural products and tariffs by a similar amount. There has been no real reduction in agricultural subsidies. Governments of the developed countries have avoided any meaningful action. Income transfers are now considered as "support payments" and "emergency" payments to U.S. farmers, permissible under the WTO, have grown rapidly particularly since the outbreak of coronavirus.

Subsidies accounted for almost 40 percent of the value of OECD farm output, the same as it was in 1986–1988. The average tariff imposed by developed countries on agricultural goods from developing countries is close to 20 percent, but the developing countries are told to eliminate all subsidies and to depend on the market price. Tariff rates for groundnuts in the United States, and meat and dairy products in the EU, are now about 100 percent. Processed food products have tariffs at least twice as high as those on unprocessed products. These barriers represent a major obstacle for developing countries to expand their exports.

It is an acceptable practice in the WTO rules on agriculture where the practice of dumping, or the sale of items at prices below the cost of production, is allowed. Developed countries are also allowed to use export subsidies.

Situation in India

Two-thirds of India's 1.3 billion-strong population depend on farming for their livelihood; however, the agriculture sector makes up only around 17 percent of the nation's total economic output, amounting to about $2.3 trillion. More than half of India's farmers are reportedly in debt, with 20,638 committing suicide in 2018 and 2019, according to India's National Crime Records Bureau. After Modi came to power in 2014, he promised to double farmers' income by 2022; however, the situation hasn't improved. The government is under pressure to bring private investments to the agriculture sector that has stagnated over the past decades. In September 2020, India's Narendra Modi imposed three bills that eased restrictions on private sector in agricultural markets to confirm to these WTO instructions, remove restrictions on hoarding, remove purchase of the FCI to distort the market forces, and remove subsidies on farm prices. The farmers fear losing the MSP guarantee that they get now under the new laws.

These laws allow big companies to capture the farming, which will harm the small and marginal farmers. These small and marginal farmers own less than 5 and 2.5 acres of land, respectively. In Punjab, and probably for North India, over 50 percent of farmers hold land of fewer than 5 acres. The Congress Party, which was in power from 1947 until 2014 with some gaps for a few years, as it depends on the rural landlords for electoral support in rural areas, was unwilling to implement comprehensive land reforms. It comprised subsidized fertilizers and irrigation, rice and wheat varieties bred to absorb high fertilizer doses, and state-led training programs to assist farmers in transitioning to new practices.

Given the expense, it was rolled out only in a few, well-endowed districts of Punjab and a few other states. Because bumper productions inevitably depress prices, farmers were guaranteed procurement through state-run *mandis* (market yards) at MSPs declared in advance. State procurement was therefore crucial to transforming Punjab into India's breadbasket.

Modi introduced the laws as watershed reforms that will usher in a new era of prosperity for farmers backed by corporate investments. On the face of it, they allow private buyers to purchase farm produce outside of the supervision of and without the payment of taxes and fees to *mandis*; limit state intervention in retail prices; and provide a framework for farming on contract to corporations. However, clauses like one that bars farmers—or anyone else—from seeking legal recourse over contractual disputes cement the fear that the laws stack the deck against farmers. Farmers fear that the laws will end the state-regulated procurement at *mandis*. The real agenda behind the laws, farmers allege, is to facilitate corporate control over agriculture and food, and Reliance and Adani Group, two of India's largest business houses, perceived to be close to the Modi government, are blamed by the farmers.

The MSP is in place to ensure guaranteed prices and to protect farmers from price fluctuations. As this has no legal backing, it could mean that the new laws will also have no provision for it. It is fixed by the central government and is offered for 23 crops based on recommendations from the Commission for Agricultural Costs and Prices (CACP). Although the government is not legally bound to pay these even when open market rates ask for a lower price. MSP is kept at 1.5 times the cost of production but ultimately the price varies. Three formulas are considered by the CACP when it comes to calculating the costs:

- A2: This takes into account money spent by farmers on things such as seeds, fertilizers, and fuel.
- A2+FL: This is an estimated value of unpaid family labor.
- C2: This considers rent and interest foregone on the land plus if farmers own any machinery.

The government insists that the new reforms are a way to modernize the regulations and have vocally talked about MSP remaining even though it is not a written law. It says it is trying to help, while farmers disagree. The average monthly income for agricultural households is 8,931 Indian rupees, which is £90.36, according to research by the National Bank for Agriculture and Rural Development in 2016. Only 35 percent of that income is actually from agriculture, meaning farmers are forced to earn money from other sources such as rent on building or land, income from interest earned on bank deposits, and interest made from investments. They are worried this could eventually leave them dependent on big corporations and that the government might not step in to help.

India hands out an estimated $32 billion in subsidies to farmers annually, according to the finance ministry, but unsupported by independent observers. With the new ordinance, any corporation can purchase directly from the farmers. Farmers fear that corporates will end up setting prices on their own terms when the state markets eventually become redundant because the corporates have taken over the buying. There is even more reason to be fearful because the MSP clause is absent and because similar things have happened before in other industries.

On the second ordinance, the concern is that allowing the corporate to engage in contracts with the farmers puts farmers at the mercy of corporate. If there is a flood situation, and the farmers cannot produce top-quality products, the corporate may not pay the farmers. This means that with this ordinance, farmers have less security on payments.

With the final ordinance, that corporate sector got the liberty to store as much as they want in their warehouses. Previously, in India, there was a law that prohibited buyers from storing for more than what is required, because these are essential items. Now, with this ordinance, corporate sector could sell the produce on their own terms during shortages, causing inflation. Every year, farmers from Punjab and Haryana sell almost their entire produce to the FCI at MSPs, thanks to well-developed market yards and efficient procurement centers, very different from Bihar's underdeveloped grain procurement infrastructure. Average monthly incomes of the farmers in Punjab and

Haryana are Rs. 18,000 and Rs. 16,000 in 2013, but it is only Rs. 3,600 in Bihar. There is no MSP in Bihar.

While Punjab and Haryana sell almost their entire rice and wheat output to FCI, the government agency's procurement in Bihar has remained at less than 2 percent of the state's total production. The FCI, the main state-run grain procurement agency, buys only rice and wheat at those prices due to a lack of storage and funds. After buying rice and wheat from farmers at MSPs, the FCI sells the staples at highly subsidized prices to the poor. The government compensates the FCI for its losses. All these are against the WTO rules and have to go. The two top Indian billionaires, who the farmers point to as poised to benefit from the Farm Bills, are Ambani (who became fourth richest person in the world in 2020, up from 40th in 2014) and Adani (who grew to be 40th richest in the world in 2020 up from 609th in 2014); both are in the business of food and agriculture, including in marketing-related infrastructures such as ports and retails.

There is a National Food Security Act. It has the aim to ensure food security for all. The state should protect rights of small and marginalized farmers and provide land reforms, minor and small irrigation systems, remunerative prices, and affordable power and crop insurance. The state should also provide provisions for procurement, storage, and movement-related interventions toward decentralized procurement. These three new Farm Bills ignore that act and shift the responsibility of state for the big corporations, without any protection for the farmers. The Farm Bills will also undermine India's public distribution system.

Hunger is widespread in India. According to the India Food Bank, about 15 percent of the population is undernourished, while an estimated 34.7 percent of children are stunted. At the same time, roughly a third of food is wasted in the country due to inefficiencies in the agricultural system. The changes in the Essential Commodities Act will make basic food items unaffordable, as the big corporations will determine prices by hoarding.

These policies, embedded in the U.S. Farm Bill, have resulted in the number of U.S. small- and medium-scale farmers dwindling and farm consolidation increasing—with agribusiness having a strong grip over farmers and farm workers' lives and agribusiness determining much of what the people eat in the United States. The result in the United States is clear: a crisis in public health, ecological health, and for rural communities. All three laws are pro-corporate. Farmer's organizations are unanimous in the demand that the only solution is to repeal the laws. Despite decades of economic growth, up to half of India's population relies on growing crops on small areas of land, typically less than 3 acres, and farmers worry that without guaranteed prices they will be forced to sell their land and lose their livelihoods.

The Modi reforms were motivated by a well-organized effort of the World Economic Forum (WEF) and its New Vision for Agriculture (NVA), part of Klaus Schwab's Great Reset, the corporate side of the UN Agenda 2030. According to Engdahl (2007, 2008), Todhunter (2019a, b, c), and Brown (2019) the new Modi laws are measures the IMF and World Bank have been demanding since the early 1990s to bring Indian agriculture and farming into the corporate agribusiness model pioneered in the United States by the Rockefeller Foundation decades ago. It allows corporations to buy farmland for the first time nationally by large companies, food processing firms, and exporters, which can invest in the farm sector. Against them, a small farmer has no chance to survive. Here we find the WEF and the Gates Foundation's radical globalized agriculture agenda.

WEF and the Corporations

Engdahl (2007, 2008, 2020), Todhunter (2019a, b, c), and Brown (2019) explained that those laws are a direct result of several years' effort of the WEF and its NVA initiative. For more than 12 years the WEF and its NVA has pushed a corporate model in Africa, Latin America, and Asia. The "big target" has been India, where resistance to corporate takeover of agriculture has been fierce ever since the 1960s Green Revolution. For the WEF Great Reset, better known as the UN Agenda 2030 for "sustainable agriculture," India's traditional farm and food system must be broken. Its smallholder family farmers must be forced to sell to large agribusiness conglomerates and regional or state-level protections for those farmers eliminated. It will be "sustainable," not for the small farmers but rather the giant agribusiness groups.

To advance that agenda the WEF created a powerful group of corporate and government interests called the NVA India Business Council. Its website at the homepage of the WEF states, "the NVA India Business Council serves as an informal, high-level leadership group to champion private sector collaboration and investment to drive sustainable agricultural growth in India." The WEF's NVA India Business Council in 2017 includes Bayer Crop Science, one of the world's largest purveyors of agriculture pesticides and now of Monsanto GMO seeds, Cargill India Pvt. of the giant U.S. grain company, Dow Agro Sciences, GMO seed and pesticide producer, GMO and agrichemical firm DuPont, grain cartel giant Louis Dreyfus Company, Wal-Mart India; India's Mahindra & Mahindra (world's largest tractor maker), Nestle India Ltd., PepsiCo India, Rabobank International, State Bank of India, Swiss Re Services, the world's largest reinsurer, India Private Limited, a chemicals maker; and the Adani Group of Gautam Adani, the second richest man in India and major financier of Modi's BJP. There is no presence of any Indian farmer organizations.

In addition to top Modi backer Gautam Adani on the WEF-NVA India Business Council, Mukesh Ambani sits on the board of directors of Klaus Schwab's WEF. Ambani, another top Modi backer, is chairman and managing director of India's largest conglomerate, Reliance Industries, and Asia's second wealthiest person worth some $74 billion. Ambani is a strong advocate of the radical farm reform as Reliance stands to reap huge gains. It is clear that the interests and welfare of India's estimated 650 million farmers are not the priority. On November 26, 2020, a nationwide general strike began that involved approximately 250 million people in support of the farmers. Transport unions representing over 14 million truck drivers have come out in support of the farmer unions. The fact the government refuses to back down suggests it will be a bitter battle or a great defeat of the farming community. Modi deregulation corresponds to the UN 2021 Food Systems Summit.

AGRA and the UN Food Systems Summit

According to Engdahl (2020), indication of the agenda in store for India's farmers is the September 2021 UN Food Systems Summit (Cordaid 2021). UN secretary-general Antonio Guterres in 2019 announced the UN would host Food Systems Summit in 2021 with the aim of maximizing the benefits of a "food systems approach" consistent with UN 2030 Sustainable Development Goals. He named Agnes Kalibata of Rwanda as his Special Envoy for the 2021 Food Systems Summit. The summit's founding statement pushes "precision farming," such as GPS, Big Data and robotics, and GMO, as solutions (Todhunter 2019a, b, c; Brown 2019).

AGRA, the Alliance for a Green Revolution in Africa, was created by the Gates and Rockefeller Foundations to introduce GMO-patented seeds and related chemical pesticides into African agriculture. A key person Gates put in charge of the AGRA, Robert Horsch, spent 25 years as a senior Monsanto executive. The Bill & Melinda Gates Foundation is also a "Contributing Partner" of the WEF. After nearly 15 years and some $1 billion in funds from Gates, Rockefeller, and other large donors, AGRA has failed to lift farmers into a better well-being. Farmers are forced by their governments to buy seeds from commercial suppliers, often tied to Monsanto and other GMO companies, as well as commercial fertilizer. The result is debt and often bankruptcy. The farmers cannot reuse the commercial seeds and, instead, are forced to abandon traditional seeds, which they could reuse.

AGRA's focus on "market-oriented" means the global export market controlled by Cargill and other major grain cartel giants. In the 1990s, under pressure from Washington and agribusiness, the World Bank demanded African and other governments in developing countries to end their agriculture subsidies, but at the same time, the U.S. and EU agriculture remains heavily subsidized. The cheap subsidized EU and OECD imports drive local farmers bankrupt, which was planned. A 2020 report on AGRA, False Promises, concluded, "Yield increases for key staple crops in the years before AGRA were just as low as during AGRA. Instead of halving hunger, the situation in the 13 focus countries has worsened since AGRA was launched. The number of people going hungry has increased by 30 percent during the AGRA years . . . affecting 130 million people in the 13 AGRA focus countries." Gates' AGRA has made African food production more globalized and dependent than ever on the will of global multinationals whose aim is cheap inputs. It forces farmers into debt and demands specific "cash crops," like GMO corn or soya, be grown for export.

The Gates Foundation's confidential Agricultural Development Strategy 2008–2011 mentioned its strategy:

> Smallholders with the potential to produce a surplus can create a market-oriented agricultural system . . . to exit poverty . . . The vision of success involves market-oriented farmers operating profitable farms . . . this will require some degree of land mobility and a lower percentage of total employment involved in direct agricultural production.
>
> In 2008 Rajiv Shah was the Gates Foundation's Director of Agricultural Development, and led the Foundation's creation of the AGRA together with the Rockefeller Foundation. Today Shah is President of Rockefeller Foundation, Gates' partner in AGRA, which foundation also financed the creation of GMO patented seeds back in the 1970s, the creation of seed banks with the World Bank. Rajiv Shah is also an Agenda Contributor at the World Economic Forum. The fact that the President of AGRA is heading the September 2021 UN Food Systems Summit exposes the links between the UN, the Gates and Rockefeller Foundations, the World Economic Forum and their web of global corporate mega companies.

India, with 1.4 billion people, perhaps half in agriculture, is the last bastion where global agribusiness has been unable to dominate the production of food. The OECD has been globalized by industrial agribusiness since decades. China has opened up and is a major player in the GMO world with Syngenta as well as the world's largest producer of glyphosate. China industrial pork factory farms, such as Smithfield Farms, where the recent African swine fever is believed to have originated, are on the way to wipe out small-scale farmers there. "The central role of the Gates-Rockefeller AGRA in the UN 2021 Food Systems Summit, the major role of the WEF in the world 'food systems' reset, and the pressures in recent months on the Modi government to implement the same corporate agenda in India as in Africa, are all no accident" (Engdahl 2020).

India Farming Protests Resonate with U.S. Agriculture

The dispute raises questions not only about agriculture but also about dwindling populations in rural India where small communities are already struggling to survive—an issue mirrored in the parts of the United States. The images of farmers marching through New Delhi recall similar scenes in Washington, D.C., during the farming crisis of the late 1970s and early 1980s, when hundreds of trucks and tractors flooded the National Mall. Thousands of farmers lost their land, in part because of government policies that caused soaring interest rates as demand for their products plunged, leading to falling land values.

In Iowa, one of the hardest-hit states, there were about 500 farm auctions a month in 1983 when families had no choice but to sell. Just as feared by those protesting in India, the American farmers lost their livelihoods and sense of identity. Rural economies in the Midwest that had been declining for decades were devastated by the farm crisis. But while many farmers who survived emerged more prosperous, the communities near them continued to struggle. There are fears that the same could happen in India if New Delhi refuses to repeal the law that favors corporate farming. India has not had a substantial industrial base to absorb the large population into gainful industrial or urban employment. Instead, vast number of rural migrants is integrated into the low-end urban and construction economy. The challenges facing India are common to many developing countries in Asia, where farmland has been gobbled up, often for factories and property development, leaving hundreds of farmers without a proper livelihood. In countries including Myanmar, Cambodia, and China, many ended up on the fast industrializing cities, doing low-paid work in service sector in massage parlors and delivery services that provide no social benefits or security.

What are the solutions? Repeal of new agricultural laws to reform Indian agriculture cannot provide any solution as these are recommended by the WTO and India government alone will be unable to rectify these unjust rules of the WTO. Withdrawal from the WTO and its replacement by bilateral trade negotiations with the major trade partners of India should be examined seriously. India has only a handful of countries as serious trade partners. The United States, the United Kingdom, European Common Market, Russia, Japan, Australia, and the Arab Gulf Co-Operation Council member countries are the important trade partners of India. It will not be difficult to have trade treaties with these countries, and other countries will follow up these treaties. In that case, India's special requirements regarding subsidies and price supports can be considered. Trade with China and Pakistan can be eliminated completely, which cannot be done at present under the WTO rules.

Recently, these agricultural laws were withdrawn but there are no positive policies implemented by the Modi government regarding the agricultural sector. There is no effort to set up *mandis* (marketing outlets) in all states. There is no effort to give the MSPs for all agricultural products. However, the corporate sector is increasing its efforts to control farmers and farm lands much to the resentments of the farmers.

Developments in India in the Twenty-First Century

Narendra Modi came to power in 2014 after the long rule of Manmohan Singh from 2004 to 2014. Modi government had great success on all noneconomic matters but great failures on every economic issues.

Since the turn of the twentieth century, India's banking sector, and public banks in particular, is struggling because of the nonperforming loans or NPL, accumulated over the years due to mismanagement and corruption in the banking industry. NPL ratios have more than doubled over the past five years. In March 2021, the Reserve Bank of India took control of Yes Bank, the country's fourth largest private lender, after the bank did not have enough capital due to the mountain of NPL.

The problems in the banking sector are the reflections of a wider problem in the Indian economy. Growth rates of the GDP were reduced in 2019–2021 due to continuous lockdowns during the COVID-19 pandemic and increasing unemployment of the people. As a result, consumptions were reduced. The enterprises could not pay back their loans.

Modi has promised to revive manufacturing industry in India and to end the crony capitalism and corruption associated with the Congress Party of Manmohan Singh. That policy was failed mainly because of the mindless policy of the Ministry of Finance, which had failed to execute the revision of the GST system in India. The sudden cancellation of most bank notes, as India has a cash-dependent economy, was a total disaster.

In November 2016, the government abruptly canceled almost 90 percent of the cash in circulation. That move was designed to eliminate "black money" and terror funding and expected to benefit ordinary Indians. However, as the economy of India depends on cash transaction mainly, reduction of money in the system caused serious difficulties for the ordinary people and the economy slowed down. Daily wages of small businesses were reduced. Consumption went down, but little black monies were recovered. It was a great failure.

Modi government declared all currency notes of some denominations are invalid and the people must change their existing currencies as soon as possible with a very low limit for each individual. That had caused chaos but failed miserably as most the currency notes came back to the banks, except possibly just 1 percent. That proved that the black boney in India was just a rumor but not a fact. The government did very little to bring back the money stacked abroad.

Demonetization was followed in June 2017 by the inefficient and inhuman execution of the GST. It was full of complicated and constantly shifting formula for calculating the taxes to be paid. It imposed heavy costs on small and medium-sized enterprises as they have to employ chartered accountants instead of doing their accounts in house as they did before. The net result is the decline of the tax revenue of the government.

The final blow came in the fall of 2018; IL&FS and other nonbanks, which were important sources of credit after traditional banks, struggling under the weight of bad debts, stopped lending to companies and households. Instead, they loaned to nonbanks, which in turn lent the money at a much higher rate, causing serious financial difficulties for small and medium-sized enterprises.

Private investment as a share of GDP was reduced to its very low levels in 2019–2021, due to the depressing situation in manufacturing and construction. The government failed to stimulate the economy, which is suffering from chronic unemployment. From automobiles to residential property, Indian consumers are spending much as their income is in short supply. Tata Motors, one of the country's largest automakers, experienced a 30 percent decline in sales between April and December 2019. Vehicle production was reduced by 13 percent in 2019. There was little confidence among the consumers and investors.

In "Make in India" campaign Modi has a limited success with cases of international companies replacing imported components with locally made ones in India or expanding their assembly operations to serve the local market in India. Apple assembles some lower-end iPhones in India and began assembling newer iPhone XRs in Chennai in October 2019. A joint venture between Hitachi and Johnson Controls, which assembles air conditioners in Gujarat, is reducing the number of compressors it brings in from China. Samsung assembles some handsets in Noida, outside Delhi. In the meantime local mobile phone manufacturers went down due to imports of much cheaper Chinese mobile phones.

Frequent lockdown due to false warning from the World Health Organization, during the COVID-19 epidemic, ruined the small and medium-sized business in India and caused massive unemployment. The government refused to infuse money in the system to provide relief to the people. Most migratory laborers went back to their villages but the government reduced the finance for the program to provide jobs for 100 days to the unemployed people in the rural areas to construct rural infrastructure. As a result, Indian growth rate for the economy declined seriously in 2020–2021. Ministry of Finance in India became the obstacle to the economy of India.

Modi's government has scaled up the tariff walls on imports from China. Since 2018, duties have doubled on Chinese goods like footwear, toys, beauty products, electronics, and furniture to protect the manufacturing industry in China. In 2021, India refused to join the Regional Comprehensive Economic Partnership, which is an attempt to create a pan-Asian trading bloc, as it is controlled by China. India's main concern was reportedly that the country's manufacturing sector would be ruined, as the agreement would only increase the imports from China without giving any advantage for India.

Following is a set of key achievements of Prime Minister Narendra Modi government: foreign equity in rail infrastructure allowed, without limit; foreign equity cap in defense raised to 49 percent; 74 percent in case of technology transfer; foreign equity cap in insurance and pension sectors increased to 49 percent; $130 billion proposed spending on railways over five years on schemes including high-speed train. All these measures are according to increasing privatization and inclusion of international finance as suggested by the IMF and World Bank.

Inequality in India

State of Food Security and Nutrition in the World (SOFI) report of 2022 suggested that from 2018 to 2020, food insecurity in India rose by 6.8 percentage points. This is due to the fact that during the COVID-19 pandemic 84 percent of the households in India experienced decline in their income as millions of people in India lost their jobs and significant number of small and medium-sized businesses had to shut down. At the same time, top 10 rich Indians increased their wealth by 100 percent and billionaires of India had experienced increased wealth by $17.15 million. A total of 40 new billionaires emerged in India when the number of billionaires increased from 102 to 142, and 46 millions of Indians, which is half of the poor of the world, are now among the very poor.

According to the World Inequality Report 2022, the bottom 50 percent of the people own only 13 percent of national income whereas the top 10 percent own 57 percent, and top 1 percent own 22 percent of national income, and over 40 percent of nation's wealth.

According to report made by OXFAM in 2022, 10 richest Indians can maintain all schools of India for the next 25 years. GINI coefficient for India, which was 74.7 in 2000, went up to 82.3 in 2021. The corresponding GINI coefficient for China is now 38.5 in 2021. Thus, India is more unequal than China. The bottom 50 percent of the people of India in 2021 have only 6 percent of the national wealth. The share in national wealth of the top 1 percent of India went up from 33.5 percent in 2000 to over 40 in 2021.

Inequality was always there in India, particularly during the British rule, but the "Reform Program" designed by the IMF-World Bank could not reduce it but made it worse. Ten richest men in the world have their wealth increased from $700 billion in 2020 to $1.5 trillion in 2021. Thus, India is following the global trend as settled by the Washington Consensus.

In a country where social safety nets for poor workers are either nonexistent or extremely inadequate and where authorities often renege on their compensation promises, academic demonstrations of the long-run benefits of trade reform are not going to be convincing. Social protection should be part of a comprehensive trade and labor reform package if reform is to be desirable as well as feasible.

Chapter 8

India

External Sector

INTRODUCTION

India, a follower of the IMF-World Bank, has no trade policy but reacts to events. India's real gross domestic product (GDP) at current prices stood at about US$ 1.82 trillion in 2021. Simultaneously, the per capita income with GDP at current prices was estimated at about US$ 1,960.96 in 2021.

India's trade and external sector has a significant impact on the GDP growth. According to data from the Reserve Bank of India, on June 2021, the foreign exchange reserves in India reached US$ 605 billion. In June 2021, the merchandise exports increased to US$ 32.50 billion, indicating broad recovery in the trade. The central government established a new mechanism to increase import screening in order to protect domestic manufacturers. The current exchange rate in June 2021 is Rs. 1 = US$ 0.013.

Historically, India has run a current account deficit, largely driven by merchandise trade deficit and partly offset by net exports of services and net receipts in the secondary income (transfers) account. With India being a net importer of goods from the rest of the world, the merchandise trade balance has been a major factor in determining the viability of India's balance of payments over the years. On the exports side, India's performances improved in 2018–2019 notwithstanding the slowdown in global trade. The improvement was led by nonoil sectors, namely engineering goods, chemicals, and drugs and pharmaceuticals. Exports of petroleum products expanded too, supported by higher international crude oil prices. Higher imports of petroleum and coal essentially reflected elevated international prices.

India's goods trade deficit turns out to be highly correlated with trends in international crude oil prices. In 2018–2019, there was a rise of 46 percent in international crude oil prices. Consequentially, net oil imports constituted three-fourth of the expansion of trade deficit of US$ 21.4 billion. Despite increase in tariff on various electronic items in recent years, electronic goods imports increased and accounted for one-third of the merchandise trade deficit in 2018–2019. A sharp increase of 25 percent in imports of machinery corresponds to the increase in domestic investment activity. With import growth (17.4 percent) exceeding export growth (11.8 percent), the merchandise trade deficit increased to 7.3 percent of GDP from 6 per cent a year ago.

According to the World Trade Statistical Review 2018 of the WTO, India was the eighth largest exporter of services in the world in 2017, though export performances has dependent on software exports, reflecting cost competitiveness of Indian companies in providing IT services. According to the World Bank (2018), India was the top remittance-receiving country in 2018, followed by China, the Philippines, Mexico, France, and Egypt.

Foreign Direct Investment

In 1991, Benin, Trinidad and Tobago, Costa Rica, and Pakistan were among the 64 countries that received more foreign direct investment (FDI) than India did. By 2020, however, India emerged as the fifth largest recipient of FDI in the world, data from the United Nations Conference on trade and development shows. In absolute terms, FDI into India increased from $97 million in 1990–1991 to more than $81,722 million in 2020–2021, according to data with the Reserve Bank of India.

Relative to portfolio investment, FDI is considered to be a stable source of external financing. Net FDI declined to US$ 17.7 billion in 2018–2019 from US$ 19.6 billion in 2017–2018. The fall was contributed by both moderation in net inward FDI and rise in net outward FDI. Net flows of FDI in the form of equity recorded a fall of 10 percent. Country-wise pattern shows that about half of FDI flows since April 2000 have been routed through Mauritius and Singapore.

As per United Nations Conference on Trade and Development (UNCTAD) estimates, the global FDI flows fell by 41 percent in 2018, although world output increased. This fall is attributed to large repatriations of retained earnings by U.S.-based parent companies from their affiliates abroad.

Real and Nominal Effective Exchange Rate

The real effective exchange rate helps measure a country's overall export competitiveness. Effective exchange rate indices summaries the movement in a country's bilateral exchange rate with its trade partners as an index. Often, these indices depict changes in the external competitiveness of a country's goods and services based on changes in the exchange rate and better capture the macroeconomic effects of exchange rates than bilateral exchange rates. The nominal effective exchange rate (NEER) index captures the change in competitiveness based on movement in nominal bilateral exchange rates. The NEER index when adjusted for price differentials across trading partners forms the real effective exchange rate (REER) index. Together, these indices serve as summary indicators in tracking changes in international price/cost competitiveness of the home country.

However, in nominal effective terms, the rupee declined by 5.5 percent during 2018–2019 as some peer economy currencies depreciated more against the U.S. dollar relative to the rupee. India's real effective exchange rate declined to a lesser extent (4 percent) during the period as relative price pressures negated some of the nominal depreciation.

INDIAN INVESTMENT ABROAD

Outbound investments from India have undergone a considerable change, not only in terms of magnitude but also in terms of geographical spread and sectoral composition. There has been a perceptible shift in Overseas Investment Destination (OID) in last decade or so. While in the first half, overseas investments were directed to resource-rich countries such as Australia, UAE, and Sudan, in the latter half, OID was channeled into countries providing higher tax benefits such as Mauritius, Singapore, British Virgin Islands, and the Netherlands.

Indian firms invest in foreign shores primarily through mergers and acquisitions (M&A). With rising M&A activity, companies will get direct access to newer and more extensive markets and better technologies, which would enable them to increase their customer base and achieve a global reach. According to the Department of Economic Affairs, India's outward foreign direct investment (OFDI) stood at US$ 2.8 billion in July 2021.

The key investments are as follows:

- Tata Steel invested US$ 1 billion in a wholly owned subsidiary in Singapore.
- Wipro invested US$ 787.5 million in a fully owned unit in the United States.
- Tata Power invested US$ 131.25 million in a wholly owned unit in Mauritius.
- Reliance Industries invested US$ 56 million in agriculture and mining-based wholly owned subsidiary in Singapore.
- Interglobe Enterprises invested US$ 51.5 million in a joint venture in the United Kingdom.

- ONGC Videsh Ltd. invested US$ 48.31 million in a joint venture in Mozambique.
- Paharpur Cooling Towers invested US$ 48 million in a wholly owned subsidiary in Singapore.
- Tata Communications invested US$ 50 million in a wholly owned subsidiary in Singapore.
- ONGC Videsh invested US$ 48.70 million in a joint venture in Russia.
- WNS Global Services invested US$ 45 million in a joint venture in the Netherlands.

In September 2021, Serum Institute of India announced to invest US$ 68 million in Oxford Biomedica, a UK-based vaccine manufacturer, to boost manufacturing of COVID-19 vaccine. In May 2021, the Serum Institute of India announced plan to invest GBP 240 million (US$ 332.38 million) in the United Kingdom to expand its vaccine business.

The 1991 industrial policy did away with the 40 percent cap on foreign equity investment. It also empowered the Reserve Bank of India to grant "automatic approval" to foreign equity investment of up to 51 percent in more than 30 industries. This list was gradually expanded over the years. During the fiscal ended March 2019, India received the highest-ever FDI inflow of $64.37 billion.

Special Economic Zones

Special economic zones (SEZs) scheme in India was conceived in 1999 following China. The basic idea is to establish the zones as areas where export production could take place free from all rules and regulations governing imports and exports to give them operational flexibility. SEZ is a specifically duty-free enclave, which shall be considered to be a foreign territory for the purposes of trade and duties and tariffs.

One of the arguments in development economics is that foreign investment, in enclaves such as SEZ, initiates the process of industrial development by creating horizontal and vertical spillover effects. Horizontal spillovers are transfers of technology and management cultures from foreign multinational firms to local industries. It comes from local suppliers of the multinational companies and the buyers. Vertical spillovers can happen when the multinational company is trying to develop local supply chains, which can promote industries in neighboring areas. There are evidences from Indonesia and China that show high degree of vertical linkages. In the 1980s China made Shenzhen the example for the world, how a SEZ can be developed into an industrial hub. From 1965 onward, India experimented with the concept of export processing zones (EPZs), but these could not gave India much spillovers. Thus, in 2000, eight EPZs were converted into SEZs with off-shore banking units as well. SEZ units are allowed to keep 100 percent of their foreign exchange earnings in special "Export Earners Foreign Currency Exchange" accounts (Kumar 2008; Aggarwal 2006, 2011).

There are significant differences in the Indian SEZs with those of China. Indian SEZs are much smaller than municipality-sized SEZs in China. Information technology (IT) SEZs are as small as 0.1 square kilometers, whereas multiproduct SEZs are at least 10 square kilometers of area.

Indian SEZs are open to both the public and private sectors. Wang (2013) finds that municipalities with Chinese SEZs experienced productivity gains while Chaurey (2016) does not find productivity gains from the SEZ in the Indian state of Himachal Pradesh.

Colonization of the Indian Economy by China

India is very similar to China and therefore it is more affected by the Chinese competition, since China has entered the WTO. In India, its textiles and clothing sector plays a substantial economic role and was accounted for 8.2 percent of Indian manufacturing value added in 2009. The Multi-fiber Agreement (MFA) was signed in 1974, and most textiles exports from developing to developed countries were subject to import quotas under MFA. China's quota was four times of that of India, and quota of four Chinese-oriented countries (China, Taiwan, Hong Kong, and Singapore) was eight times of that of India. There was a definite pro-Chinese bias in the MFA, and it was carried forward in the WTO as well since 2001. Therefore, in 2002 and 2005, India was faced with the removal of a secure import quota in the markets of the developed countries, but Chinese exports have no restrictions in the markets of the developed countries. Thus, India is affected badly twice. China's WTO membership intensified competition for developing countries on their traditional export markets. Due to the dismantling of the MFA, increased Chinese export competition was particularly destructive in the textiles sector. Between 2000 and 2005, China's share of U.S. and EU textiles imports doubled, increased by 5123 percent in the United States and by 98 percent in the EU. In 2013, China accounted for 29 percent of global textile exports. That had nearly destroyed export markets of all non-Chinese countries; India was the main victim.

India-China Conflict in Trade

India-China bilateral trade in the year 2019 has reached US$ 92.89 billion. India's exports to China were US$17.97 billion, and India's imports from China were US$74.92 billion. One can easily see the difference. India rejected China's demand to grant it market economy status, with the background of near-war situation between the two armies along the Line of Actual Control (LAC). New Delhi will continue to treat its neighbor as a nonmarket economy, which allows it to impose steep antidumping duties on imports from China. World Trade Organization (WTO) members are allowed to apply antidumping measures on any company if it exports a product at a lower price than its home market and if the product threatens to affect badly the local industry. So far, at least 50 percent of the manufacturing jobs in India were destroyed by Chinese exports to India.

"China joined the WTO in December 2001 after years of negotiations on the condition that it will be treated as a non-market economy by other member countries for anti-dumping proceedings. A non-market economy refers to a country which has a complete or substantially complete monopoly of its trade and where all domestic prices are fixed by the state. While the 15-year period ended in December 2016, the European Union and the US have desisted from granting market economy status to China, citing wide-ranging price control on export commodities by China" (Horn, Reinhart, and Trebesch 2019). After the expiry of China's accession to WTO, it must be treated in same way as any other WTO member and regardless of the domestic law of that particular member; imports from China PR must be demonstrated on the basis of Chinese prices and costs. India, however, said since Chinese producers failed to file relevant information to prove the market economy status, it will continue to treat it as a nonmarket economy. Jayant Dasgupta, former Indian ambassador to the WTO, said, "If 80% of the companies are directly or indirectly controlled by the state and the banks are controlled by the Chinese Communist Party, then how can China claim that its trade partners should give it market economy status" (Dhar 2020).

India initiated 18 antidumping proceedings in 2019, most of them against China, according to the WTO website. However, China remains one of India's largest trading partners and a major source of intermediate products for its industry. India's exports to China rose to $17.1 billion in 2019, while imports rose to $68.3 billion. Imports from China began expanding quite rapidly from 2003 to 2004. In 2019–2020, China accounted for nearly 14 percent of India's imports and was by far its largest source of goods imports (Khosla 2020).

India's depends on China in two product groups, namely telecom and electronics products and pharmaceutical intermediates (Active Pharmaceutical Ingredients (APIs)). India imports more than 90 percent of the APIs for several antibiotics and vitamins from China. Three other sectors are important. The first is the motorcycle industry, which in 2018–2019 sourced 85 percent of its imports of parts and components from China. More than 90 percent of imports of silicon wafers and solar lanterns in 2019–2020 were from China. The third sector is textiles composed of natural, synthetic and artificial woven yarn. India's imports from China are mainly capital goods, railway equipment, and power plants. Although India produced these but private sector of India imports these because of their low costs. Indian imports include consumer durables. Imports of intermediates like APIs have also been sizeable. The share of imports of these products from China as a proportion of total imports increased to 57 percent in 2017 from 37 percent in 2003. The share of intermediate goods imports from China, including APIs, but increased by nearly 34 percent in 2019. India is critically dependent on China in many areas and that this dependence cannot be reduced quickly. India's exports are mainly raw materials and intermediates while capital and consumer are insignificant. Thus, it has the colonial pattern in trade (Dhar 2020).

India's imports from China in 2019 composed of high and medium technology products. Only 12 percent of the manufactured products that India imported from China in 2019 were low technology. The reason is the privatization and liberalization of import tariff. The average import duties on industrial products decline to below 9 percent in 2008 from 33 percent in 2000 under WTO instructions. India also had to remove all the quantitative restrictions on imports, such as import licensing, in 2001. More important reason is the faith in the Government of India on the marketplace. The public sector companies established to produce capital goods and ingredients of generic medicines (APIs) were neglected, and India government is now privatizing even profitable public sector companies and banks. Some of the biggest importers from China are close friends of Prime Minister Modi and his financiers. Successive governments have deepened import liberalization through free trade agreements (FTAs). India's three major FTAs, with the Association of South East Asian Nations (ASEAN), Korea, and Japan, respectively, have resulted in a widening trade deficit (Dhar 2020, 2018). Trade with China constitutes more than 40 percent of India's total trade deficit. India's anti-dumping duties on Chinese goods are being evaded by misclassification of products by the officers of the Government of India, thus there are Chinese agents in very powerful positions in India (Dhar 2019)

Impact on Micro, Small, and Medium Enterprises (MSMEs)

Very poor-quality Chinese products dominate the unorganized retail sector. This sector comprises domestic industries producing better-quality products. The solution is to use antidumping measures to promote these industries, which used to provide massive employment but now at least 50 percent of the jobs were destroyed by Chinese exports to India.

Textile Industry

Goods and Services Tax (GST) on synthetic fibers of 18 percent has increased the import of similar fabrics from China. Chinese fabric is manufactured into garments in Bangladesh and imported at cheap rates into India. It is difficult to impose any tariffs on imports from Bangladesh. However, actions can be taken on the brand names of some Western companies that buy from Bangladesh. That requires withdrawal from the WTO.

Bicycle Industry

There are preferences for cheap Chinese bicycles over Indian ones mainly because of the price advantages. The government can use the Public Procurement (Preference to Make in India) Order, 2017.

All these and more industries were defeated by cheap low-quality imports from China, reducing manufacturing units into importers and destroying jobs in India. India freed imports, thereby strangling its domestic industry. The tariffs on finished goods were often less than those for intermediate inputs. This discourages manufacturing industry and employment in manufacturing. Many now believe service industry jobs can replace industrialization. However, with 12.5 percent annual growth between 2007 and 2016, services added only 3 percent to India's employment. On the contrary, growth of services sector creates inequality of incomes and shifts employment for the highly educated section of the population. India's attractive domestic demand with a large market has attracted FDI. Sixty percent of FDI inflows are in the service sector, where few jobs can be created. Nearly half of FDIs have taken over local industry. They downsized these industries and reduced employment to increase efficiency; 92 percent of FDI in pharmaceuticals and 60 percent in chemical sector was M&A driven (Dhar 2020).

Chinese steel companies also have big plants in India. A majority of power companies in India use China-made power equipment, and TBEA, one of the biggest equipment exporters, has set up a China-dedicated industrial park in Gujarat. One key example is China's overwhelming presence in India's mobile phone market, where four out of the top five brands are Chinese. Xiaomi, the market leader, has seven factories in India and plans to invest more than $500 million to expand its retail presence here. Xiaomi's rival, BBK Electronics, which sells phones under three different brands—Oppo, Vivo, and OnePlus—has two factories in UP. Chinese share in India's imports grew from 11.6 percent in 2013–2014 to 16.6 percent in 2017–2018. In a decade to 2017–2018, China's imports in India rose by $50 billion. India registered a trade deficit of $157 billion in 2017–2018. Chinese government gives an effective rebate of 17 percent to its exporter companies (Dhar and

Joseph 2019). This results in Chinese goods being 5–6 percent cheaper than their Indian counterparts, making them lucrative for Indian importers. On account of costlier energy, finance, and logistics, Indian goods are costlier by about 9 percent in the global market. Chinese industry gets loans at 6 percent, compared to 11–14 percent in India. Logistics costs are 1 percent of the business in China, compared to 3 percent in India. Of the 803 licenses provided by the Bureau of Indian Standards (BIS) to foreign manufacturers selling in India under the Foreign Manufacturer Certification Scheme (FMCS), 294 licenses for 55 products have been granted to Chinese manufacturers. A similar scheme has also provided 9,274 registrations for information technology and electronics products. Of this, 5,857, or 64 percent, registrations have been granted to Chinese manufacturers. As much as 75 percent of the APIs used in the formulations of essential drugs in the National List of Essential Medicines (NLEM) are sourced from China (Dhar 2020, 2019; Rao and Dhar 2018).

Cheap Chinese imports have resulted in 35 percent closure of power looms in Surat and Bhiwandi. Bicycle imports from China saw a rise of 58 percent in volume and 47 percent in value in April to October 2017 over the previous year. Further, underinvoiced bicycles constitute 85 percent of the total bicycle imports from China in 2017–2018. Apart from affecting bicycle manufacturers, it is gradually killing the unorganized industry of small bicycle parts manufacturers that provide employment to many skilled and unskilled workers (Impact of Chinese Goods on Indian Industry, 145th report of Parliamentary Standing Committee on Commerce; Rao and Dhar 2018).

India, particularly the politicians, officers, and the business community, has surrendered to China already and only look at its profit by being an economic colony of China. So far India has not taken any serious efforts to reduce imports from China but has gone to the extreme to implement the WTO rules, which will only benefit China and open the economy for further colonization by China.

Chapter 9

India

Illegal Transfer and Crony Capitalism

PRIVATIZATION

Governments in developing countries and transition countries normally take the route of strategic sales, which means direct asset sales to selected owners known to the government because those countries do not have any efficient stock market. Literature based on empirical evidences suggests that privatization even carried out in a very honest way through the stock market could have very limited effects on efficiency. The costs are very high. Unemployment goes up. Wages go down. Prices go up. Social activities of the public sector enterprises disappear.

A 2012 study published by the European Commission argues that privatization in Europe had mixed effects on service quality and has achieved only deterioration of employment and working conditions.[36] Privatizations in Russia and Latin America had created very corrupt oligarchs, which has discredited privatization in these regions, leading to rise in the level of economic inequality and a collapse of the economy. A 2009 study published in *The Lancet* medical journal has mentioned that at least a million people died as the result of mass privatization in the former Soviet Union and in Eastern Europe during the 1990s. In India, a survey by the National Commission for Protection of Child Rights (NCPCR) on free medical services to the Economically Weaker Section in Private Hospitals, revealed although they were allotted land at subsidized rates, private hospitals do not care for the poor. Oxfam India says, "The privatization of public services . . . implies limited or no access to essential services for people living in poverty." Most public sector enterprises before privatization used to have hospitals or clinics for their workers but since privatization these mainly have disappeared.

There are other reasons to support public sector enterprises. An elected government accountable to the people is motivated to safeguard the people of the nation; profit motive cannot be a substitute for social welfare. If a publicly owned company providing an essential service to all citizens is privatized, its new owner can reduce the social obligation to increase profit. In most cases, privatization leads to asset stripping.

Privatization of Public Sector in India

India used to have a mixed economy in which both private and public sectors exist especially in the areas of banking, telecom, road transport, education, health care, manufacturing, and education, among others, but recently Prime Minister Narendra Modi declared on February 24, 2021,

> "Government has no business to be in business. The government's focus should be on projects related to the welfare and development of the people." He was influenced by the philosophy of the IMF-World Bank, not by the philosophy of the welfare state.

Jain (2021) examined Chapter 9 of the Economic Survey, 2019–2020. This chapter narrated the efficiency gains from privatization by analyzing the before and after performance of 11 Central Public Sector Enterprises (CPSEs) that were privatized. Performance indicators used are net worth (equity capital and profits), net profit (profit after tax), gross revenue, return on assets (profit after tax to assets), return on equity (profit after tax to net worth), net profit margin (profit after tax to operating income), sales growth, and gross

Table 9.1. Money in the Swiss banks from India (Millions of US$)

1996	5,211
1997	4,863
1999	5,985
2004	5,088
2005	5,766
2006	7,223
2007	8,885
2008	8,257
2011	3,393
2012	2,566
2013	2,648
2014	2,234
2015	1,448
2016	800
2017	524

Source: BIS, 2019.

profit per employee (profit to the number of employees) but not on employment, wage rate, pensions, medical supports, educational supports for the children of the worker, and other benefits to the workers.

The performance of these 11 CPSEs is then compared for 10 years before and after privatization. Based on this analysis, the chapter pushes for aggressive privatization.

Selling away profitable CPSEs is similar to selling off the family's silver. The main objective of the disinvestment policy is to fill up the fiscal deficit gap. Of the 11 privatized firms, almost six firms have experienced minuscule benefits or adverse effects on performance. The survey uses only successful private firms such as Vedanta, Moser Baer, Mahindra & Mahindra, and Ashok Leyland, among others, as the "peer" firms. These firms are structurally and functionally very different from state-owned enterprises. There are many private firms that have failed to repay their loans from the banks, which is the main reason for the crisis in the banking sector of India. Any evaluation should incorporate employments, regional imbalances, and operating in areas and sectors where the private sector is unwilling to enter (Jain 2021).

Former governor of the Reserve Bank of India in an address in 2014 mentioned, "Our provision of public goods is unfortunately biased against access by the poor. While the poor do not have the money to 'purchase' public services that are their right, they have a vote that the politician wants. One of the greatest dangers to the growth of developing countries is the middle income trap, where crony capitalism creates oligarchies that slow down growth" (Raghuram Rajan's address at the 20th Lalit Doshi Memorial Lecture on August 11, 2014, in Mumbai). However, India has chosen to create crony capitalists.

GAUTAM ADANI AND THE CONCENTRATION OF POWER IN INDIA

When the Indian government approved the privatization of six airports in 2018, it allowed companies without any experience in the sector to bid. Gautam Adani, with no history of running airports, got all six, which showed how the central government favored politically connected business tycoons. He is also its largest private sea ports operator and thermal coal power producer. He has a growing share of India's power transmission and gas distribution markets and announced that his Adani Green Energy would invest $6 billion to build solar plants with a capacity of 8 GW, one of the largest renewable projects in the world. Along with Reliance Industries chairman Mukesh Ambani, Mr. Adani controls most valuable parts of the economy in India. Since 2014 Adani's net worth has increased by about 230 percent to more than $26 billion as he won government tenders and built infrastructure projects across the country. It is not new. During the Nehru era, Birla and other Marwari business community members got the upper hand in getting all licenses, permits to import, and quotas in the name of planning. They maintained their hold even after 1992, but the arrival of Modi means now Gujarati business community got most of the privileges. Adani's total bonds are worth $7.8 billion. Total outstanding loans are $22.2 billion. If he fails, the banking system of India would be in great danger.

Crony Capitalism of Gandhi Family

Robert Vadra, the husband of Priyanka Vadra, daughter of Rajiv Gandhi, has been accused of taking an interest-free loan of Rs. 65 crores and huge bargains on land from Delhi Land and Finance in exchange for political favors for a development company DLF. In addition, there are questions about the authenticity of balance sheets of companies owned by Robert Vadra, which claim that Corporation Bank had provided an overdraft of Rs. 7.94 crores for his businesses. All this money belongs to the public, and crony capitalism has resulted in the misuse of public funds for the gain of an individual's businesses.

Air India Sale

With the successful sale of Air India to the Tata group, Prime Minister Narendra Modi's government has restarted the long-stalled privatization program. The acquisition gives the Tata Group 141 planes and 900 slots at overseas airports, the most valuable of which are at London's Heathrow Airport.

Before 2005, both Air India and Indian airlines were profitable companies, but they were merged, new 111 planes from Boeings and Air Bus were purchased, and profitable routes were given away to the private airlines. All these unnecessary activities increased deliberate massive losses, and the call for privatization was increased.

Before, during the Vajpayee administration, government managed to sell as many as 12 public sector units. Indian Petrochemicals was bought by Mukesh Ambani's Reliance Industries during that time. Some of the important privatization in future include Bharat Petroleum, Shipping Corporation of India, Container Corporation of India, and HLL Lifecare. Apart from this, six steel plants are also listed for sale, including Neelachal Ispat Nigam, Durgapur Steel Plant, Salem Steel Plant, and Rashtriya Ispat Nigam, also known as Vizag Steel. The government also wants to reduce the number of public sector banks in the country through sale to the private sector.

If crony capitalism under the Congress-led United Progressive Alliance was characterized by scams like captive coal block allocation, some politicians and small-time crooks received very valuable coal mines. BJP in turn has helped some companies to escape from the bankruptcy process when they could not repay the loans from some banks.

The Case of Thermal Power Projects

By 2018, almost 34 private thermal power plants across India were unable to compete with rivals with cheap coal from their own captive coal blocks and, when the Supreme Court cancelled all coal block allocations in 2014, were in problem with the banks. Tata, Adani, and Essar were among these companies.

Rajshekhar (2020) wrote, in 2010, these companies demanded tariff reductions, arguing that a price increase in Indonesian coal required that. In June 2017, the Department of Revenue Intelligence found out overinvoicing of imported coal by Adani Mundra, Tata Mundra, and Essar Salaya, but the Union Ministry of Power rescued them (Rajshekhar 2020).

In the case of Essar Oil, a serious corruption can be detected. A group of Indian oil companies, led by ONGC Videsh, purchased a share in Rosneft's Vankor oilfield. The deal, initially settled in August 2015 at $900 million for a 15 percent stake, became in September 2015 at $1.25 billion. Over the next 12 months, Indian oil companies purchased another 34.9 percent at the same valuation. In the second deal, Rosneft overpaid for Essar's oil refinery at $1.456 billion, when Essar had valued its oil business (not including the port) at $1.08 billion. Rosneft paid another $26.6 million for the adjacent Vadinar port and related infrastructure. The deal valued Essar Oil at 12.5 times EBITDA (earnings before interest, tax, depreciation, and amortization). At the end, Rosneft made $6 billion from the sale of its oilfields (Vankor and an oil subsidiary called TNYGD) (Rajshekhar 2020). Essar made a profitable deal instead of losing its refinery in bankruptcy proceedings. Business groups close to the government continue to obtain finance despite their difficult financials.

Rafale Aircraft Case

Rafale aircraft was rejected on technical ground by the IAF in 2011; because of bribes it came back to the competition. It gave a contract of $50,000 crore to Anil Ambani, brother of Mukesh Ambani, although he has no experience in aircraft manufacturing. Before, France supplied materials for Chinese nuclear weapons when China had no nuclear reactors both in 1964 and in 1967. France gave the first Chinese nuclear reactor only in 1992. France during the Pakistani invasion on Kargil in 1999 blocked the missile launching facility in Mirage fighter of India electronically. They can do the same for Rafale in future conflict. Morocco and Egypt also purchased Rafale, and Pakistani pilots are getting trained in France in Rafale. They can be transferred to Pakistan along with their Rafale in any future conflict with Pakistan.

Size of India's Black Economy

There are no official estimates of India's black economy. In 2011 the government had commissioned a joint study to estimate Indian entities' unaccounted wealth both at home and abroad. The final report has not been submitted. India was ranked fifth largest exporter of illicit money between 2002 and 2011, with a total of $343.04 billion. India is fifth in the world on illicit outflows.

Other Estimates

According to Global Financial Integrity (GFI), a Washington-based think tank, Indians send away $462 billion in overseas tax havens between 1948 and 2008. Money stashed away in tax havens by Indians, according to former CBI director A. P, Singh, can be as high as $500 billion (see Table 9.1 and 9.2).

Table 9.2. Illicit Flow, GFI Report, December, 2011

Rank	*Country*	*Illicit Outflow (Billions of US$)*
1	China	2,467
2	Mexico	453
3	Russia	427
4	Saudi Arabia	366
5	Malaysia	338
6	Kuwait	269
7	United Arab Emirates	262
8	Venezuela, BR	171
9	Qatar	170
10	Poland	160
11	Nigeria	158
12	Kazakhstan	123
13	Philippines	121
14	Indonesia	119
15	India (US$104 billion)	104
16	Ukraine	92
17	Chile	84
18	Argentina	83
19	Islamic Republic of Iran	66
20	Egypt	60

Source: Global Financial Integrity.

An amount of $1.4 trillion can be parked in undisclosed overseas accounts, according to a BJP task force report of 2011.

Other Estimates

$462 billion (about Rs28.6 lakh crore): According to Global Financial Integrity (GFI), a Washington-based think-tank, Indians salted away $462 billion (about Rs 28 lakh crore in current exchange rates) in overseas tax havens between 1948–2008.

$500 billion (about Rs 31.4 lakh crore): Money stashed away in tax havens by Indians, according to former CBI director AP Singh.

$500 billion (Rs 31.4 lakh crore) and $1.4 trillion (Rs 86.8 lakh crore): Parked in undisclosed overseas accounts, according to a BJP task force report of 2011.

The author of the GFI report, Dev Kar, a former International Monetary Fund economist, said that almost three-quarters of the illegal money that comprises India's underground economy ends up outside the country.

(GFI means Global Financial Integrity, an organization based in Washington D.C.)

GFI estimates that as much as $510 billion has flowed out of India illicitly between 2004 and 2013, of which $332 billion went out between 2010 and 2013. In 2013, for instance, about $83 billion was estimated to have been siphoned out of the country, and the only comfort was that it was significantly lower than the $93 billion taken out of the country in 2012. The think tank has estimated that over $1 trillion was siphoned out of developing nations in 2013 alone and over $7.8 trillion in the decade up to 2013.

Some the main findings of the report are as follows:

- India lost a total of $462 billion in illegal capital flows between 1948, a year after independence, and 2008.
- The flows are more than twice India's external debt of $230 billion.
- Total capital flight out of India represents some 16.6 percent of its GDP.
- Some 68 percent of India's capital loss has happened since the economy opened up in 1991.
- "High net-worth individuals" and private companies were found to be primary drivers of illegal capital flows.
- The share of money Indian companies moved from developed country banks to "offshore financial centers" (OFCs) increased from 36.4 percent in 1995 to 54.2 percent in 2009.

India's underground economy has been estimated to account for 50 percent of the country's GDP—$640 billion at the end of 2008. This is the list of 28 "Nationalist" business men who looted money from Indian Banks:

(1) Vijay Mallya, (2) Mehul Choksi, (3) Nirav Modi, (4) Nishan Modi, (5) Pushpesh Baidya, (6) Ashish Jobanputra, (7) Sunny Kalra, (8) Arti Kalra, (9) Sunjay Kalra, (10) Varsha Kalra, (11) Sudhir Kalra, (12) Jatin Mehta, (13) Umesh Parikh, (14) Kamlesh Parikh, (15) Nilesh Parikh, (16) Vinay Mittal, (17) Eklavya Garg, (18) Chetan Jayantilal, (19) Nitin Jayantilal, (20) Dipti Bein Chetan, (21) Saviya Saith, (22) Rajiv Goyal, (23) Alka Goyal, (24) Lalit Modi, (25) Ritesh Jain, (26) Hitesh Nagenderbhai Patel, (27) Mayuriben Patel, and (28) Ashish Suresh Bhai. Total looted amount stands at Rs.10,000,000,000,000 (only Rs. 10 trillion).

In comparison, the total funds held by all foreign clients of Swiss banks rose about 3 percent to CHF 1.46 trillion or about Rs. 1,000 billion in 2017, according to the official annual data released today by Swiss National Bank (SNB), the central banking authority of Switzerland. According to the SNB data, the total funds held by Indians directly with Swiss banks rose to 999 million Swiss franc (Rs. 6,891 crore) in 2017, while the same held through fiduciaries or wealth managers increased to CHF 16.2 million (Rs. 112 crore). These figures stood at CHF 664.8 million and CHF 11 million, respectively, at the end of 2016 (1 crore is equal to 10 million).

As per the latest data, the Indian money in Swiss banks included CHF 464 million (Rs. 3,200 crore) in the form of customer deposits, CHF 152 million (Rs. 1,050 crore) through other banks, and CHF 383 million (Rs 2,640 crore) as "other liabilities" such as securities at the end of 2017. The funds under all three heads have risen sharply, as against a huge plunge across all categories in the previous year, the SNB data showed. The funds held through fiduciaries alone used to be in billions till 2007 but began falling after that amid fears of regulatory crackdown. The total funds held by Indians with Swiss banks stood at a record high of CHF 6.5 billion (Rs. 23,000 crore) at 2006 end but came down to nearly one-tenth of that level in about a decade (1 crore is equal to 10 million).

Swiss Banking Association Report

2006 details of bank deposits in the territory of Switzerland published by Switzerland National Bank (SNB) by nationals of following countries:

Top five
India—$1,456 billion
Russia—$ 470 billion
United Kingdom—$390 billion
Ukraine—$100 billion
China—$ 96 billion

India has more money in Swiss bank than all the other countries combined. Second best Russia has four times lesser deposit. The United States is not even there in the counting in top five.

India has around 450 billion dollars' worth of coal deposits and 170 billion dollars' worth of iron ore deposits, looted by state politicians. According to Indian government, there are around 100,000 places in India where people are doing illegal mining. Dishonest persons, scandalous politicians, and corrupt IAS and IPS officers have deposited in foreign banks in their illegal personal accounts a sum of about $1,500 billion, which have been misappropriated by them. This amount is about 13 times larger than the country's foreign debt. This huge amount has been appropriated from the people of India by exploiting and betraying them.

According to the latest SNB data, funds parked by Indian individuals and enterprises in Swiss banks, including through India-based branches, fell by 5.8 percent in 2019 to 899 million Swiss francs (Rs. 6.625 billion). The data for "total liabilities" of Swiss banks toward Indian clients take into account all types of funds of Indian customers at Swiss banks, including deposits from individuals, banks, and enterprises. This also includes data for branches of Swiss banks in India as well as nondeposit liabilities.

A viral message on social media claims that WikiLeaks has released a list of top black money holders in Swiss banks. Incidentally, all the individuals named in the list are Indians. "Indigestible news: Indians black money in Swiss bank is Rs. 358,679,863,300,000 (estimated to be 1.3 trillion dollars) this money belongs to 2000 Indians who have kept there to evade from tax, This money is enough for India to become 10 America and become one of the most powerful developed country in the world for next 100 yrs," reads the concluding paragraph of the message.

WikiLeaks published first list of black money holders in Swiss bank; the top most 30 members are all politicians (money is in crores; 1 crore is equal to 10 million; as in 2019).

1. Asadudhin Ovaisi (568,000)
2. Moidin Bava (7,800)
3. U. T. Khadar (158,000)
4. Siddaramayya (82,000)
5. Sonia Gandhi (155,040)
6. Mallikarjun Karge (28,900)
7. Roshan Beg (9,000)
8. Mohammed Haris Nalpad (15,000)
9. Pranab Mukherjee (75,000)
10. Mani Shankar Aiyar (50,000)
11. Shashi Tharoor (5,900)
12. Ahmed Patel (220,000)

13. Aajam Khan (76,888)
14. K. J. George (582,114)
15. Ambika Soni (19,800)
16. D. K. Shivakumar (135,800)
17. Chidambaram (8,200)
18. Manmohan Singh (14,500)
19. Lalu Prasad Yadav(28,900)
20. G. Parameshwarappa (9,000)
21. Kalanithi Maran (15,000)
22. A Raja (35,000)
23. Kanzhimoli (5,900)
24. Rahul Gandhi (189,008)
25. Mayawati (168,009)
26. Mamata Banerjee (257,500)
27. Akhilesh Yadav (300,089)
28. Digvijay Singh (220,060)
29. Sashi Kala(154,700)
30. Karunanidhi (12,870)

WikiLeaks published another list of black money holders in Swiss bank, as in 2019. The top most 25 members are as follows (they are all businessman) (money is in crores; 1 crore = 10 million):

1. Ambani (568,000)
2. Adani (7,800)
3. Amit Shah (158,000)
4. Rajnath Singh (82,000)
5. Arun Jaitley (15,040)
6. Smriti Irani (28,900)
7. Yadiyurappa (9,000)
8. Ravi Shankar Guruji (15,000)
9. Baba Ramdev (75,000)
10. Janardhana Reddy (50,000)
11. Nalin Kohli (5,900)
12. Devendra Fadnavis (220,000)
13. Lalit Modi (76,888)
14. Sushma Swaraj (582,114)
15. Narendra Modi (19,800)
16. Harshad Mehta (135,800)
17. Ketan Parekh (8,200)
18. Katta Subramanya Naidu (14,500)
19. Lalu Prasad Yadav (28,900)

20. J. M. Scindia (9,000)
21. Kalanithi Maran (15,000)
22. Karunanidhi (35,000)
23. Vasundhara Raje (5,900)
24. Raj Foundation (189,008)
25. N. Chandrababu (168,009)

The data from the BIS are available from the year 1996. Going by this data, the liabilities of Swiss banks toward Indian nonbanks had reached a peak of US$8,885 million in the year 2007, just before the global financial crisis. But following the global financial crisis, these liabilities had continuously decreased ever since except in the year 2013 when they increased marginally.

Contribution of Mauritius

In February 2008, R. Prasad, the then chairman of the Central Board of Direct Taxes (CBDT), led a team of tax sleuths to Port Louis, the capital city of Mauritius. Backed by a team from the Ministry of External Affairs, Prasad made an attempt to convince Mauritius officials to renegotiate the double tax avoidance agreement (DTAA), which was resulting in massive tax losses to India. Prasad's attempt was unsuccessful, but what he discovered in the process was startling: a handful of persons acted as directors for about 30,000 companies located in that island nation. Also, companies there exist only on paper, as addresses of many of those begin with a mere post box number.

Mauritius and many other tax havens act as buffers to bring back India's black money as white. Now, the Supreme Court-appointed Special Investigation Team (SIT) on black money wants such tax treaties to be redrafted. The government had to hand over to the apex court a complete list of 627 Indians who have accounts in HSBC Bank, Geneva.

While tax havens like Mauritius will help black money come back into the country as white, Indians continue to send illicit money abroad. This is done through various methods, "Hawala" (illegal private money traders) transactions—where money is transferred abroad without any real movement of funds—being one of them, although, according to a finance ministry white paper on black money released two years ago, "Hawala" transactions have actually dwindled over the past decade.

The classic example of such a hurdle is seen in the case of Pune-based stud farm owner Hasan Ali Khan, who was raided by the IT department seven years ago. Documents and data in his laptop established that he had a Swiss bank account with a whopping $8 billion in deposits. Ali was sent to jail, but the ED that probes money laundering cases found out from the Swiss authorities that Ali's accounts had been emptied.

The maximum amount of money associated with a client connected to Mauritius was $24.2 million. Total amount from Swiss Bank HSBC was $141 million (Source: World Bank). Mauritius has been the biggest source of Foreign Investment in India over the last 15 years. In fact, Mauritius accounted for one-third of all inflows of investment into India over the last 15 years. In the same time, the United States only accounted for 6.2 percent of investment.

Why Mauritius Is More Important Than Switzerland

Black money sent abroad is not the same as black money held abroad. Funds are moved out of India not to be stashed away in Swiss banks but to be brought back as foreign investment.

In the case of India, this mostly happens through sham corporations registered in Mauritius. While the money comes back as investments, the earnings on such investments are not taxed in India because India and Mauritius have a double tax avoidance treaty.

The primacy of the small island to the subcontinent is apparent from this statistic: Between 2000 and 2012, 38 percent of the FDI in India came from Mauritius, while only 6 percent came from the United States. Mauritius accounted for $8,059 million of $18,286 million of FDI in India in 2012–2013. If the government were serious about tackling the black economy in India, it would achieve more by closing the loopholes in the Mauritius route.

Forty percent of the total FDI coming into India comes from Mauritius. There is no taxation on capital gains in Mauritius so that if an entity sets up a paper company there, our Double Taxation Avoidance Agreement (DTAA) becomes in fact a double nontaxation agreement. Income Tax Department had the power to examine and verify whether the resident status of a company in Mauritius was genuine or not. The BJP government withdrew that power by Circular 789 of April 2000, under which a simple certification from the Mauritius government is now accepted. This means that India no longer has the power to question the residential status of a company there.

Mauritius-based funds investing in India get a tax breather. They have now been virtually exempt from the indirect transfer provisions of the income tax law. The finance ministry has now specified "Mauritius" as an eligible country for its funds to be registered with SEBI as category I foreign portfolio investor (FPI). The budget had exempted category I FPI from the ambit of indirect transfer provisions under income tax law. This move will benefit both regulated and unregulated funds domiciled in Mauritius.

Singapore has become an alternative to Mauritius. Shifting to Singapore will allow category II FPIs to escape the higher tax liability imposed on them in Mauritius. Foreign funds are making changes to their structures to reduce their tax outgo. India-focused funds that use Mauritius for favorable tax treatment are planning to route their funds through Singapore, another tax haven, to escape higher tax liability after the Union budget removed some exemptions for those based in Mauritius.

Shifting to Singapore will ensure that category II FPIs are not saddled with higher tax liability as the city state is still exempt from indirect transfer provisions. Mauritius made in 2019, Rs. 4.37 trillion worth of portfolio investments into India. While a majority of foreign funds were exempted from indirect transfer provisions in 2017, the Finance Bill of 2020 has removed exemptions for category II FPIs, which include hedge funds and funds that are set up in countries not compliant with the Financial Action Task Force (FATF) norms to combat money laundering and terror financing. Mauritius is not an FATF jurisdiction. The other big issue is the retrospective nature of the provisions. Investments made between September 2019 and February 1, 2020, by FPIs that don't fall in category I will also attract indirect transfer tax provisions.

The Role of the United Kingdom

Investments routed through Mauritius are estimated to have cost India between $10 billion and $15 billion over the last 20 years in lost capital gains tax, dividends tax, and tax on interest and royalty payments. The system has been used not only by foreign investors but also by Indian nationals, who essentially send their funds on a round trip.

Britain's overseas territories have topped a list of the world's most significant tax havens ahead of Switzerland, the Netherlands, and Luxembourg. The British Virgin Islands were ranked as the "greatest enabler of corporate tax abuse," with the Cayman Islands in second place and Bermuda third.

The United Arab Emirates (UAE) was a new entry into the top 10 after an investigation found it had benefited from $250 billion (£180 billion) of multinational funds routed through the Netherlands. The report said the UAE had emerged as a new destination for multinational corporations operating in Africa and the Middle East. South Africa was highlighted as one of the biggest losers from firms shifting profits to the low-tax UAE.

Global Alliance for Tax Justice wrote, "The biggest economies in the world were helping companies avoid $245billion in tax," and "to trust the OECD in light of its findings is like trusting a pack of wolves to build a fence around your chicken coop." OECD countries were responsible for 39 percent of the world's corporate tax abuse risks. Their territories and former colonies—such as the United Kingdom's independent territories and Jersey, Guernsey, and the Isle of Man, which are crown dependencies—were responsible for 29 percent. Countries graded by the OECD as "not harmful" are responsible for 98 percent of the world's corporate tax abuses risks. Britain's overseas territories and crown dependencies continued to facilitate capital flight from many of the world's poorest nations, allowing multinational corporations to avoid legitimate claims on their profits.

The total amount of black money deposited in foreign banks by Indians is unknown. Some reports claim a total of US$1.06—1.4 trillion is held illegally in Switzerland (in WikiLeaks); other reports, including those reported by the Swiss Bankers Association and the Government of Switzerland, claim these reports are false and fabricated, and the total amount held in all Swiss bank accounts by citizens of India is about US$2 billion. In February 2012, the director of India's Central Bureau of Investigation said that Indians have US$500 billion of illegal funds in foreign tax havens, more than any other country. In March 2012, the government of India clarified in its parliament that the CBI director's statement on $500 billion of illegal money was an estimate based on a statement made to India's Supreme Court in July 2011. In March 2018, it was revealed that the amount of Indian black money currently present in Swiss and other offshore banks is estimated to be US$1.5 trillion. As per data released by the Department of Industrial Policy and Promotion (DIPP), two of the topmost sources of the cumulative inflows from April 2000 to March 2011 are Mauritius (41.80 percent, US$54.227 billion) and Singapore (9.17 percent, US$11.895 billion). It is obvious that tax evaders routed through these money in order to conceal from revenue authorities.

Investment in the Indian stock market through participatory notes (PNs) or overseas derivative instruments (ODIs) is other ways in which the black money generated by Indians is reinvested in India. The investor in PNs are legally held by the Foreign Institutional Investors, like Foreign Pension Funds, Gold imports through official channel and smuggling is a major conduit to bring back the black money from abroad and convert into local black money as the gold commands high demand among the rural investors particularly. Also fictitious high-value round-trip travels, by diamonds and precious stones exporters and importers, are a channel for illegal transactions. Also, fictitious software exports can be booked by software companies to bring black money into India.

In February 2015, balances for the year 2006–2007 in HSBC's Geneva branch were obtained by French newspaper *Le Monde* and included the names of several prominent businessmen, diamond traders, and politicians. The balance against the 1,195 names stood at US$3.6 billion.

The 2016 Panama Papers were obtained by International Consortium of Investigative Journalists, originally from Mossack Fonseca, a Panama-based law firm with offices in more than 35 countries. The list consists of names of 500 Indians such as Amitabh Bachchan, Aishwarya Rai, Niira Radia, K. P, Singh, Garware family, Harish Salve, and others.

WTO-induced privatization of public assets generated these gigantic flows of illegal monies from India. However, India is not the only country in this matter. One has to blame corruptions, lax administration, and implicit support from the developed countries along with the drive to comply with the WTO's agenda for a market economy.

Role of Dubai and the UAE

While the vast majority of financial, business, and real estate transactions in Dubai are not associated with illegal activity, part of what underpins Dubai's prosperity is a steady stream of illicit proceeds borne from corruption and crime. Dubai is now a major gold trading hub. Meanwhile, both Emirati leaders and the international community continue to turn a blind eye to the problematic behaviors, administrative loopholes, and weak enforcement practices that make Dubai a globally attractive destination for dirty money (Page and Vittori).

Corrupt and criminal actors from around the world operate through or from Dubai. Afghan warlords, Russian mobsters, Nigerian kleptocrats, European money launderers, Iranian sanctions-busters, and East African gold smugglers all find Dubai a conducive place to operate. Dubai's property market is a magnet for tainted money. Built to attract foreign buyers, the emirate is dominated by towers of upscale flats and man-made islands studded with luxury villas. Now one of the world's largest gold hubs, Dubai is also a place to launder illegally mined gold, especially from conflict-prone parts of East and Central Africa. Opaque business practices and regulatory loopholes allow this laundered gold to enter world markets on a massive scale. With approximately 30 free trade zones, Dubai is a haven for trade-based money laundering. Operating with minimal regulatory oversight or customs enforcement, these zones allow businesses to disguise the proceeds of crime via the over- and underinvoicing of goods, multiple invoicing, and falsifying of other trade documentation (Vittori 2021).

The central government of the UAE, Dubai officials, and Emirati law enforcement agencies largely possess the technical knowledge and capacity to tackle these challenges. Emirati regulators, officials, and law enforcement agents are aware of how Dubai is being used as a conduit for illicit financial transactions. Dubai, and the UAE, is strategically important to the United States, the United Kingdom, and other countries. In its April 2020 report on the UAE, the intergovernmental Financial Action Task Force (FATF) specifically called out Dubai for its limited number of money-laundering prosecutions and convictions. The European Commission said in 2020 that it would place the UAE on the EU's anti-money laundering and counterterrorist financing list if it has not made significant progress in the fight against money laundering and terror financing by June 2021. Currently, the UAE is in a probationary period after the European FATF identified several shortcomings.

We provide below a typical example of these illicit activities. Members of the royal families of Saudi Arabia, Kuwait, and the UAE reportedly helped launder funds from the Malaysia Development Berhad (MDB) through their sovereign wealth funds and state-owned enterprises, apparently with help from certain Western banks. Chinese officials then allegedly offered to help bail out the Malaysian prime minister at the center of the scandal, Najib Razak, in return for Chinese stakes in various railway and pipeline projects—a charge the Chinese government denies. Moldova is the poorest country in Europe, and yet between $20 billion and $80 billion allegedly were laundered through its banks from 2010 to 2014. According to reporting by the Organized Crime and Corruption Reporting Project (OCCRP), shell companies were created in the United Kingdom, Cyprus, and New Zealand in which a fake "lender" company would use a Moldovan court to collect debts from a defaulting fake Russian "debtor." The Russian shell company would then allegedly wire the money through a Moldovan bank to accounts of the "lender" in a bank in Latvia; from there, the funds were wired to 5,140 companies in 96 countries. Although the United States, the United Kingdom, and the European Union could have done more to help prevent this immense theft, it nonetheless demonstrates how weaker jurisdictions like Moldova and Latvia can be used for massive money laundering scenarios.

COMMENTS

Illegal money transfer is the direct result of privatization and the drive to create a market economy as desired by the WTO. That has cause extreme in equality. In India, privatization has started in 1993 under the instruction of IMF-World Bank, and it was intensified after the WTO was created. The WTO wants to create a worldwide market economy as a part of the Washington Consensus. Market system automatically creates inequality, as the market is ruthless to distribute resources to them who by any means can control the resources in a fully privatized economy. The result can be extreme inequality.

In India, 10 percent of the people control 77 percent of the resources of the country. In the United States, 1 percent can control more than 90 percent of the resources.

The dominance of large corporations in global markets has implications for how trade policy affects inequality. The gains from international trade are most frequently captured by large corporations, often at the expense of small enterprises, women entrepreneurs, rural agriculturists, and fisheries. Such small organizations face various obstacles to gain from the international trade, including limited information, lack of financing, prohibitive entry costs, and underrepresentation in trade policy decision-making. Small firms are thus often unable to compete with larger foreign corporations, as the latter have the capacities to overcome such obstacles by influencing the politicians to monopolize competitive advantages.

Trade policy also increases inequality through market access and entry conditions. International trade is increasingly regulated through nontariff measures, like legal restrictions, which affect most traded goods and have a greater influence on trade than tariffs. Product standard based on health criteria restricts exports from countries that lack quality control and appropriate infrastructure. Such nontariff measures influence international trade and can have serious effects on inequality, both within and between countries.

International trade can further affect inequality by promoting structural transformation. It has been instrumental in the transformation of many unplanned countries in East Asia from agricultural to manufacturing economies. This process has contributed to the creation of a thriving middle class in many emerging newly industrialized countries but at the same time destruction of the rural economies. Farmers became unskilled workers in the city often doing menial works. This has further intensified within country income inequality. A planned economy in place of a market economy would be the solution, but the WTO is totally against planning.

Chapter 10

China's Hard Power

After occupying Tibet, East Turkestan, Inner Mongolia, and Manchuria, China now is trying to occupy the entire South China Sea and the islands in it. At the same time, it is threating Taiwan continuously that sooner or later China will occupy it. Although none of the countries in the UN supports the claim of China, but China does not care. It does not allow Vietnam or the Philippines to explore oil and gas in those islands and sometimes it gives warning to passing ships that they are entering Chinese territories.

China's geopolitical strategy is to use its competitive advantage of soft power to outmaneuver the United States, and other countries such as India, Japan, Vietnam, or the Philippines, in acquiring natural resources and to allow for continued growth of its economy while gaining political influence in various countries and regions throughout the world.

China's application of unrestricted warfare is apparent when the security and military aspects of China's involvement in Afghanistan are well known. China enjoys protection of its projects in Afghanistan because of its close relationship with Pakistan. This implies that Pakistan's national intelligence agency, Inter-Services Intelligence Directorate, or ISI, exerts its influence over the Taliban to allow the Chinese projects to continue unimpeded. While Chinese workers in Afghanistan have been attacked, the level of violence is very low when compared to attacks on the United States, India, and UN personnel and facilities.

It is unlikely that there will be peaceful development of China overall, as there appears to be no desire for peace and stability but rather a development of good, old-fashioned militarism and imperialism. In the first place, the economic "miracle" of the Chinese economy is based on the fierce exploitation of its working class and farmers and on an export drive to destroy the manufacturing capacity of most of the countries of the world by offering cheap debt facility and cheaper manufactured products. The economic colonization accompanied by a strong geopolitical strategy to project Chinese power, both military and financial, are the building blocks for the new Chinese empire, in which the new international business order is facilitating the Chinese expansion. Taiwan is about to be a new victim.

Relations between China and India deteriorated after India gave refuge to the Dalai Lama in 1959, followed by India's humiliating defeat in the 1962 war over a disputed border and Chinese aid to Pakistan. India still claims that China occupies 38,000 square kilometer of its territories and, for its part, Beijing still lays claim to the northeastern Indian province of Arunachal Pradesh.

There is no evidence that Tibet was a part of China before China colonized it in 1949. The same is true of Taiwan and Eastern Turkistan. If the Manchus are not Chinese, as Sun Yat Sen declared in 1911, Manchuria, which China received as a gift from Stalin in 1950, was never a part of China either.

CHINA'S FALSE CLAIM ON FORMOSA

In 1947, Kuomintang forces of Chiang-Kei-Seik, defeated by Mao-Tse-Tung, were allowed to invade Formosa by the United States. They massacred the local population, who are not ethnic Chinese but a mixed population of Japanese, Chinese, Portuguese, and the indigenous proto-Malays. However, now China claims that Formosa, renamed as Taiwan, is an inalienable part of China and China wants to reclaim it as soon as possible. History cannot support that Chinese claim.

We need to learn the history of Formosa or Taiwan.

From 1368 to 1644, China had the Ming Dynasty of the Chin or Han Chinese tribe. At that time, Formosa was occupied first by the Dutch and then by the Portuguese. For a brief period from 1645 to 1662, a half-Japanese general of the Ming Dynasty, Tei Seiko, after being driven from China by the invading Manchus from the north, occupied that island. However, the Portuguese soon regained control of the island, which they had renamed as Formosa, or the beautiful island. The Machu Empire only ruled Formosa for eight years between 1887 and 1895, but Manchus were not Chinese either.

The Manchu Empire of China managed Formosa for just that brief period of time and, in 1895, gladly ceded it to Japan. After that, China had forfeited its rights to the island permanently or until the signing of another international treaty. The present-day Beijing government claims that the 1943 Cairo Declaration and the 1945 Potsdam Declaration recognized China's sovereignty over Formosa. That is not factually correct. The Cairo Declaration had nothing new on the question of Chinese territorial sovereignty over Formosa. Furthermore, both the Cairo and Potsdam Declarations were not valid international treaties but, to quote Justice Radha Binod Pal, a "victor's justice," where Japan never took any part (Ushimura 2003).

The People's Republic of China, which came into being in 1949, was at war with the UN in 1951 over Korea and was not invited to sign the San Francisco Treaty in which Japan formally renounced "all right, title and claim to Formosa." The Republic of China or Kuomintang was unable to represent China in that treaty. Accordingly, to follow the UN principle of self-determination, Formosa belongs only to Formosans, not to China.

The history of Tibet, Manchuria, East Turkistan, and Formosa, dating back more than 2,000 years, has been one of independence from China. At no time, since the founding of the nation in 127 BC, have the Tibetans conceded their sovereignty to a foreign power. East Turkistan was occupied from time to time, but those periods of occupation were brief. Manchuria was not occupied by China until 1950. Formosa, except for seven years, was never a part of China.

China has no limit to its demands on lands, islands, rocks, and reefs in the South China Sea, disregarding any international laws and conventions. China only recognizes might, not logic. Legitimate claims by other nations of East Asia have no meaning in the dictionary of China. China has claimed sovereignty across most of the South China Sea. It grants itself rights that cannot apply to an international shipping route. In fact, China imposes its demands by building military structures on uninhabited archipelagos, islets, rocks, and reefs that are already possessed by other countries in the region, including Japan, Vietnam, the Philippines, Malaysia, and Indonesia. Chinese citizens are encouraged to fish everywhere under the protection of China's coastguards, and to engage in prospecting for oil, with the installation of a drilling platform off the coast of Vietnam. In a direct head to head with Vietnam, Malaysia, Brunei and the Philippines, Taiwan, and Japan, Beijing claims possession of the Paracel and Spratly Islands, the Scarborough Shoal, and the Senkaku Islands. It also appears to be extending its own territorial waters so much that there is practically nothing left for the rest of Southeast Asia.

China's aim to make Asia its exclusive property, keeping Japan at bay and excluding U.S. military presence, is just one part of a greater mission. China intends to extend its military power through Burma, Africa, and Pakistan up to the Arabian Sea, on to the Persian Gulf and into the Middle East and Africa. China's defense budget is second only to that of the United States, giving it great purchasing power and increased military capabilities.

Recent outbreak of coronavirus and resultant thousands of death all over the world is blamed on China that either China has developed this virus in its laboratory in Wuhan or it suppressed the information so that other countries could not take action beforehand. The result is worldwide shutdown and mass unemployment and bankruptcy. Most companies are having the problem of very low demand and reduced share price. China is taking advantage of that. It is buying up companies after companies everywhere particularly in the developing countries.

China recently created a new type of imperialism. In the name of Belt and Road Initiative, it is giving huge loans to a number of countries for infrastructure projects at very high interest rates. All materials for these projects including labor force would come from China, although the recipient countries could supply most of these particularly the labor forces to reduce the borrowings. When the country will be unable to pay back these loans, China will take very long-term lease of important ports, airports, mines, or islands. Recently Sri Lanka when unable to repay its loan to China gave lease of an airport, Humbantota, for 90 years to China. Maldives has taken from China a loan of $250 million, which is the same as its GDP. Kenya gave up Mombasa port to China, after failing to repay its debt to China.

These are nothing when we consider Pakistan, which has taken $40 billion loan from China with a guaranteed rate of return of 30 percent, which it cannot repay. Therefore, Pakistan has given away Gwadar port in Baluchistan for a joint military base with China. This is imperialism in another name.

Both China and the United States thus correspond to the classical pattern of colonialism. They both want to capture territories to promote their business interests. In the case of American Empire the desire is to protect its overseas investments and particularly the oil industry worldwide. China wants to capture resources of the world to promote its industry in future as a matter of national honor and prestige to wipe out "the century of humiliation" and to humiliate other countries. Taiwan is a victim of that strategy.

DOMINATION THROUGH TRADE AND LENDING

China wants to dominate the world. It has a long-term strategy. It first wants the world dependent on it by removing all competitors in the supply line of the world. With the money it earns it buys all politicians, all journalists, all judges, and all industrial leaders. The steps are as follows:

(1) It has started its campaign first in Asia, by creating the Asian financial crisis in 1998.
(2) It then tried to take care of all Western countries.
(3) By joining WTO, it got the legitimacy to control the World.
(4) Trump made an attempt to stop that plan, but he lost the game as by that time China has total control on the media, the judges, and politicians in

the United States and other Western countries and some of the parts of the United Nations itself.

When China joined the WTO, it was forced to change some of its laws but there was not any genuine commitment, but China never observed those commitments in reality and only signed the Protocol of Accession to the WTO. The objective of these commitments was to transform China into a market economy but in reality, China is still a controlled economy. Supachai Panitchpakdi, director general of WTO from 2002 to 2005, and Mark Clifford, former editor of *Business Week*, wrote a book, *China and the WTO*, where they asserted that WTO has created a set of rules for China to transform itself to market economy like the other members after it would join WTO. However, China has violated all premises of a market system (Ezell and Atkinson 2015). China joined the WTO in 2001 in Doha Conference of the WTO. WTO is based on the so-called Washington Consensus, which promotes nondiscrimination, transparency, the primacy of rule based, market-based rules, in accordance to the theory of comparative advantage. China on the other hand developed a policy regime based on mercantilism, which is against the policy of the WTO (see Table 10.1).

Table 10.1. Conditions of the WTO and China's Behavior

Conditions of the WTO	*China Applied This Rule to Itself*
Technology transfer as a condition for market access	No
The Government Procurement Agreement	No
State industries purchases based on pure commercial considerations	No
Reduction of share of the state industries in the economy	No
Foreign banks receives same treatment as domestic banks	No
Telecommunication market open to foreign producers	No
Foreign film distribution liberalized	No
Substantial reduction of export subsidies	No
Progress toward the implementation of Washington Consensus	No
Reductions of intellectual property theft and violations	No
Removal of technical barriers to trade agreements	No
Nonmanipulation of technology standards	No
No currency manipulations	No

Sources: (Ezell and Atkinson 2015; OXFAM report on WTO 2019; Webster 2013).

In table 10.1 we summarize the violations of China (Ezell and Atkinson 2015; Oxfam Report on WTO 2019; Webster 2013):

Currency manipulations to keep of the exchange value of yuan low promotes export subsidies and helped China to have a massive trade surplus. In its policy of "innovative mercantilism," it discriminates against foreign firms and provides supports for the domestic firms. It induces foreign firms to collaborate with the Chinese firms to promote technology transfer.

In a document "National Medium and Long Term program for Science and Technology Development 2006–2020," China identified 402 key technologies from intelligent automobiles to integrated circuits and high-performance computers where foreign companies are encouraged to transfer technologies in exchange for market access and contracts. That was extended for aircraft, missiles, and multiple target nuclear missiles as well. In the "National Guideline for Development and Promotion of the Integrated Circuit Industry," China had a plan to invest at least $100 billion in the semi-conductor industry to create a closed loop system where design, manufacturing, assembly, packaging, and all activities will be combined in a planned size of $140 billion by 2020. China wants to eliminate the U.S. semi-conductor industry within 20 years from 2006. China wants to combine invisible hand of the market with the visible hand of the government. In its "National and Regional IC Funds," China already allocated at least $100 billion to invest first in state-owned firms, which in turn will invest in private equity firms, particularly to buy foreign semi-conductor firms. One major example is China Tsinghua Unicorn Groups purchase of Micron Technology in 2015 for $23 billion. For economic development, China embraced industrial policy, state-owned industries, and techno-nationalism. China ignores the core principle of the WTO; it does not accept nondiscrimination toward foreign companies, *most-favored nation* status to charge the minimum possible tariffs for WTO member countries, and transparency. If a company uses at least 60 percent Chinese components, it receives government subsidy. China accepted conditions at the time it joined the WTO that it would not put any condition of research and development on new investment, but in new investments in automobile and steel sector, these conditions regarding research and development are still there. China does not care about the WTO standard but has its own standard regarding all information technology products.

Ezell and Atkinson (2015), Oxfam report on WTO, and Webster (2013) mentioned a number of commitments, which China disregarded.

Commitment No. 1: Prices in Every Sector Must Be Determined by Market Forces

Section 9 of China's WTO Protocol of Accession provides that China "shall allow prices for traded goods and services in every sector to be determined by market forces, and multi-tier pricing practices for such goods and services shall be eliminated."

Exceptions to this requirement are quite limited and are set out in Annex 4 of the Protocol. The products covered in Annex 4 are certain agricultural products, certain pharmaceuticals, natural gas, and processed oils. Except these, China committed to allowing prices to be set by the market immediately in 2001. Even today in 2021, many key prices are being determined by the government in China.

Commitment No. 2: All Subsidies to Be Notified to the WTO and Prohibited Subsidies to Be Eliminated

Under Section 15 of WTO Accession Protocol, China agreed to notify to the WTO any subsidy granted by China. China also committed itself to eliminate all subsidy programs. These obligations are disregarded by China. Subsidies are not revealed at all or inadequate publicity of subsidies is given. China still provides export subsidies and subsidies to use of local products. China committed to make available to all other WTO members, all laws, regulations, and other factors affecting trade in goods, services, TRIPS, or the control of foreign exchange. Unfortunately, China has disregarded those obligations it committed to join the WTO.

Commitment No. 3: State-Owned Enterprises (SOEs) to Operate Free of State Influence

Under Section 6 of China's Accession Protocol, and Article XVII GATT 1994, China agreed that these SOEs would import or export based on market conditions on prices, quality, marketability, and availability. However, China has disregarded this rule of the WTO. There are government subsidies, which are illegal under the WTO rules, for the SOEs. Overcapacities in the SOEs resulted in a flood of exports of steel, glass, cement, and other building materials to other countries in the excuse of the *Belt and Road Initiatives*.

Commitment No. 4: Nondiscrimination in Procurement

WTO rules suggest that foreign individuals and organizations shall be treated equally to domestic individuals and organizations regarding the procurement of inputs and goods and services. China disregarded this rule and refused to accept the *Government Procurement Agreement* (GPA). FIEs face discriminations in public procurement unless they have Chinese partners. FIEs cannot bid for public contracts in certain sectors important for China, like railways, constructions, steel, engineering, and design sectors. Tenders are not publicly announced. There is discrimination against foreign equipment and technology through *the Steel and Iron Industry Development Policy*, and China encourages the use of local companies and local technology.

Commitment No. 5: Nondiscrimination in General

China when it has joined the WTO has agreed to change all laws that are inconsistent with the GATT "Most Favored Nation" (MFN) and National Treatment rules. China in the *Strategic Emerging Industries* encourages innovation in high-technology areas and discriminates against foreign firms and products.

Commitment No. 6: Technical Barriers to Trade (TBT)

China disregarded the TBT rules of the WTO. China has not harmonized technical regulations, standards, and conformity evaluation procedures, which creates difficulties for foreign companies to enter the Chinese market. China does not use international standards.

Commitment No. 7: Intellectual Property Rights (IPR)

China violates these TRIPS rules totally; it does not accept intellectual property rights of foreigners and foreign companies.

Commitment No. 8: Market Access

In China, there are still restrictions for foreign companies to enter the Chinese market. There are prohibition to invest in certain strategic sectors and requirements for local content and joint venture. Steel companies and mining sector are prohibited for foreign investment.

Commitment No. 9: Nontariff Measures

Foreign business organizations in order to enter the market in China must transfer their technology to the Chinese partner company. There are also requirement to balance trade and foreign exchange by which a foreign company must export similar in value to its import requirements.

Commitment No. 10: Judicial Review

The judicial system in China is biased against foreign companies. According to the WTO rules, China must implement all administrative actions relating to the implementation of laws, related to Article X:1 of the GATT 1994 and the TRIPS agreement; China has never respected its commitments to the WTO.

COMMITMENTS FOR SPECIFIC AREAS

Automotive Sector

In China, industrial plans of foreign companies require substantial investments in R&D facilities in China with local contents, which are not allowed in the WTO regime.

Banking Sector

According to the WTO rules, China should treat foreign banks in the same way as it treats domestic banks. However, it is not doing that.

Telecommunications

China should have opened its telecommunications sector to foreign companies but it has not done. It has many restrictions for foreign companies like very high level of capital investments and Chinese partners and technology transfer requirement. These are not allowed under the WTO rules but so far China ignored these requirements.

The Film Industry

China have not liberalized the distribution of foreign films.

Agriculture

China has today more than $100 billion subsidies for agriculture sector including domestic subsidies and export subsidies. It does not allow free market access. It has arbitrary import restrictions, although India has introduced its three new agricultural laws to be in line with the WTO rules. China refuses to do so.

Retail industry

China has restriction of foreign retail outlets, which is against the WTO rules.

Legal services

In China, foreign legal services are restricted, which is against the WTO rules.

The fertilizer industry

In China, there are discriminatory tax and import controls, which are against WTO rules.

Import and export regulations

In China there are still export control, import controls, and deliberate dumping efforts to promote exports.

UNFAIR TRADE PRACTICES

China ignored rules of fair trade and reciprocal treatment in international trade. For year after year, China used dumping subsidies, exchange rate manipulations, industrial planning, forced technology transfer, and discriminations against foreign companies and got away with. "China's average tariff rate is nearly three times higher than the average United States rate. The United States charges a 2.5 percent tariff on Chinese cars, while China charges a 25 percent tariff on cars from the United States" (Ezell and Atkinson 2015). President Trump imposed 25 percent tariff on Chinese exports, but now a pro-Chinese Biden was installed as the president of the United States and most tariffs are expected to be removed.

In 2018 alone, the Trump administration had found dumping or unfair subsidies on 13 different products, including steel wheels, cold-drawn mechanical tubing, tool chests and cabinets, forged steel fittings, aluminum foil, rubber bands, cast iron soil pipe and fittings, and large-diameter welded pipe. In January 2018, the Trump administration found the China's overproduction of steel and aluminum. Belt and Road program of China is nothing but to export these excess products of China. The United States has a $375 billion deficit balance of trade in 2017 alone.

Belt and Road Initiative (BRI)

Belt and Road Initiative (BRI), or China's effort to develop infrastructure in the developing countries, is an attempt to extend China's empire throughout the world by fair means or foul. China uses BRI funds to drown the developing countries in debt and then take over ports, land, mines, and other strategic assets. BRI was started in 2013 and became the foreign policy strategy of Xi Jinping. In 2017, BRI was written into the constitution of the Chinese Communist Party, and 138 countries and 30 international organizations have agreed to participate, with declared Chinese investments to some $8 trillion.

There are many examples of corruption in the Belt and Road. Bangladesh shut down a highway project, contract of which was given to the China Harbour Engineering Company but then it was revealed that the company reputedly offering a Bangladeshi official a bribe. The United States arrested the representative of China's CEFC Energy Company for illicit payments to officials in Chad and Uganda. A 2017 McKinsey survey found that at least 60 percent to 80 percent of Chinese companies in Africa admitted to paying bribes (CSIS 2020; McKinsey 2017).

In much the same way, Djibouti in East Africa lost control of a container terminal built as part of BRI projects, after the project had debt equivalent to 88 percent of its GDP of $1.72 billion. Similarly, Venezuela owes China around $20 billion, according to estimates by China's Commerce Ministry.

BRI is a vehicle to expand China's military capability beyond its geographical limits in a very clever way. China has the management control of Haifa port in Israel; it means that the U.S. Mediterranean fleet cannot go to the port of Haifa. China is about to build a rail line connecting Haifa with the Red Sea as an alternative to the Suez Canal.

The China-led Asia Infrastructure Investment Bank, or AIIB, is the vehicle to finance One Belt One Road (OBOR). So far, it has provided $1.73 billion to support infrastructure projects in seven countries, including Pakistan, Bangladesh, Tajikistan, Indonesia, Myanmar, Azerbaijan, and Oman. Apart from AIIB, China also has a $40 billion Silk Road Fund and a New Development Bank to fund the OBOR initiative.

"Chinese aid activity in the Pacific region has been predominantly in infrastructure development, fuelled largely by loans rather than grants. Pacific countries are among the most vulnerable countries in the world to potential debt sustainability problems and by extension possible 'debt trap' diplomacy" (Cerutti and Zhou 2018). Three small Pacific economies, Tonga, Samoa, and Vanuatu, are among those most heavily indebted to China. Regarding the global debt sustainability issues of Chinese projects, the Pacific islands are very important, as they also changed their diplomatic relations from Taiwan to China in return for massive bribes (Wroe 2018; Dziedzic 2019; Whiting, Zhou, and Feng 2019; ABC News, 19 November 2018; Riordan 2018).

The Pacific islands, in 2017, received aid equal to 5.2 percent of their gross national income; sub-Saharan Africa received only 3 percent of its gross national income. Pacific islands have limited scope to grow their way out of any existing debt. China is an important creditor to all four. In 2011–2018, China made official loan commitments totaling US$6 billion (about 21 percent of regional GDP) (CSIS.org 2020; Dornan and Brant 2014; ABC News, 7 August 2019).

Africa and China

In Africa, BRI projects are designed to expand Chinese colonies in resource-rich countries. Elaine Dezenski analyzed a vital connection between Chinese capitalism and large-scale corruption; she argues that BRI exports "corruption, opacity, and waste" (Dezenski 2020). All projects have delays, financial implosions, and negative public sentiment. A large portion of these deals were being made with countries that had credit ratings classified as "junk." Making big deals with countries like Pakistan, Sri Lanka, and Malaysia showed the initial propensity of the Belt and Road to emphasize quantity over quality, expediency over transparency.

There are growing fears among African countries over the "debt trap." Djibouti is said to have debt to China, which is the equivalent of 75 percent of its GDP. China owns 72 percent of Kenya's external debt, which stands at US$50 billion (Bandiera and Tsiropoulos 2019).

Kenya is the country, which was one of the first to sign a memorandum of understanding with China under its BRI and has benefited from being a recipient of its funds. Kenya owes $6.5 billion to China, 21.9 percent of its total external debt. It is already using a third of its revenue to service that borrowing (see Table 10.2).

Kenya's standard gauge railway (SGR) connecting Mombasa to Nairobi, the biggest investment in Kenya since its independence, is a flagship BRI project in East Africa. It is also a textbook example of the kind of early BRI lending that is credited with fueling budget deficits that pushed the nation's debt to 61.7 percent of GDP at the end of 2019, up from 50.2 percent at the end of 2015, according to the IMF—from a manageable debt level to an unsustainable debt problem.

Over the next three years from 2020, Kenya has to pay US$60 billion to the China Exim Bank alone. For the Mombasa port and the SGR connecting to Nairobi, the Kenyan government borrowed Sh227 billion from China. Kenya may lose the control of Mombasa port if it defaults on the SGR loans from the China Exim Bank (Horn, Reinhart and Trebesch 2019).

African states spent $100.8 billion on infrastructure in 2018. Approximately 38 percent came from the African governments themselves, while 25.7 percent came from China. Some countries have already started to push back on the terms of Chinese lending. Bagamoyo in Tanzania was going to be the biggest port in East Africa, but the agreement, signed in 2013 with China Merchants Holdings International, has stalled. Although China accounts for a relatively small share of Tanzania's external debt, Beijing has been among the largest investors in Tanzania in recent years. Tanzania owes around $2 billion to China, 9 percent of its total external debt. In Uganda, several Turkish companies have opened manufacturing plants and other businesses, while the government has drawn up a short list of companies from China, France, Portugal, Turkey, Austria, and South Korea to begin work on its Kampala-Jinja smart motorway.

African countries are cancelling or postponing now BRI projects over rising debt concerns. Zambian government has revoked a Chinese company's license to operate coal mines. Ugandan government has postponed the construction of the Kampala-Entebbe Expressway. Sierra Leone government cancelled the US$318 million Mamamah International Airport project under the BRI. Tanzanian government has postponed lending from China for its new Bagamoyo port project (Knowledge@Wharton 2020; Hurley, Morris, and Portelance 2018; Dezenski 2020).

Of the 49 countries that China claims have signed memorandums of understanding (MOUs) of officially expressed support for the BRI, 34 (nearly 70 percent) are located along the coast of Africa—16 in the west, 8 each in the north and east, and 2 in the South. These include, it says, Djibouti Port, three Egyptian ports—Port Sudan, Port Said-Port Tewfik, and Port Ain Sokhna—Zarzis Port in Tunisia, and El Hamdania Port in Algeria. An oil refinery in the north of Sudan is located close to the railway line connecting Port Sudan and Dakar Port. Gabes, a hub for petrochemical and phosphate industries in Tunisia, has been connected by rail to the port of Zarzis. An industrial park in Ethiopia is located near the Addis Ababa-Adama highway, which connects with the Addis-Djibouti rail line connected to Djibouti port. This enables China to use the maritime route to transport raw materials such as phosphate, copper, cobalt, gold, iron ore, cocoa, bauxite, coal, lithium, steel, granite, and marble back to the mainland and finished goods and Chinese labor to Africa (Dezenski 2020; Brazys and Vadlamannati 2018).

Recipients of BRI cash would lose control of assets if they could not repay their debts. Countries rich in natural resources, like Angola, Zambia, and Republic of the Congo, or with strategically important infrastructure, like

Table 10.2. General Government Gross Debt (% of GDP)

	2015	*2016*	*2017*	*2018*
World	80.6	83.6	83.1	82.8
MICs	44.5	47.4	48.6	49.8
Mongolia	62.1	87.6	85.3	89.0
Montenegro	76.8	78.0	79.7	80.9
Pakistan	65.7	70.0	69.1	67.6
LICs	36.1	40.4	41.9	41.6
Maldives	73.1	83.1	96.5	109.0
Djibouti	72.1	86.6	88.1	87.5
Laos	65.8	67.8	69.0	70.3
Kyrgyzia	65.0	62.1	64.2	65.5
Tajikistan	33.4	44.8	51.8	56.8

Source: UNCTAD.

ports or railways such as Kenya, are most vulnerable to the risk of losing control over important assets in negotiations with Chinese creditors (Smith 2020; Brazys and Vadlamannati 2018; World Bank 2018; IMF, Debt Limits Policy 2015).

CHINA AND ASIA

In BRI, most of its investment contracts have been negotiated in secret. It is called "debt-trap diplomacy." When Sri Lanka defaulted on the loan to build Hambantota Port and a Chinese company got a 99-year lease in return, the evidence of China's strategic designs became clear. Center for Global Development, in Washington D.C., warned that "23 of 68 countries benefiting from Belt and Road investments were significantly or highly vulnerable to debt distress" and identified eight countries—Djibouti, Kyrgyzstan, Laos, Mongolia, Montenegro, the Maldives, Pakistan, and Tajikistan—to be particularly at risk. Debt problems will create an unfavorable degree of dependency on China as a creditor. Increasing debt, and China's role in managing bilateral debt problems, has already exacerbated internal and bilateral tensions in some BRI countries" (Hillman 2018). However, a new study from Chatham House, the very biased pro-Chinese British think tank, blames Sri Lanka's IMF bailout; Chinese investment was "not used to repay port-related debt, but to pay off more expensive loans, generally to Western entities" (Chatham House – International Affairs 2020).

According to the World Bank, between 2010 and 2016 nearly $36 billion was given to Malaysia by Chinese state-owned firms. Multiple infrastructure projects, including the East Coast Rail Link project and a massive port city called Melaka Gateway, were started, Chinese firms bought up multiple Malaysian ports, and mega-projects, such as the $100 billion, were being built with Chinese direction and financial backing. Then it was discovered that over $7.5 billion of government money had disappeared. Via Belt and Road projects, China had tried to help the embattled prime minister to cover evidence of financial irregularities by artificially inflating the costs of infrastructure projects, so the excess could be justified for other reasons. In return, Malaysia was to give Chinese companies big shares in national railway and pipeline projects and to give permission for the Chinese navy to use two Malaysian ports (IDA Lending Terms: World Bank 2018).

Laos is among the poorest countries in Southeast Asia, though it has been expanding rapidly with GDP growth averaging 8 percent over the past decade. Since 2013, the IMF has been raising doubts about the ability of Laos to service its debts if it moves ahead with its plans to build the China-Laos railway, in addition to other major capital projects. The financial terms for many elements of the project remain a secret, although one source has reported that a $465 million loan from China Exim Bank for the joint company building and operating the railway would be provided. The Laotian government has also reportedly signed a $600 million loan agreement with China Exim Bank for a hydropower project (Chin and Gallagher 2019).

For Mongolia, China Exim Bank agreed in early 2017 to provide financing under its $1 billion line of credit at concessional rates for a hydropower project and a highway project from the airport to the capital. However, the hydropower project has stalled. If reports that China would provide $30 billion in credit to BRI-related projects over the next 5 to 10 years are true, then the prospect of a Mongolia default is extremely high, regardless of the concessional nature of the financing (Bandiera and Tsiropoulos 2019)

Tajikistan is evaluated by the IMF and World Bank as a "high-risk" country regarding debt. Despite this, it is planning to borrow from China to pay for infrastructure investments in the power and transportation sectors. Most significantly, a $3 billion portion of the Central Asia-China gas pipeline (Line D) will pass through Tajikistan, financed through Chinese foreign direct investment (FDI). Most recently, Tajikistan issued $500 million in Eurobonds to pay for a new hydropower-generating facility. China is Tajikistan's single largest creditor and accounts for almost 80 percent of the total increase in Tajikistan's external debt over the 2007–2016 period (Horn, Reinhart and Trebesch 2019).

Kyrgyzstan is a poor country with significant new BRI-related infrastructure projects under construction, financed by loans from China. By the end of March 2017, public and publicly guaranteed debt amounted to roughly 65 percent of GDP, of which external debt represented about 90 percent of the total debt. China's Exim Bank is the largest single creditor; roughly, 40 percent of the country's total external debt belongs to it. Kyrgyz and Chinese authorities have plans for construction of a chain of hydropower plants, a China-Kyrgyzstan-Uzbekistan railway, additional highway construction, and completion of the Central Asia-China gas pipeline, with loans from China (Bandiera and Tsiropoulos 2019).

The most high profile of the BRI ventures in Pakistan is the Gwadar Port project. It is the main feature of the $62 billion China-Pakistan Economic Corridor (CPEC), with at least $33 billion of this amount would be invested in energy projects. China will reportedly finance roughly 80 percent of that amount. China is charging high interest rate for the loans taken by Pakistan. That could lead to public debt ratios well above 70 percent. The CPEC is a road link between Pakistan's Gwadar port near Karachi to Xinjiang in China, and a stretch of it passes through the Gilgit-Baltistan region, which Pakistan invaded and occupied in 1947. India cannot join Belt and Road because it would mean accepting that parts of Kashmir that Pakistan occupied are essentially Pakistan (Horn, Reinhart, and Trebesch 2019).

In the Maldives, there is a similar concern that Beijing is using debt-trap diplomacy to build a strategic advantage in the region. Chinese investors due to China's unbalanced economy are eager to invest in Sri Lanka and the Maldives and many more countries with minimal due diligence, as investments in China have become unproductive. China is now thus exporting its unproductive investment abroad (Asia Maritime Transparency Initiative 2020).

China in Europe

A very important project in Europe is to provide a railway link from the port of Piraeus in Greece to Eastern Europe. China, through its China Ocean Shipping Company, bought a 67 percent stake in the port's Pier I from the Piraeus Port Authority SA in January 2016.

Montenegro's debt problem is enormous. The World Bank estimates that public debt (including guarantees) as a share of GDP might climb to 83 percent in 2018 in the absence of fiscal adjustment. The source of the problem is one very large infrastructure project, a motorway linking the port of Bar with Serbia that would integrate the Montenegro in transport network with those of other Balkan countries. The Montenegro authorities concluded an agreement with China Exim Bank in 2014 for the latter to finance 85 percent of the estimated $1 billion cost for the first phase of the project. The estimated cost has since risen to $1.1 billion, or over 25 percent of GDP. The road is being built in three phases, and the IMF believes the nonconcessional terms would likely result in debt default (Horn, Reinhart, and Trebesch 2019).

The United States has been worried about China's intentions. Developing the economies of South and Central Asia is a long-standing U.S. goal that intensified after the start of the U.S.-led war in Afghanistan and President Barack Obama's pivot to Asia, but the American efforts are at their minimum for development projects. Several countries in Central and Eastern Europe have accepted BRI financing, and Western European states such as Italy, Luxembourg, and Portugal have signed provisional agreements to cooperate on BRI projects. There are fears that the BRI could make partner countries vassal states.

Empire of China

The winner of the new international business order is China, which has dominated the markets of most of the developed countries. The result of that victory also has promoted Chinese imperialism in Asia. This chapter analyses the history of some of the victims of China.

China's geopolitical strategy is to use its competitive advantage of soft power to outmaneuver the United States, and other countries such as India, Japan, Vietnam, or the Philippines, in acquiring natural resources and to allow for continued growth of its economy while gaining political influence in various countries and regions throughout the world.

China's application of unrestricted warfare is apparent when the security and military aspects of China's involvement in Afghanistan are examined. China enjoys protection of its projects in Afghanistan because of its close relationship with Pakistan. This implies that Pakistan's national intelligence agency, Inter-Services Intelligence Directorate, or ISI, exerts its influence over the Taliban to allow the Chinese projects to continue unimpeded. While Chinese workers in Afghanistan have been attacked, the level of violence is very low when compared to attacks on the United States, India, and UN personnel and facilities.

It is unlikely that there will be peaceful development of China overall, as there appears to be no desire for peace and stability but rather a development of good, old-fashioned militarism and imperialism. In the first place, the economic "miracle" of the Chinese economy is based on the fierce exploitation of its working class and farmers and on an export drive to destroy the manufacturing capacity of most of the countries of the world by offering cheap debt facility and cheaper manufactured products. The economic colonization accompanied by a strong geopolitical strategy to project Chinese power, both military and financial, are the building blocks for the new Chinese empire, in which the new international business order is facilitating the Chinese expansion.

Since China resumed its threats against Taiwan, India, Vietnam, and the Philippines, and increasingly threatened Japan, both France and Germany have been trying to overturn the arms embargo on the People's Liberation Army for purely commercial reasons. That demonstrates the influence of Chinese finances and the lure of the Chinese markets for the European powers.

To the south of China, the country is largely underwriting the construction and development of a 1,850-kilometer network of roads, rivers, and ports in Vietnam and Laos, circumventing the natural defensive barriers of the foothills of the Himalayas in India, which will directly connect Chinese Kunming to Thailand. That facilitates the movement of the Chinese military to the Southeast Asia region whenever it needs and provides markets and natural resources for the Chinese economy.

Around India and Pakistan to the west of China, within the framework of Chinese imperialism major development is also occurring. As the United States and India enjoy an increasingly warmer relationship, Pakistan will probably look closer to China for technical and military assistance.

China already supplies Pakistan with nuclear technology, including nuclear weapons.

According to the Asian Studies department at the Brooking Institute, the nuclear program in Pakistan is essentially the result of Sino–Pakistani relations. Some news agency reports suggest that Chinese security agencies knew of the transfer of nuclear technology from Pakistan to Iran. Worldanalysis.net shows that one of the most significant recent projects is the construction of a major port complex at the naval base of Gwadar on the Arabian Sea, giving China strategic access to the Persian Gulf and a naval outpost on the Indian Ocean.

Relations between China and India deteriorated after India gave refuge to the Dalai Lama in 1959, followed by India's humiliating defeat in the 1962 war over a disputed border and Chinese aid to Pakistan. India still claims that China occupies 38,000 square kilometer of its territories and, for its part, Beijing still lays claim to the northeastern Indian province of Arunachal Pradesh.

China's recent demand that Arunachal Pradesh of India is a part of China has provoked a very adverse reaction from the Government of India and the Indian media in general. Once again, India has failed to turn the tables against China. India should have said, China has no border with India at all, but Tibet has. By not recognizing the fact that China is occupying Tibet illegally India has once again, in practice, accepted the Chinese occupation of Tibet, Manchuria, and Eastern Turkistan or the Pakistani occupations of Baluchistan and North West Frontier Province (NWFP).

There is no evidence that Tibet was a part of China before China colonized it in 1949. The same is true of Taiwan and Eastern Turkistan. If the Manchus are not Chinese, as Sun Yat Sen declared in 1911, Manchuria, which China received as a gift from Stalin in 1950, was never a part of China either. However, the world has ignored this Chinese imperialism and even gives recognition to China as being one of the five controlling powers of the world affairs as a permanent member of the UN Security Council (Richardson 1984; Marshall 2004).

China has no continuous history as a nation-state. Before 1279, only the central part of what is China today was pure Chinese—that is, inhabited by the Han Chinese tribe. During 1279–1368, China was a part of the Mongol Empire and it ceased to exist as a sovereign state. From 1368 to 1644, China had the Ming Dynasty of the Han Chinese tribe but was occupied by the Manchus in 1644 until 1911.

Chinese Empire of Tibet

Tibet has a history of at least 1,300 years of independence. The first recorded contacts between Tibetans and Chinese date back to the seventh century, following the unification of Tibet under King Songtsen Gampo and the marriage of a Chinese princess to Songtsen Gampo in 641. This marriage alliance was sought after Tibetan armies had captured towns in Sichuan province. In 821, a treaty recognizing them as two independent nations ended almost 200 years of war between China and Tibet.

During the thirteenth and fourteenth centuries both China and Tibet came under the influence of the Mongol Empire. The Mongol's militarily conquered China while the Tibetans and the Mongols established the historically unique "priest patron" relationship, also known as CHO-YON. The Mongol aristocracy had converted to Buddhism and they sought spiritual guidance and moral legitimacy for the rule of their vast empire from the Tibetan theocracy. As the patrons of Tibet, the Mongols promised to protect Tibet against foreign invasion. The Mongol Empire came to an end in the mid-fourteenth century. Today, a part of Mongolia, which is not occupied by China, is an independent country, not a part of China, and Mongols are not Chinese. By the fifteenth century, political authority in Tibet had passed into the hands of contending religious hegemonies that were eventually replaced by a system of rule under the Dalai Lamas. In China, the native Ming Dynasty overthrew the Mongols. During the Ming Dynasty both Tibet and China existed as separate and fully sovereign states.

Tibet and the British

The British, after 1911, convened a tripartite conference to discuss Tibet's border with the British India in Simla in 1914 (Aitchison 1929). The Tibetans arrived at the conference with written proof of Tibet's historical independence. The Chinese delegation—present only to witness the treaty between Britain and Tibet—argued that Tibet's subjugation by the Mongols and the Manchus became an integral part of China and should therefore be ruled as part of the new Republic of China of Sun Yat Sen from Peking. That was also the beginning of the border dispute between China and India. However, although Tibet was not really subjugated by the Mongols and Manchus, it was certainly influenced by them. Neither Mongols nor Manchus were Chinese. In fact, China itself had been occupied for a long time by both the Mongols and the Manchus (van Walt van Praag 1987).

The fact that both Tibet and China came under Mongol political influence does not indicate unification of the two countries, as China claims. Iraq, Turkey, most parts of Russia and Eastern Europe, the Indian subcontinent, northern Burma, North Vietnam, and Korea were all part of the vast Mongol Empire. Would that mean these areas belong to China? British India included Burma until very recently. The British Empire also used to control Sri Lanka, Malaysia, Iraq, and Burma. Does that mean India should now legitimately claim Sri Lanka, Iraq, Malaysia, and Burma as its integral parts? Such is the absurdity of the Chinese claim. The most important point is that Manchus, like Mongols, are not ethnic Chinese and suggestions that Tibet became an integral part of a "Chinese" Empire during the Manchu Empire are just absurd. Tibet continued to conduct itself as a fully sovereign nation, recognized by the British Empire until its occupation by Communist China in 1949 (van Walt van Praag 1987).

Today however, China disputes the legal status of the Simla Convention and the resultant McMahon line—the border between India and Tibet accepted by the British, the true significance of which lies in its recognition of Tibet as an independent nation with which binding agreements such as the Lhasa Treaty of 1904 could be negotiated. Throughout the Nationalist (Kuomintang) period from 1912 to 1949, no Chinese government was able to exert any influence over Tibet. During the Second World War, Tibet remained neutral, despite strong pressure from the United States, Britain, and China to allow the passage of raw materials through the country. When Nepal applied for membership of the UN in 1949, it cited its treaty and diplomatic relations with Tibet to demonstrate its full international personality (van Walt van Praag 1987).

Chinese Invasion of Tibet

The invasion of Tibet by troops from the People's Liberation Army in 1949–1950 is described in official Chinese histories as a "peaceful liberation." The Seventeen-Point Plan for the Peaceful Liberation of Tibet in 1951 was signed between the Communist government and Tibetan officials in May 1951, which apparently "enjoyed the approval and support of the people from every ethnic group in Tibet" (Information Office of the State Council of The People's Republic of China 1992). If Tibet was part of China, then there was no need for the agreement, which was forced upon the Tibetan delegation in China for signature, and then China announced to the world that Tibet was liberated.

Human Rights Violations in Tibet by China

"In fact, discrimination and the suppression of traditional practices in eastern Tibet drove hundreds of Tibetans up into the mountains to conduct guerrilla warfare, while thousands more fled west to Lhasa to escape Chinese persecution. In March 1959, growing Tibetan resistance exploded in an uprising against the Chinese occupation. The 14th Dalai Lama fled into exile in northern India, and the subsequent Chinese crackdown in Tibet was brutal. . . . Tibetan sources suggest as many as 430,000 were killed in the Uprising and subsequent years of guerrilla warfare" (Tibet Support Group 1994).

From 1951 to 1959 China broke every promise that it made toward Tibet, resulting in the Tibetan uprising against China in March 1959. The Dalai Lama and 100,000 Tibetans escaped into exile. From that day onward, Tibet effectively became an occupied country.

Despite promising not to get involved with the existing system of government and society in Tibet by signing the Seventeen-Point Plan for the Peaceful Liberation of Tibet, China did interfere in eastern Tibet—reneging on the treaty altogether in 1959. China has renamed two of Tibet's three provinces as parts of the Chinese provinces of Qinghai, Gansu, Sichuan, and Yunnan and has renamed the remaining province of U' Tsang as Tibet Autonomous Region (TAR). On October 28, 1991, U.S. Congress under a Foreign Authorization Act passed the resolution wherein they recognized "Tibet, including those areas incorporated into the Chinese provinces of Sichuan, Yunnan, Gansu and Qinghai, AN OCCUPIED COUNTRY under the established principal of international law." The resolution further stated that Tibet's true representatives are the Dalai Lama and the Tibetan government in exile as recognized by the Tibetan people in the US State Department Authorization Act of 1991.

Some 1.2 million Tibetans are estimated to have been killed by the Chinese since 1950. Reprisals for the 1959 National Uprising alone involved the elimination of 87,000 Tibetans by the Chinese count, according to a Radio Lhasa broadcast of October 1, 1960. Tibetan exiles claim that 430,000 died during the uprising and the subsequent 15 years of guerrilla warfare. In its 1959 and 1960 reports, the International Commission of Jurists concluded that "there was a prima facie case of genocide committed by the Chinese upon the Tibetan nation." These reports consider events before the Cultural Revolution of Mao Tse-Tung, during which much of Tibet's own cultural assets were destroyed and thousands of Tibetans killed (Tibet Support Group 1994).

Up to 260,000 people died in prisons and labor camps between 1950 and 1984. Since September 1987, approximately 3,000 people are believed to have been imprisoned for political offenses such as giving out leaflets, writing letters, or talking to foreigners about the Tibetans' right to independence. From March 1989 to May 1990, the Chinese administered a campaign of torture against Tibetan dissidents in prison. During 1994–1995, three nuns died shortly after release from custody as a result of ill treatment and torture in detention. Beatings and torture are still regularly used against political prisoners today. Detainees are held in substandard conditions, malnourished, forbidden to talk, denied medical treatment, and often held in solitary confinement. According to the Tibet Support Group (1994), "The Chinese have refused to allow independent observers to attend so-called public trials. Prison sentences are regularly decided before the trial. Less than 2% of cases in China are won by the defense."

Tibetan was replaced by Chinese as the official language and despite official pronouncements there was no practical change in this policy. It is difficult for Tibetans to gain employment in the state sector without proficiency in Chinese. Secondary school children are taught all classes in Chinese. Religious practice was forcibly suppressed until 1979, and up to 6,000 monasteries and shrines were destroyed. In 1995 the Chinese authorities rejected the child recognized by the Dalai Lama as the rebirth of the Panchen Lama and installed their own candidate. There are an estimated 300,000 troops stationed on Tibetan territory and three nuclear missile sites. Near Lake Kokonor, the largest lake on the Tibetan plateau, there is a 20-square-kilometer dump for radioactive pollutants and China has admitted depositing nuclear waste (Tibet Support Group 1994).

Demographic Change in Tibet

China is filling up Tibet with ethnic Han Chinese in an attempt to destroy the ethnicity of the Tibetans. This policy has much more potential to destroy Tibet as a nation than the millions who have died from Chinese policies, the destruction of more than 6,000 Buddhist monasteries, the arrest and torture of Tibetan monks, the destruction of Tibetan forests, and the stationing of nuclear weapons and waste dumps in Tibet.

Samdhong Rinpoche, the prime minister of the Tibetan government-in-exile, estimates that 7 million ethnic Chinese now live in Tibet, where there are only 2.3 million Tibetans. In towns like Lhasa and Chengdu, 75 percent of the people are ethnic Chinese. According to the Tibet Support Group (1994), it was this influx of Chinese nationals that destabilized the economy. Forced agricultural modernizations in Tibet were the cause of extensive crop failures and the country's first recorded famine (1960–1962), in which 340,000 Tibetans died. Tibetan farms and grazing lands have been confiscated and incorporated into collectivized and communal farms.

The resettlement of Chinese migrants has led to Tibetans becoming the minority in many areas, including Lhasa. This in turn has created high unemployment among Tibetans. Official figures put the number of non-Tibetans in the TAR at 79,000. Independent research puts the figure at 250,000–300,000, and for the whole of Tibet 5–5.5 million Chinese to 4.5 million Tibetans. In Kham and Amdo, the Chinese outnumber Tibetans many times over.

As with previous railways built by China in Mongolia and East Turkistan, the more recently built Tibet railway would greatly speed colonization of the area. The railway will improve China's military maneuverability, enable rapid troop deployments, and facilitate the expansion of People's Liberation Army bases and increases in nuclear weapons stockpiles and missile deployments on the Tibetan plateau.

China's Empire in East Turkistan

East Turkistan, another colony of China, is bordered by Kazakhstan to the north, Tibet and India to the south, and Afghanistan and Pakistan to the West. It is China's largest province of 640,000 square kilometers—one-sixth of the present Chinese territory. However, it was not a part of China until 1949 and the people of that land are not Chinese either. About 96 percent of its population is Turkic peoples of Tajik, Kyrghyz, Uzbek, or Kazakh, similar to their relatives in the former Soviet Union, commonly known as Uyghurs. The invasion of East Turkistan by the Han Chinese started in 104 BC, and the country was occupied several times by Chinese soldiers, but none of these occupations lasted for long. There were six invasions from 104 BC to 751 AD, but during that period the Chinese invaders sustained their control for only 157 years. Arab, Turkic, and Tibetan forces repulsed the Chinese occupiers in 751 AD. East Turkistan later became a part of the Mongol Empire briefly. In 1876, the Manchu Empire occupied East Turkistan. The people in the southern part of East Turkistan established an Eastern Turkistan Islamic Republic in 1933 and then, in 1944, established the second Eastern Turkistan Republic (Starr 2004; Millward 2007)

East Turkistan was occupied by China in 1949, and its name was changed to Xing Kiang in 1955. Communist China has been exercising a colonial rule over the land since then. The people there, just like the people in two other colonies of China in Tibet and Manchuria, have to undergo unimaginable suffering and have been subjugated to inhuman conditions under the repressive alien rule. The year 1999 saw mass arrests, and murders of the people of East Turkistan become most widespread. This policy was especially sinister in the regions of Hotan, Kashgar, Aksu, and Ili. As recently as 1999, some 2,500 people were killed. According to Amnesty International, currently at least 250,000 people are in prison.

Chinese Empire of Manchuria

In 1639, the 5th Dalai Lama established another CHO-YON relationship with the Manchu emperor, who, driven out of Manchuria by the Russians, occupied China and established the Manchu Dynasty in 1644. Manchu officials or *Ann bans* were stationed in Tibet from 1728 until the fall of the dynasty in 1911. *Ann bans* were instructed not to interfere in the internal policies of Tibet and to refrain from exploitation. In 1911, Sun Yat Sen declared Manchus to be foreigners, deposed the Manchu emperor of China Pei Wei, and proclaimed China to be a republic.

Manchuria had been a Russian territory since the sixteenth century. Russia had developed industrial cities like Harbin in Manchuria and Port Arthur in Korea. The settlement of Han Chinese in Manchuria was prohibited until late into the nineteenth century. In 1905, Japan according to the Portsmouth Treaty took over Manchuria from Russia but allowed some pro-Japanese warlords of China to rule over it from 1918. In 1931, Japan took complete control over Manchuria, renamed it Manchuko, reestablished Pei Wei as the sovereign emperor of China, and in his name they tried to occupy the rest of China. The Soviet Union took over Manchuria in 1945 after the surrender of Japan to the United States but gave it away to China in 1950 without any consideration for the wishes of the people in Manchuria (Rearden 2012). Despite claims of Chinese propaganda, millions of non-Chinese people living in areas presently under the People's Republic of China suffer all kinds of discrimination. The most disturbing effect of Chinese policy toward people in these areas is the demographic transformation that has been imposed upon them. In virtually every area, new Chinese immigrants have become the majority community. Manchuria has been completely absorbed, and the distinct Manchu culture that was vibrant until 1949 does not exist at all anymore.

China's False Claim on Formosa

In 1949, Kuomintang forces of Chiang-Kei-Seik defeated by Mao Tse-Tung invaded Formosa. They massacred the local population, who are not ethnic Chinese but a mixed population of Japanese, Chinese, Portuguese, and the indigenous proto-Malays. However, now China claims that Formosa, renamed as Taiwan, is an inalienable part of China and China wants to reclaim it as soon as possible. History cannot support that Chinese claim (Davidson 1903; Takekoshi 1907).

From 1368 to 1644, China had the Ming Dynasty of the Chin or Han Chinese tribe. At that time, Formosa was occupied first by the Dutch and then by the Portuguese. For a brief period from 1645 to 1662, a half-Japanese general of the Ming Dynasty, Tei Seiko, after being driven from China by the invading Manchus from the north, occupied that island. However, the Portuguese soon regained control of the island, which they had renamed as Formosa, or the beautiful island. The Machu Empire only ruled Formosa for eight years between 1887 and 1895, but Manchus were not Chinese either.

The Manchu Empire of China managed Formosa for just that brief period of time and, in 1895, gladly ceded it to Japan. After that, China had forfeited its rights to the island permanently or until the signing of another international treaty. The present-day Beijing government claims that the 1943 Cairo Declaration and the 1945 Potsdam Declaration recognized China's sovereignty over Formosa. That is not factually correct. The Cairo Declaration had nothing new on the question of Chinese territorial sovereignty over Formosa.

Furthermore, both the Cairo and Potsdam Declarations were not valid international treaties but, to quote Justice Radha Binod Pal, a "victor's justice" (Ushimura 2003), where Japan never took any part.

The People's Republic of China, which came into being in 1949, was at war with the UN in 1951 over Korea and was not invited to sign the San Francisco Treaty in which Japan formally renounced "all right, title and claim to Formosa." The Republic of China or Kuomintang was unable to represent China in that treaty. Accordingly, to follow the UN principle of self-determination, Formosa belongs only to Formosans, not to China.

The history of Tibet, Manchuria, East Turkistan, and Formosa, dating back more than 2,000 years, has been one of independence from China. At no time, since the founding of the nation in 127 BC, have the Tibetans conceded their sovereignty to a foreign power. East Turkistan was occupied from time to time, but those periods of occupation were brief. Manchuria was not occupied by China until 1950. Formosa, except for seven years, was never a part of China.

CHINESE EMPIRE IN VIETNAM, THE PHILIPPINES, AND INDONESIA

China has no limit to its demands on lands, islands, rocks, and reefs in the South China Sea, disregarding any international laws and conventions. China only recognizes might, not logic. Legitimate claims by other nations of East Asia have no meaning in the dictionary of China. China has claimed sovereignty across most of the South China Sea. It grants itself rights that cannot apply to an international shipping route. In fact, China imposes its demands by building military structures on uninhabited archipelagos, islets, rocks, and reefs that are already possessed by other countries in the region, including Japan, Vietnam, the Philippines, Malaysia, and Indonesia. Chinese citizens are encouraged to fish everywhere under the protection of China's coastguards and to engage in prospecting for oil, with the installation of a drilling platform off the coast of Vietnam. In a direct head to head with Vietnam, Malaysia, Brunei and the Philippines, Taiwan, and Japan, Beijing claims possession of the Paracel and Spratly Islands, the Scarborough Shoal, and the Senkaku Islands. It also appears to be extending its own territorial waters so much that there is practically nothing left for the rest of Southeast Asia (O'Neill 2018).

In April 2012, there was a clash between China and the Philippines over Scarborough Shoal, one of the Spratly Islands in the South China Sea. The confrontation between the naval vessels of the two countries continued for almost two months and in the middle of this the United States and the

Philippines carried out a joint military drill in the vicinity. Japan, Australia, and South Korea all sent their personnel to participate in this drill.

China deployed an armada of 80 military and civilian ships, along with support aircraft, to install a billion-dollar oil rig on Vietnam's continental shelf well within its 200-mile exclusive economic zone (EEZ). According to Rodis (2012):

> When Vietnam responded by dispatching 30 of its ships to defend its sovereign territory, China used high-powered water cannons to disperse them and even rammed its vessels straight into Vietnamese ships causing damage to the Vietnamese ships and injury to those on board. Vietnam may have the will to fight but clearly lacks the 'suitable' might to defend itself against China.
>
> Vietnam is mindful about what happened on March 14, 1988 when four ships of the Chinese People's Liberation Army Navy [PLAN] landed on Vietnam's Johnson South Reef and faced Vietnamese defenders on the reef who refused to leave. The Chinese ships fired at will at the sailors and pounded the reef with heavy shells. When the dust settled, several Vietnamese ships were destroyed and 64 Vietnamese sailors lay dead. The Johnson South Reef Massacre was recorded by the Chinese Navy and shown all over China as an example of China's might.

China's attack against the Philippines was initiated when China moved a giant oil rig to the Recto Bank—just 85 nautical miles from Palawan. The U.S. Energy Information Administration (USEIA) has estimated that there could be approximately 11 billion barrels (bbl) of oil reserves and 190 trillion cubic feet (tcf) of natural gas reserves in the West Philippine Sea. Ayungin is the gateway to the Recto Bank, and China intends to occupy Ayungin Shoal (Robis 2014).

China's occupation of the Philippines mining industry is another issue. One of China's mining companies is operating in the Philippines "located near the Scarborough Shoal in the coastal town of Masinloc where China's Wei-Wei Group has set up a US$100 million nickel processing plant. In nearby Botolan, Zambales, China's Jiangxi Rare Earth and Rare Metals Tungsten Group Company Limited operates a US$150 million nickel exploration and cobalt processing project" (Rodis 2012).

There is an estimated US$1 trillion in untapped mineral resources in the Philippines. Chinese mining companies, many of them operating illegally, have been exporting precious minerals such as gold and nickel out through the island country's porous coastal ports, where there are no customs officials. If China can occupy the Scarborough Shoal, smuggling precious metals from the Philippines to a Chinese base will be easy. In 1996, China occupied the Mischief Reef—75 miles from Palawan. Vietnam, Malaysia, and the Philippines have separately protested against Chinese land reclamation at numerous reefs in the Spratly Islands. The fear is that they could be used for air, naval, or logistic bases to strengthen China's territorial claims a long way from its mainland (O'Neill 2018).

Around the Great Natuna Island, in Indonesia there is a growing of alarm, over China's claim to maritime rights in the sea surround the island. In February 2021, China allowed the coast guards to enforce the Chinese rights on the island using all kinds of weapons. That area has fishing resources and a possible natural gas reserve. Natuna Island is located 1,800 kilometers south of China's mainland. This island is located within the so-called "Nine-Dash line" drawn by China itself to demonstrate its claim. In January, 2021, about 50 Chinese fishing boats operated inside the exclusive economic zone of Indonesia. Indonesia objected to the United Nations but without any effects. The Natuna archipelago has a population of about 80,000. Japan is providing assistance to Indonesia worth about 830 million yen to construct docks so that Indonesia can build up a fisheries-zone free of Chinese occupation. Thus, after Vietnam and Philippines, Indonesia is now a victim of Chinese colonialism.

China and the Asian Financial Crisis on 1998

After 1998, IMF-World Bank tried to hide China under a strange argument of crony capitalism. If that would be the correct analysis, then the crisis would be repeated every year. However, that was not the case. The countries affected by that crisis changed their trade pattern to survive from the Chinese attack on their economies. They used to be export-oriented economies. Now they, since 1998, became the suppliers of raw materials and primary products to China.

To analyze that history, we can start from the background of that crisis. Between 1970 and 1996 the "Tiger" economies of Southeast and East Asia through their industrial and trade policies narrowed the gap between output per person in those countries and that of the most advanced countries. Between those years, the gross national product per head in South Korea went up by elevenfold, of Hong Kong by fourfold, and that of Thailand went up by 3.5-fold. In 1970, Korea's real income per head, at the purchasing power parity, was only 15 percent of the U.S. level. By 1995, it became 40 percent of the U.S. level. Thailand's income per head has risen from 11 to 28 percent of the U.S. level over the same period. The instruments used to achieve these very positive results are high rate mass education, prudent industrial policies, high savings rate, promotions of exports, realistic exchange rates, and appropriate intervention in the market. East Asian economies with currencies linked to the U.S. dollar enjoyed high levels of competitiveness particularly against Japan. The Thai economy expanded at an average rate of 8.4 percent a year between 1990 and 1995. Rapid growth initiated high inflows of foreign capital. Thailand had a current account deficit of about 7 percent of its GNP between 1990 and 1995 financed by these capital inflows.

In 1994, China devalued its currency by about 50 percent. As a result, Southeast and East Asian countries lost their competitiveness and started to have declining growth rates of their economies.

The Asian economic crisis started in the middle of 1997 when a large conglomerate of South Korea defaulted in its debt repayment and the stock market of Thailand started collapsing along with its currency. Very soon, one country after another was experiencing a combination of mass depreciation of their currencies, sharp downfall of stock prices, floods of outflows of foreign capital, and bankruptcies of big and small companies. Within a year the so-called "Tiger" economies of East Asia were reduced to countries with mass unemployment, social upheavals, political disturbances, and were begging for assistance from the IMF and the rich developed countries. By the end of 1996, sharp depreciation of currencies has caused rise in the price of imports and increased foreign debts in local currencies for the corporations and banks. Authorities increased rates of interest to stop outflows of capital. The result is reduction of consumption and investments and deep economic downturns. Reductions of money supply and public expenditure as suggested by the IMF as the prices of economic assistance led to the reductions of investments and consumptions. Financial and credit functions became paralyzed, and the currency crisis became an economic crisis.

As these countries of East and Southeast Asia are closely interlinked through trade and investments during the era of high-speed economic growth, economic crisis spread from one to other quickly. Real economic growth in Southeast Asia in 1998 was reduced to −6.9 percent, compared with 8.2 percent in 1995 and 7.1 percent in 1996. Inflation was 21 percent in 1998 in Southeast Asia, compared with 5.6 percent in 1997 and 6.6 percent in 1996. South Korea, Indonesia, Thailand, and Malaysia all had negative growth rates in 1998. There were growing nonperforming loans in the banks as the companies depend on the banks rather than the stock markets. Asian countries have liberalized their capital accounts of the balance of payments and relaxed restrictions of their financial markets. That had caused significant inflows of foreign institutional funds of short-term nature. By the end of 1996, the share of short-term liabilities to total liabilities was above 50 percent, and the ratio of short-term external liabilities to foreign reserves was above 100 percent in South Korea, Indonesia, and Thailand. However, anticipations of future bailout provided international banks strong incentives to take on even more risks.

The ratio of short-term debts to foreign reserve was 54 percent in 1994 in South Korea, 177 percent in Indonesia in 1996, 100 percent in Thailand in

1996, 79 percent in the Philippines, 41 percent in Malaysia in 1996, but only 24 percent in 1996 in China.

The ration of short-term debt and debt service to foreign reserve was 85 percent in 1994 in South Korea, 294 percent in 1996 in Indonesia, 137 percent in 1996 in the Philippines, 123 percent in Thailand in 1996, 69 percent in 1996 in Malaysia, but only 38 percent in China.

China also protected its balance of payment capital account against any sudden outflows. Ratio of foreign liabilities to assets in 1996 reached 1103 percent in Thailand, 375 percent in South Korea, 424 in Indonesia, 172 percent in the Philippines, 148 percent in Malaysia, but 120 percent in China. In the presence of rapid currency depreciation if foreign banks refuse to extend the credit lines to domestic banks, these imbalances may cause serious financial problem and that had happened in 1997 in Southcast Asia. Since 1990, China was devaluing its exchange rate and in 1994 it devalued yuan by about 50 percent, which along with its policy export subsidies drove out exports from the ASEAN countries. In 1997 and 1998, China's exports were growing at some fantastic rates. Table 10.3 and 10.4 demonstrate how China destroyed the export market of the ASEAN countries causing the 1998 financial crisis.

(Categories of goods whose exports to the United States fell by over US$1 million in 1995–1996 and whose exports by China to the United States increased)

Table 10.3. Trade Destruction Caused by China (US$ million)

Categories of Goods Exported	*Decrease*	*Increase in China*
Malaysia:		
Skirts, knitted, synthetic fibers	3,130	2,230
Nightshirts, pajamas, of cotton	5,040	43,230
Clothing for infants, synthetic fibers	3,820	4,810
Men's or boys overcoats, car coats	2,170	31,960
Women's overcoats, car coats	1,180	1,1640
Tin alloys	3,600	7,560
Fittings for loose-leaf binders	7,740	22,120
Lamps	1,110	121,160
Thailand		
Frozen fish	5,180	22,890
Silicon dioxide	1,340	7,380
Tubes, pipes, hoses, of plastic	1,980	2,440
Gloves	3,810	13,860
Footwear	2,310	28,780
Soles of footwear	1,790	12,700
Seats, etc.	1,720	19,210

Source: MITI and JETRO, Japan.

Table 10.4. Export Growth Rates in East Asian Economies (%)

	1997							*1998*		
Months	6	7	8	9	10	11	12	1	2	3
South Korea	9.6	19.3	14.0	13.4	5.2	3.8	1.7	–0.3	19.9	6.6
Thailand	–5.1	0.7	0.7	9.9	10.7	–0.5	–1.4	–11.8	–4.9	–10.5
Malaysia	1.2	4.5	2.5	0.9	–2.6	–2.4	–11.0	–23.2	8.9	–12.9
Indonesia	6.8	12.7	8.8	8.7	1.9	5.0	0.5	–2.2	–6.5	11.5
China	25.3	25.1	13.4	23.4	17.1	23.0	4.7	8.4	23.5	9.5

Source: JETRO, Japan.

From 1996 to 1997, the nominal GDP per capita dropped by 43.2 percent in Indonesia, 21.2 percent in Thailand, 19 percent in Malaysia, 18.5 percent in South Korea, and 12.5 percent in the Philippines. Hong Kong, Mainland China, Singapore, and Japan were also affected but less significantly.

Besides its economic impact, the Asian financial crisis also resulted in political repercussions. The prime minister general of Thailand, Yongchaiyudh, and the president of Indonesia, Suharto, resigned. An anti-Western sentiment was triggered, especially against George Soros, who was blamed for triggering the crisis with large amounts of currency speculation by some individuals.

The impact of the Asian financial crisis was not limited to Asia. International investors became less willing to invest in and lend to developing countries, not only in Asia but also in other areas of the world. China gains from that. Oil prices also fell due to the crisis. As a result, some major mergers and acquisitions in the oil industry took place to achieve economics of scale. Russia was seriously affected.

The IMF generated several bailout packages for the most affected countries during the financial crisis. It provided packages of around $20 billion to Thailand, $40 billion to Indonesia, and $59 billion to South Korea to support them, so they did not default.

The bailout packages are structural adjustment packages. The countries that received the packages were asked to reduce their government spending, allow insolvent financial institutions to fail, and raise interest rates aggressively. The purpose of the adjustments was to support the currency values and confidence over the countries' solvency. However, it has nearly destroyed the affected countries in their economies and their trade patterns. They became dependent to China more and more as China took over their export markets and they were reduced to supplier of raw materials or semi-finished products to China.

China's aim to make Asia's seas its exclusive property, keeping Japan at bay and excluding U.S. military presence, is just one part of a greater mission. China intends to extend its military power through Burma, Africa, and

Pakistan up to the Arabian Sea, on to the Persian Gulf and into the Middle East and Africa. China's defense budget is second only to that of the United States, giving it great purchasing power and increased military capabilities.

Recent outbreak of coronavirus and resultant thousands of death all over the world is blamed on China that either China has developed this virus in its laboratory in Wuhan or it suppressed the information so that other countries could not take action beforehand. The result is worldwide shutdown and mass unemployment and bankruptcy. Most companies are having the problem of very low demand and reduced share price. China is taking advantage of that. It is buying up companies after companies everywhere particularly in the developing countries.

Every nation in the world talks of peace. Throughout the twentieth century, countries have enthusiastically praised the virtues of "stability," "peace," and "good relations," yet they have all been caught up in the irrationality of actively prepared for and fomented war. Among growing economic chaos, there is unlikely to be a "peaceful rise" to Chinese imperialism—just preparations for war to expand China's economic interest through its militarism.

China recently created a new type of imperialism. In the name of BRI, it is giving huge loans to a number of countries for infrastructure projects at very high interest rates. All materials for these projects including labor force would come from China, although the recipient countries could supply most of these particularly the labor forces to reduce the borrowings. When the country will be unable to pay back these loans, China will take very long-term lease of important ports, airports, mines, or islands. Recently Sri Lanka when unable to repay its loan to China gave lease of an airport, Humbantota, for 100 years to China. Maldives has taken from China a loan of $250 million, which is the same as its GDP. Kenya gave up Mombasa port to China, after failing to repay its debt to China.

In Africa, similarly, a number of countries leased out their mines. China has a plan to invest $60 billion in Africa, 75 percent of that in oil-related industries. Sudan has taken $6.4 billion, Kenya has taken $8 billion, Republic of Congo has taken $7.3 billion, Ethiopia has taken $13.5 billion loan from China, and Angola has taken $25 billion from China. These are nothing when we consider Pakistan, which has taken $40 billion loan from China with a guaranteed rate of return of 30 percent, which it cannot repay. Therefore, Pakistan has given away Gwadar port in Balochistan for a joint military base with China. This is imperialism in another name (Toh 2017; Kesling and Emont 2019).

Big corporations in the Western world control the mass media. For example, Walmart, the biggest retail chain stores in the United States, which receives most of its supplies from China, is owned by Rupert Murdoch, who also owns some of the most important newspapers and television channels in the United States, the United Kingdom, Australia, India, and East Asia. The result is a continuous pro-Chinese propaganda in the media, which is blaming the democratically elected Taiwanese leaders for provoking China by not accepting the Chinese colonialism. With the interests and ambitions of the Kuomintang Chinese and China have now merged, it will not take long for the United States to discard Taiwan to its fate in order to please China and to protect the commercial interests of the American companies in China.

Both China and the United States thus correspond to the classical pattern of colonialism. They both want to capture territories to promote their business interests. In the case of American Empire the desire is to protect its overseas investments and particularly the oil industry worldwide. It can correspond somehow to the theory of Lenin. Chinese Empire does not correspond to the theory of Lenin at all. China wants to capture resources of the world to promote its industry in future as a matter of national honor and prestige to wipe out "the century of humiliation."

How China Won in Afghanistan

The United States ran away from Afghanistan. Pakistan and Taliban are in control of Afghanistan. Americans left all their weapons and armed cars in Afghanistan to be used by Taliban and Pakistan. The question is who really won the war? Why India is so passive after investing more than $3 billion in Afghanistan?

The war had started in 1947 when Britain gave Afghan areas in the cast of Durand Line to newly formed country Pakistan. These areas are the Pashtun-speaking areas in the North West Frontier Province and Baluchistan. These areas were taken by the British government as lease from Afghanistan in 1893 just like Hong Kong was leased from the Manchu Empire of China in 1893. Britain had no authority to give these areas to Pakistan. That was the reason Afghanistan objected the entry of Pakistan in the United Nations. Britain rescued Pakistan at that time, and Afghanistan lost those areas. Baluchistan became an independent country in August 1947 but Pakistan invaded it in March 1948 and absorbed it. Britain had not objected it but encouraged Pakistan before to annex Jammu and Kashmir. Pakistan invaded Jammu and Kashmir in October 1947 with active participation of the British army. Captain Brown, the commander in charge of the Gilgit Scout, raised the flag of Pakistan on the northern areas of Jammu and Kashmir and Lord Mountbatten refused to allow the Indian army to attack the Pakistani-British forces to drive them away from Northern Kashmir. He asked Nehru, then the acting prime minister of the Dominion of India, to go to the United Nations, where Britain refused to support India.

In both 1965 and 1971, Britain supported Pakistan, which it has created. Afghanistan was in relative peace as King Zahir Shah was in power with the support of the United States-United Kingdom and the Soviet Union. When in 1994 Zahir Shah was ousted by his son-in-law Daud Khan, the problem for Afghanistan had started. Benazir Bhutto wrote in her autobiography that Nassurullah Baber, the governor of Punjab, came to her father J. A. Bhutto, then the prime minister of Pakistan, suggesting that Pakistan should now invade Afghanistan, which Pakistan did in some subdued clandestine manner.

The Pakistani invasion of Afghanistan became open and intense when Nur Mihamed Taraki, the leader of the Afghan Communist Party, removed Daud Khan in a socialist revolution and became the president of Afghanistan in a Socialist government in 1976. Pakistani forces dressed up as Pathan tribesmen, as they did in 1947 in Kashmir, entered Afghanistan. CIA and MI6 were both involved in that. In 1979 in a coup organized by the deputy of Nur Mohamed Taraki, Hafezul Amin, he killed President Taraki and became the president. That coup was supported by the CIA and MI6. Amin started killing the members of the Afghan Communist Party and expelled Vice President Babrak Karmal to Czechoslovakia. In the meantime Pakistani forces in Pathan dress advanced inside Afghanistan taking advantage of the chaos. By October 1979, the situation became very grim and the Afghan Communist Party asked the Soviet Union for help. In the meantime, these Pakistanis attacked and killed several Soviet teachers and agricultural specialists in Afghanistan. There was a meeting of the Political Bureau of the Communist Party of the USSR in October 1979 to discuss the problem of Afghanistan, where a decision was taken for the Soviet army to go to Afghanistan to help the country and to deter the Pakistani invasion. According to that decision, the Soviet army entered Afghanistan in December 1979, which the Western countries and their media had termed as Soviet invasion of Afghanistan.

From 1979 to 1992 Afghanistan became a battle ground between Muslim warriors from different countries mainly Pakistan and the Afghans and their Soviet supporters. Zbnew Brijhinski declared that the United States will make Afghanistan a Vietnam for the USSR. In Vietnam, the United States was defeated because of continuous weapons supplies by the Soviet Union. The United States and its allies also started doing that to the Muslim warriors through Pakistan.

By 1985 the situation in Afghanistan was stabilized. War was only in the border areas of Pakistan. In the cities the life was normal. Thus, Gorbachev thought that the Afghan army could take care of their own country. He announced gradual withdrawal of the Soviet army and by 1989, all Soviet soldiers left Afghanistan.

Deathblow of Afghanistan came in 1992, when the Soviet Union disappeared and new president of new Russia Yeltsin abolished the Communist

Party of Russia and cut off all supplies to Afghanistan. Afghanistan appealed to India for help, but India refused fearing the United States and the United Kingdom. Pakistan army took advantage of the situation and occupied Afghanistan completely through an unofficial army of the Muslim warriors called Mujahedeen. Thousands of people, members of the Afghan Communist Party, Shias, non-Pashtuns like Hazera, Tajik, and Uzbeks were killed by the Mujahedeen army. Most parts of Afghanistan built by the Soviets were destroyed. Pashtuns are about 40 percent of the people of Afghanistan, and the rest are non-Pashtuns. Taliban formed in 1996, by Bill Clinton, the president of the United States, when the Mujahedeen government could not make a deal with the American company UNICAL to construct a gas pipeline from Turkmenistan to Pakistan. Taliban army is of Pashtun origin; they are equipped and trained by Pakistan.

After 9/11 attack on New York and Washington, the United States invaded both Afghanistan and Iraq but at the same time allowed the Taliban to escape to Pakistan. The United States so far gave more than $20 billion to Pakistan to maintain its supply routes to Afghanistan. Pakistan provided full training and other facility to the Taliban and other terrorist groups including Al-Qaeda. Bin Laden was living in Pakistan in the military town of Abbottabad, where he was killed by the American marine.

The United Kingdom was involved through Turkey and Pakistan. When Turkey was sending weapons to Yugoslavia and Pakistan was sending 400,000 Arabs terrorists to Yugoslavia to kill the Christians to create communal riots, British media was supporting these Muslim terrorists against the Serbians who were trying to maintain the unity of their country. British soldiers were giving training to the Turkish and Chechen to create Islamic countries in the former republic of the USSR, Chechnya, and in the breakaway parts of the former Yugoslavia, Bosnia, and Kosovo. Clinton started bombing Yugoslavia to force it withdraw from Bosnia and Kosovo. Clinton sent his special adviser for South Asia Robin Raphael to Afghanistan to congratulate Taliban in 1996. British ambassador to Turkey in 1990, Richard Moore became a professor in a major Turkish University. In 2021, he is now the head of the MI6, the British spy network. He was the British ambassador to Pakistan from 1995 to 1998, when Taliban was formed. Is that the reason British and the American media is implicitly supporting Taliban today?

During the time of "great game" Britain had supported and equipped two countries on both sides of the Russian Empire, Japan and Turkey. Britain had invaded Russia to take over Crimea in 1853. It equipped Japan with battleships to occupy Port Arthur of Russia in Korea and in 1905 sea battle with Russia. Turkey was the main source of terrorists who destroyed Syria and formed the ISIS, which has links with Pakistan and Taliban. All the deals between the United States and Taliban-Pakistan took place in Qatar, a former

British and Turkish colony, and the home of Al-Jazeera was formed with the support of the BBC, the British government-supported media. British has an airbase in Qatar. British chief of staff General Nicholas Carter openly supported Taliban recently. British foreign secretary came to Pakistan soon after the takeover of Afghanistan by Taliban-Pakistan, to give more than 90 million pounds of financial aid to Pakistan. British prime minister Boris Johnson is the great-grandson of a Turk, Ali Kamal Bey, who changed his surname, after immigrating to the United Kingdom.

President Biden gave away Afghanistan to China via Pakistan on a plate along with millions of dollars worth of equipment, aircrafts, and military cars. Now Afghanistan is under the effective control of Pakistan that actively supported Taliban against the forces of the former vice president Abdullah Saleh and the Tajik leader Masood. Pakistan is now revived with the support of the United States and the United Kingdom. Sons of Biden and John Kerry along with Kamala Harris have extensive financial links with China. China is close to Pakistan and is interested in the mineral resources of Afghanistan, discovered by the Soviet geologists.

That created immediate threat to India. However, India is passive without having any strategy or foreign policy. The inaction of India is surprising given the fact that Afghan government repeatedly asked India recently for support but India refused. Thus, forces of darkness won in Afghanistan again.

ORIGIN OF THE CORONAVIRUS: CHINA'S UNRESTRICTED WARFARE

Coronavirus created all over the world a fear of death. How this virus was originated? The standard explanation from the Chinese was that virus originated in the wet market of Wuhan from bat meat and pangolin meat and gradually spread all over Wuhan and other areas of China and then all over the world. However, serious doubts are now raised in the non-Chinese world. The reason is bat was not sold in the wet market of Wuhan. There is active research going on in the Institute of Virology in Wuhan on various deadly viruses, under the control of the Chinese military. Questions are raised whether accidentally virus was released from that institute or was it deliberate.

According to *NTD News*, a web magazine, since last December 2019 China imported masks and other personal protection materials worth millions of dollars from all over the world creating worldwide shortage, although China itself is the biggest producer of these items. Since November 2019, China knows about coronavirus, when one Chinese died in early November 2019 in Wuhan. The first foreign victim was in December 2019 in Thailand, which receive millions of Chinese sex tourists every year. Prof. Liebar of Harvard University Biology Department was arrested for receiving $1.2 million to support the Institute of Virology in Wuhan, the center of coronavirus. Thus, a conspiracy angle cannot be ignored.

According to *Epoch Times*, a web magazine (youtube.com/watch?v GDD7dtDaymM&t 316s), China has created this virus as a part of its strategic plan to create chaos in the world, which will serve its purpose of defeating the United States on a world scale. Wuhan is the largest city in Central China. Institute of virology is controlled by the Chinese army. Chinese president Xi also came from the Chinese army. Thus, it is important to know to what direction their research is going.

On December 3, 2019, an unknown pneumonia virus was detected in the wet market of Wuhan, which sells all kinds of wild animals including snakes and domestic cats and dogs for food. One person was infected and died. It was told that the virus came from bat, but that market does not sell any bats. That market was closed down on January 26, 2020. Chinese government still insisted that the source of this new virus was that wet market.

In the British journal called *Lancet*, on February 24, 2020 a Chinese scientist Dr. Chaolin Huang in 2020, who is the deputy director of a specialized hospital in Wuhan for the victims of this new virus, published an article, which is the result of research by his team conducted for the period between December 1, 2019, and January 1, 2020. He and his team claimed that the virus obtained from the victims is unrelated to the wet market in 14 out of 41 cases, and there were no bats in the wet market at all.

Prof. Judy Mikovits of the Institute of Antiviral Mechanism, of the Utah State University, United States, where she was the director, explained this new virus is 100 percent mutation of SARS virus, which created fear in 2002–2003 worldwide (*Epoch Times*). There is a spike protein, which can unlock the natural protection of human cells, but spike protein cannot naturally invade human cells, unless it was enhanced to do that artificially. Thus, this new virus must be manufactured. A group of Dutch scientists with Dr. Van Doremalen (2020) published their finding in March 13, 2020, in the *New England Journal of Medicine* that HCOV-19 (which is also called SARS-COV-2) is similar to SARS-COV-1. That supports the earlier finding of a group of Indian scientists with the lead scientist, Prasant Pradhan, and eight other scientists of the School of Biology of IIT Delhi, that the unique insertion in the 2019-nCOV of spike protein of HIV-1 gp 120 and HIV-1 Gag gives this virus ability to destroy body's natural immunity (Pradhan 2020).

On January 3, National Health Commission of China gave the order to the Wuhan Institute of Virology that all their documents and samples collected by Shi Zheng Li and her team should be destroyed. Who is this Shi Zheng Li? She had studied up to master's level in the Institute of Virology in Wuhan.

Then she did her PhD in the University of Montpelier in France. France had collaborated with China on many scientific areas including China's nuclear explosion in 1964 when China has no nuclear reactor but France supplied the materials to China. France helped to create the Institute of Virology in Wuhan.

In 2002–2003, Shi Zheng Li discovered the SARS virus and in 2010, she and her team found out that spike protein can help the coronavirus to move from one species to another by adding a component from the HIV virus. That was published in China in Chinese language.

On October 2013, in the British journal *Nature*, Shi Zhang Li and her team published an article that a new virus, which causes pneumonia, can be extracted from bats (2013). On November 2015, in the British journal *Nature Medicine*, she and her team published another article showing a synthetic virus that can go from one species to another and she did an experiment on monkeys (Shi Zhang Li 2015). This is the origin of the coronavirus.

That caused concern in the scientific community. Prof. Simon Wain Hobson of the Institut Pasteur of Paris expressed his fear explicitly on this type of research of Shi Zheng Li. As a result, French government curtailed all collaboration with the Institute of Virology of Wuhan. President Obama stopped financing research on genetic manipulations.

Shi Zhang Li (2015) and her team added a new component HIV-gp41 to this synthetic virus, which she has published in the *Nature Medicine* in 2015, which removes the protection of the human cells and helps the passage of the spike protein in the human cells, which makes this new virus deadly. The argument of the Institute of Virology of Wuhan on January 24 was that 2019-nCOV virus is identical to the virus BAT Cov Ra TG 13, which came from bats. The Institute of Virology of Wuhan patented that virus (Shi Zheng Li 2017, 2015; Anderson 2020).

The director of Wuhan P4 Lab in Wuhan, Wang Yan Yi, is now suspected of releasing that new virus either deliberately or accidentally. French government initially supported that P4 lab in Wuhan whose director was Yuan Zhiming and former vice president of that P4 Lab was Jiang Mianheng, who is the son of the former Chinese president Jiang Zemin who in 1989, at the time of the visit of Gorbachev to China, killed 8,000 students demanding democracy, in the Tiananmen Square in Peking.

Shi Zheng Li is now disappeared; she had created the 2019 –nCov virus, which is now infamous as coronavirus, by adding a component of HIV virus to the SARS virus, thus making it deadly (Shi Zheng Li, https://www.nature.com/articles/nm.3985/). Jiang Zhicheng, grandson of that killer ex-president of China Jiang Zemin, got the exclusive right to manufacture and sell an antidote of coronavirus named Remdesivir from his pharmaceutical company in China.

The question is why on earth the Chinese researchers rather than doing research on how to cure people will put their energy on how to kill massive number of people with this invisible weapon of a virus. Behavior of the Chinese government caused suspicion. Why did it ask the overseas Chinese to buy up masks, gloves, and other personal protective items from most countries in December 2019 and send these back to China, causing worldwide shortages of these items that China itself produces and exports. Does that mean China knew about the possible pandemic, which would be caused by coronavirus, in advance? Why does China not export Remdesivir, the possible cure for the pneumonia caused by the coronavirus? Why both Peking and Shanghai, both not far from Wuhan, have so few people affected by coronavirus, when the major victims are from Italy, the United States, and Spain, which are thousands of miles from Wuhan? Why did, in last November and December 2019, millions of Chinese tourists go out of China to these countries? Why did some beautiful Chinese girls go to Italy in January 2020 and ask Italians to hug them? Are these all just coincidental?

Two senior officers of the Peoples Liberation Army of China, Qiao Liang and Wang Xiangsui (1999), wrote a book named *Unrestricted Warfare or Warfare beyond Bounds* in 1999, about how to defeat a technologically superior enemy through a variety of means, all banned by the international law, which China does not care (https://www.c4i.org/unrestricted.pdf; 1999). These means can put the enemy in a condition that no direct military action would be needed. It is known as Fourth Generation Warfare, which suggests that there should not be any difference between combatants and civilians. This is totally unacceptable in India according to Kautilya in his Arthashashtra, but the Western countries and China do not care about any ethics in war (Basu and Miroshnik 2021). That is the reason Prithviraj Chauhan was captured by Muhammad Ghori, who was defeated before by Chauhan but according to the ethics of war in India was released with honor (Talbot 2015).

Thus, releasing a deadly virus can serve the purpose of China in another way. Most companies and airlines are in serious financial problem with their share prices are going down and they will be bankrupt soon. China can take advantage of this by buying up most of these companies in distress. India government took a preemptive action against these types of Chinese attacks on companies in India under financial stress but other countries are yet to take any action. Rothschild at the time of the Battle of Trafalgar spread a rumor in London that Napoleon won the battle. As a result, share prices in London stock market collapsed and Rothschild purchased them all. China may do the same in very near future. Lives of a million people are too insignificant for that strategy of a war without any ethics.

After the Russian operation on Ukraine another view was developed. According to the Russian army sources there are 32 biological research laboratories in Ukraine and a few in Mongolia created by the United States. They have stored and developed extremely dangerous pathogens, specially suited for the Slavonic and Mongolian races. Dr. Fauchi, the chief medical adviser to the president of the United States, gave so far millions of dollars for research to the Wuhan Institute in China. Thus, a question is raised whether the United States was responsible for the spread of the COVID-19 virus all over the world, as China claimed.

BELT AND ROAD INITIATIVE (BRI): COLONIALISM WITH CHINESE CHARACTER

China has a foreign debt of about $1.6 trillion but China at the same time is offering huge loans to a number of countries as a part of its BRI program, which was interpreted by many as the imperialism with Chinese characteristics.

Total BRI loans today in 2022 are about 6 percent of the global GDP. Total amount of loans is $1.5 trillion to 150 countries. In 2017, total BRI loans are about 15 percent of the GDP of the borrowing countries. For some countries like Congo, Laos, and Zambia it is more than 20 percent of their GDP, for Laos at least 45 percent of its GDP.

In 2020, we have the following account of the total loans taken by countries: Venezuela with $62.2 billion, Pakistan with $30 billion, Brazil with $29.7 billion, Kenya with $27 billion, Angola with $25 billion, Ecuador with $18.4 billion, Argentina with $17.1 billion, Ethiopia with $13 billion, Sri Lanka with $5 billion, Maldives with $600 million, Africa as a whole with $153 billion, and Central Asian countries with $4.1 billion (College of William and Mary, How China Lends).

In Southeast Asia and Latin America, where China is relentlessly expanding its power, Xi Jinxing has declared how the Belt and Road seeks to create a "community of common destiny" and has reiterated its focus on "the fundamental issue of development, releasing the growth potential of various countries and . . . delivering benefits to all." In reality, the BRI became an instrument for Chinese imperialism.

Chinese companies in sectors such as aluminum, steel, and cement have created massive production and overcapacities. The way out was to invest into big extractive and infrastructure projects abroad to find out the export outlets. China also exports its surplus labor by not employing the local people.

China wants to import foreign raw materials, especially minerals, fossil fuels, and agricultural commodities, for its industries. Africa has all these natural resources and as a result, it is now a main target of investments from China. Already China has become the continent's biggest trade partner. In Africa, China had lent at least $95.5 billion between 2000 and 2015.

While exports from and import to a country is not imperialism but the Chinese loan can be interpreted as imperialism; when China offers gigantic loans at exploitative costs and when the recipient country will be unable to repay the loan, China normally takes over their ports or airports or mines. Hambantota port in Sri Lanka, Gawadar port in Pakistan, and Mombasa port in Kenya are the examples. In Zambia, having invested there for its rich copper mines, China has moved men and machinery to the country, replacing Zambian with Chinese workers. These examples show that China's trade policy exhibits a pattern of exploitation. Colonialism is back—but this time with Chinese characteristics (Akol Nyok and Thayer 2020; Etzioni 2020).

Lang (2010) explained, following Lenin's formulation of imperialism, about the recent behavior of China. For Lenin, imperialism is: (1) the concentration of production and capital has developed to such a high stage that it has created monopolies, which play a decisive role in economic life; (2) the merging of bank capital with industrial capital and the creation, on the basis of this finance capital, of a financial oligarchy; (3) the export of capital as distinguished form of commodities acquiring importance; (4) the formation of international monopolist capitalist associations, which share the world among themselves; and (5) the territorial division of the whole world among the biggest capitalist powers.

Lang (2010) highlights the following five new aspects of the new imperialism: (1) the monopolies play a decisive role not only in economic life but also in cultural and political life; (2) financial oligarchy is achieved through no ordinary banks, but investment banks, with their financial products and leverage tools; (3) the scale of capital export has escalated to the free flow of capital at the will of the new imperialists; (4) much more sophisticated international monopolist capitalist associations, for instance, Monsanto, one of the four biggest grain dealers, and Wall Street, are sharing the world among themselves; and (5) in tandem with the territorial division, there emerges a geopolitical capital division, and hence a new configuration of "economic colonization" is completed.

Chapter 11

Soviet and Russian Contributions

Chinese Communist Party won the war in 1949 against the Nationalist Chinese Army because of massive Soviet support. The Soviet Union gave away East Turkistan, Inner Mongolia, and Manchuria to China. Thus, both political and economic relations were very close between the Soviet Union and China from the beginning in 1949 until 1960. The Soviet government organized manpower and resources to support China to start its Five-Year Plan of national economic development during 1953–1957. The USSR started sending equipment and technology, along with scientists and engineers, to China. The Soviet Union became China's largest trading partner, which is still true with a gap between 1960 and 1992.

In 1950, the Soviet Union provided a loan of $300 million to China, which is in addition to $520 million longer-term loan to assist its first Five-Year Plan, and thousands of Soviet scientists and engineers came to China to develop its economy (Hoeffding 1963). Thus, the development of science and technology in China the years until 1960 was due to the Soviet Union. China broke away from the Soviet Union in 1960 due to its political differences with the Soviet Union and the refusal of the Soviet Union to give nuclear weapons technology to China, which came to China ultimately in 1964 from France. Since 1992, due to the destruction of the Soviet Union, the new Russian politicians were supporting China by all means (Kaple 2016). After 1992 Russia reestablished its close relationship with China, and China has taken advantage of that in developing both its economy and military power.

India, from 1947 to 1953, had hardly any relationship with the Soviet Union. Stalin refused to meet the first ambassador of India to the Soviet Union, who was the sister of the prime minister of India, Nehru, but at the same time provided food aid to India (Mastney 2010). India's relationship started with the arrival of Khrushchev and Bulganin in India in 1955. The

Soviet Union helped India in India's Five-Year Plans and its industrial development. Destruction of the Soviet Union has not affected that relationship with India as that close relationship continued with Russia, despite of the serious efforts of the president of the United States, Clinton, during the early 1990s to obstruct that relationship (Brzezizinski 1997). However, India although has taken advantage of that close relationship with Russia in its military sphere but has failed so far to utilize that relationship in the economic front.

Given this introduction, this chapter explains the reasons for these different outcomes of the Russia-China relationship as opposed to the Russia-India relationship.

SOVIET CONTRIBUTION TO CHINA

Construction of modern industrial plants, agricultural development in China by Russian scientists, and educational development of the Chinese, all these the Soviet Union did to China to establish the foundation of a modern economy on a nearly destroyed country ravaged by continuous wars since 1930s. For the first 10 years of China's existence after the communist takeover almost half of China's trade was with the Soviet Union. China had little foreign exchange at that time, and there was the embargo from most of the Western countries. The equipment and technology provided by the Soviet Union was worth 2.5 billion rubles until 1960 (Borekov and Koloskov 1980; Zhang, Zhang, and Yao 2006).

The Soviet Union was exporting the entire industrial plants to China along with iron and steel, crude oil, and other petroleum products. Every types of industrial factories, textile, machinery, mining equipment, chemical and pharmaceutical firms and agricultural machinery were built in China by the Soviet Union. The reason that China after 1978 started exporting all kinds of products to the world market was that these Soviet-made factories created products that were in demand in both the domestic market and in the international market. China was paying in terms of its exports to the Soviet Union in terms of fabrics, clothing, and footwear, products of the Soviet-made factories. The trade relationship was at its top in the year 1959; it declined from that year.

> Soviet assistance to Chinese industrial projects took several forms, including the transfer of entire designs; shipment of manufacturing technology and equipment; deployment of experts to instruct Chinese during construction, installation, and debugging of equipment; and training and instructions of Chinese technical and administrative cadres and workers during trial production. (Borekov and Koloskov 1980)

Eastern European countries provided product designs and manufacturing technology for instruments and wireless components (Peng 1989). Because China accepted Soviet product designs, technology, and other technical data, this meant that China also adopted Soviet technology and industrial standards (Filatov 1980; Zhang, Zhang, and Huang 2000; Zaderskov 2003). For example, the First Automobile Factory in Changchun received Soviet equipment and technology and produced quality Jie Fang trucks (Dong 1997; Fan 1999).

At the time of its inception, the People's Republic of China completely lacked expertise in the field of computing technology. As to Soviet assistance to the development of the institute for computing technology of the Chinese Academy of Science, the Institute of Computing Technology in China was founded in 1959. The computers developed by this institution played an important part in developing nuclear weapons and missiles, even today. Overall, the Soviet Union played a very important role in transferring computing technology to China (Chinese Academy of Science 1961;Cheng 1965; Fan 1986; Zhang, Zhang, and Huang 2000; Zhang and Zhang 2003).

In 1960 China closed down all Soviet consulates and asked the Soviet scientists and engineers to leave China, accusing that the Soviet Union had tried to kill Chinese leaders. While Khrushchev wanted to have a friendly relationship with the Western countries, Mao Tse-Tung wanted continuous war against the capitalist countries. At the same time China was having a great famine in which possibly 10 million people were starved to death, as China had insufficient foreign exchanges to buy grains from Canada and Australia, its traditional suppliers, and there was a great drought and crop failure. China's shifted from the Soviet model of economic growth, in terms of investment in heavy industry, and this was replaced by "Great Leap Forward" policy of Mao in which rural small-scale industries and rural development got prominence. Famine is the result of the failure of that policy. In October 1962, perhaps to divert the attention of the critics Mao had decided to invade India when the United States and the Soviet Union were about to start the Third World War over Cuba. The Soviet response was to send MIG aircraft to India in November 1962 to help defend India. That was the end of the Soviet-China friendship.

In 1969 there was a short war between the Soviet army and China when China attempted to invade Siberia. Since 1960 China was becoming friendly toward both Germany and France, for technology. France supplied the nuclear weapons materials to China by which China conducted its first nuclear tests in 1964 and hydrogen bomb test in 1967. China had nuclear power plants with the help of France only in 1992, as the Soviet Union created facilities for nuclear research in China but refused to help China on the matter of nuclear weapons (Norris 1996; Martin 2013; Reed and Stillman 2009: Arnold 2001).

China and Russia since 1992

In 1992 Russia and China identified each other as "friendly states," in 1994 declared bilateral relations of "constructive partnership," and in 1996 at the highest state level declared the construction of "partnership relations of strategic interaction." Finally, in 2001 the long-term policy of strategic partnership between Russia and China was legitimized in a program bilateral document—the Treaty of Good Neighborhood, Friendship and Cooperation.

This section examines the key features of China's defense technological and industrial base (DTIB). China's DTIB is now dominated by 10 conglomerates, including the Aviation Industry Corporation of China (AVIC) and China North Industries Corporation (NORINCO).

Within the aim of obtaining foreign technology, "science and technology diplomats" act as the overseas arm of the International Cooperation Department of China's Ministry of Science and Technology (MOST). China bribes foreign scientists, professional associations, and ethnic Chinese scientists employed in foreign universities to obtain foreign technology (Fedasiuk, Weinstein, and Puglisi 2013)

The Chinese embassy and consulates in Russia were the agents to acquire technology of Russia. PRC diplomatic staff was most interested in early-stage technology projects developed by Russian government-backed researchers. These researchers are working at the Russian Academy of Sciences, primarily at institutes in the Far East Branch. China is acquiring expertise in aerospace, nuclear energy, new energy, drones, and 5G. Chinese diplomats were particularly interested in acquiring Russian projects related to information technology and advanced materials. China views the Russian science community as a breadbasket from which to acquire technology (Hewson 2010; Cliff, Ohlandt, and Yang 2011).

The contribution of nonstate defense enterprises such as Shaanxi Baoji Special Vehicles to state sector-led R&D and production processes continues to grow. Russia constitutes the single most important foreign partner of China where the development and production of arms is concerned.

Prominent high-technology enterprises such as Lenovo and Huawei collaborate closely with the Russian state sector (Rubin et al. 2022).

Sino-Russian defense-industrial collaboration is extensive and is crucial to Chinese efforts to develop and produce advanced weapon system. China has access to components, subcomponents, and systems of a "dual-use" nature. The contribution of Russian industry is essential due to the gap resulting from inability of China's engine development program. This need will be greatest in sectors such as aerospace where the pace of technological progress is comparatively rapid. China's defense industry is still very weak when it comes to key technologies such as jet engines and electronics. China continues to be one of Russia's biggest arms buyers, acquiring more than US$3.6 billion worth of arms from Russia during 2012–2016 (Johnson 2017; Bitzinger 2017)

Science and Technology (S&T) Parks

In 2006, the Changchun Sino-Russian Science and Technology Park was established for the S&T cooperation and innovation. It was supported by the Chinese Academy of Sciences, in cooperation with the Russian Academy of Sciences, Siberian Branch, and the Novosibirsk state of the Russian Federation. In 2018, the Shaanxi Provincial Government, the Russian Direct Investment Fund, and the Sino-Russian Investment Fund established the China–Russia Innovation Park, for information technology and biomedical and artificial intelligence enterprises. In June 2016, the Sino-Russian Investment Fund and the Skolkovo Foundation built a medical robot center to manufacture medical robots in China with academic support from scientists from the Russian Academy of Sciences' School of Design and Technology (Surnin 2020).

In 2016, the China–Russia Silk Road Innovation Park was founded in the Xixian New District of Xian. In 2018, the Harbin in Manchuria became a major center for Sino-Russian technological cooperation uniting the resources of Moscow, Yekaterinburg in Russia, and Harbin and Shenzhen in China. In 2019, the Russian Direct Investment Fund and the China Investment Corporation financed the $1 billion project located in Shanghai Jiaotong University and the Moscow Aviation Institute, the China-Russia Joint Aviation Academy. In September 2018, the first China–Russia Industry Innovation Competition was held in Xixian New District, on the subjects of AI and high-end manufacturing, including a flying robot project, and robot based on functional electrical stimulations (Danilin 2020; Heifetz 2020).

The Chinese Academy of Sciences has more than 67,900 scientists engaged in research activities, while the Russian Academy of Sciences includes 550 scientific institutions and research centers across the country employing more than 55,000 scientists. In 2016, the Russian and Chinese academies of sciences signed a road-map agreement to work on joint projects. These projects include a concentration on brain functions that will include elements of AI, genetics, psychophysical innovations, and neurodegenerative diseases (Eliseev 2016; Heifetz 2020).

Huawei began collaborations with Russian universities, and in 2019 the company started cooperation on AI with Russia's National Technology Initiative and the Siberian Branch of the Russian Academy of Sciences. Russian institutions have received several technological requests from Huawei, which has two research centers in Moscow and St. Petersburg (Rubin et al. 2022; Dudley 2020).

Russia has manifest strengths in industrial automation and defense applications. The Russian Robotics Association has collaborations with the China Robotics Industry Alliance and the China Electronics Society. In 2017, Harbin Institute of Technology and the Engineering University of the Russian Federation started their joint research on robotics and intelligent manufacturing (Hannas, Mulvenon, and Puglisi 2013; Korolev 2016, Katyrin 2019). In September 2018, Sistema PJSFC and CapitalBio Technology, two life science companies and the Russia–China Investment Fund, created the innovative biotechnology laboratory in Russia for genetic and molecular research.

CHINA'S SPACE PROGRAM

The space industry is a critical element of the overall national strategy of China. It was developed by the Soviet Union in 1950s and 1960s and after 1992, thousands of Russian scientists and engineers went to China to develop China's space program. Since 2016, China's space industry made space infrastructure, the completion and operation of the BeiDou Navigation Satellite System, the completion of the high-resolution earth observation system, steady improvement of the service ability of satellite communications and broadcasting, the conclusion of the last step of the three-step lunar exploration program ("orbit, land, and return"), the first stages in building the space station, and a smooth interplanetary voyage and landing beyond the earth-moon system by Tianwen-1, followed by the exploration of Mars, all supported by Russia (Puglisi 2020).

China became the third country in the world after the Soviet Union and the United States, which was able to send a man into space and return him all because of Russia. China makes no secret of the fact that Shenzhou is based on the Soyuz. With such a system, including a manned spacecraft, upper stage, and fuel tankers, Sergei Korolev planned to send astronauts to the moon in the 1960s. Shenzhou uses the CZ-2F launch vehicle, which is actually an enlarged Soviet UR-200 rocket with four-side boosters (Bitzinger and Popescu 2017).

The collapse of the Soviet Union played an important role, providing the PRC with rapid access to the technology of Russia. In the mid-1990s, China bought a descent module for a Soyuz spacecraft from Russia and docking equipment from Ukraine. Almost simultaneously with these supplies, the Chinese scientists began training in Russia. In the late 1990s, Russian officials confirmed the transfer of technology related to manned cosmonautics to the Chinese side (Malykh and Gafarova 2019).

The RSC Energia near Moscow, which produces the Soyuz spacecraft, supplied the China with a descent module. Chinese specialists have also repeatedly visited Russian space industry enterprises, including the Samara-based Progress Space Center, where Soyuz rockets for launching the eponymous spaceships are serially produced. The Shenzhou, which was launched for the first time in unmanned mode, turned out to be practically a copy of the Soyuz.

Besides Russia, China borrows the last remaining relevant space technologies from Ukraine, in particular, "block E" of the descent lunar module, on which in the late 1960s-early 1970s the USSR planned to land the first cosmonaut on the surface of moon.

INDIA-RUSSIA ECONOMIC COOPERATION

Economic ties were the cornerstone of Indo-Soviet relations. In 1959, the Soviet Union gave a $375 million interest-free credit payable over 50 years with the exports from India. Before that since 1955, a number of scientists and engineers came to India to support the Five-Year Plans of India. The Soviet Union helped India to be industrialized. The Indo-Soviet Treaty of Friendship and Cooperation of 1971 stressed upon "economic, scientific and technological cooperation." That cooperation continued until 1991 when the Soviet Union collapsed. Thus, by all means, in 1991, India was much more technologically developed than China. However, because of its obsession of neutrality between the two competing powers, the Soviet Union and the United States, and the hostility of the private sector, India could not take advantage of this technological development over China.

The repayment of Soviet Union credits did not involve any foreign exchange unlike the repayment of American and Western loans. Instead the Soviet loans could be repaid through exports from India. For the Western loans the country had to keep on borrowing to pay off the earlier debts (Allen 1960; Bhatia 1984).

"The average repayment to Western countries during 1958–1960 to 1962–63 was only 142.5 crores per annum but roused to Rs 427.5 crores for 1971–72. Interest constitutes 30 to 40 percent of the total debt-service payments to the western countries. It is estimated that in 1972–73 out of a total western aid of Rs 626 crores, Rs 502.4 crores were used for repayment and interest on loans and only Rs 123.6 crores for investment purposes in India" (Mehta 1975).

The benefits that India got from Soviet type of assistance were that India had no balance of trade or balance of payment problem with the Soviet Union. Indian second Five-Yeas Plan was ruined because of the steel plants India purchased from Britain and Germany. In 1966 India wanted to import wheat, but India was forced by the United States to borrow from the IMF and planning was stopped from 1966 to 1969, causing bankruptcies for large private sector industries deprived of government contract due to the IMF policy of reduction of public expenditure (Rothermund 1969).

Although the India-Russia ties in general survived the upheavals of the early 1990s, economic relations began to cool in the post-Soviet period due to the increasing hostility of the Democratic Party president Clinton who tried his best to persuade Russia not to give any technology to India and imposed sanctions on India several times. The current annual bilateral India-Russia trade remains confined to under US$ 10 billion. This section analyzes the current state of economic relations between India and Russia. It analyzes the major issues that prohibited development of economic ties between the two countries.

The Soviet Union played a significant role in India's development and industrialization. It granted generous assistance to India in the form of low-priced economic credits that were repayable in rupees over a very long period and in terms of exports from India. It also supplied military equipment, which the West refused to supply, and other key commodities like oil, fertilizer, and metal, among others.

The Soviet assistance helped India to achieve economic self-sufficiency; the Western countries refused to help. Some of most important public sector companies like Steel Authority of India, Bharat Heavy Electricals Limited (BHEL), Oil and Natural Gas Corporation (ONGC), and Hindustan Aeronautics Limited (HAL) were also set up with mainly Soviet cooperation.

The economic cooperation between India and the Soviet Union began after the first visit of India's first prime minister Jawaharlal Nehru to the Soviet Union in 1955 (Pradhan 2019). The Soviet Union supported the development of India's basic and heavy industries, which include steel, oil, power and power equipment, coal, mining machinery, heavy machines, precision instruments, pharmaceuticals, fertilizer, and so on. The Soviet Union transferred technology without any reservations along with the help of setting up research and development organizations for the education and progress of technologies. The Soviet Union constructed a steel plant at Bhilai. After the Bhilai Agreement, the United Kingdom offered to build Durgapur Steel Plant and Germany offered Rourkela Steel Plant at a much higher rate of interest for the credit, which is of very short term. As a result Indian second plan was nearly destroyed because of the lack of foreign exchanges, but the conservatives of India celebrated the British and German steel plants as signs of neutrality (Eldridge 1969; Gibert 1970).

Another soviet contribution was the development of oil industry in India. The Government of India approached Western countries for help in oil exploration but none obliged, but with the help of Soviet Union, India created the Oil and Natural Gas Commission (ONGC) (Mehta 1975). Soviet cooperation in Indian drugs has helped India to break the monopoly of international drug companies and to organize a government-owned Central Engineering and Design Bureau. Soviet Union helped India to manufacture MIG aircraft and other weapons, which the West denied. On top of this, the Soviet Union supported India to procure submarines, frigates, bombers, attack and transport helicopters, air defense systems, and tanks from the Soviets (Pradhan 2019; Rothermund 1969). The Soviet Union supplied India with US$35 billion in equipment between 1960 and 1990, most without immediate payment, and to be paid in Indian rupees at concessionary interest rates (Gidadhubli 1999).

There was no outflow of resources or capital from India to the Soviet Union. However, the remittances made abroad on *account of dividends, royalties*, and *technical know-how* by the private sector were made to the United States, the United Kingdom, and other Western countries. India was in serious financial problem with little foreign exchange to import essential items when suddenly the Soviet Union disappeared as trade with the Soviet Union used not to cost any foreign exchange. India without any thinking went to the IMF, which took advantage of the situation and declared that self-sufficiency means self-denial and privatization is the virtue that will solve India's economic problem. IMF suggested the same solution for new Russia, which came out of the Soviet Union. Trade between India and Russia collapsed in 1992, when the Soviet Union was the largest importer of Indian goods in 1989 at around US$ 2,881 million (Dhar 2007)

Currently, Russia constitutes a mere 1 percent of India's total trade, and India accounts for only 1.2 percent of Russia's overall trade (2015–2016). India's exports to Russia in 2015 were worth only US$ 1,588 million. That signified the dismal state of the bilateral trade relations. India-Russia overall trade in 2015–2016 amounted to US$ 7.83 billion. India's bilateral trade with the United States was about US$ 100 billion, with China about US$ 70.73 billion, and the EU over 105.2 billion euros for the same period.

OIL AND NATURAL GAS DEVELOPMENT

Indo-Russian energy cooperation, particularly in hydrocarbons, continued after 1992. This is manifested in ONGC's investment in Russia's Sakhalin-1 hydrocarbon project in 2001. Recent developments include investments made by Indian companies like Indian Oil Corporation Limited (IOCL), Indian Oil Corporation Limited (OIL), and Bharat Petro Resources Limited (BPRL) in Russia's oil and gas sector. This includes acquisitions of stakes in Russia's Vankorneft, Taas-Yuryakh, among others (Kundu 2016; Tembekar 2015).

Nuclear Energy

Russia has completed construction of four nuclear reactors in 2022, with nine more planned. The India–Russia nuclear cooperation agreement allows India to reprocess the spent fuel from Russian reactors and, very likely, any other spent Russian fuel used in non-Russian-origin reactors, particularly spent fuels from Bangladesh reactor being built by Russia. India's Department of Atomic Energy (DAE) and Russia's Rosatom signed in 2014 on the serial construction of nuclear power units in India by using Russian technology. It has the plans for the construction of more than 12 nuclear power units in India. Moreover, India, Russia, and Bangladesh signed a civilian nuclear deal in 2017 to build a nuclear power plant in Rooppur in Bangladesh (Roy Chaudhury 2017).

The Russian Far East is an area of active bilateral energy cooperation. In 2015, India's Tata Power made an agreement with the Russian Ministry of Far East Development for investment projects in the energy sector in the region.

The Russian-origin equipment in the Indian military has created a "lock-in" effect, which created a sense of trust in key strategic circles. Indo-Soviet defense ties began in the 1960s and have persisted ever since, maturing from a buyer-seller dynamic to codevelopment of weapon systems. India has purchased US$70 billion worth of arms from Moscow since 1991, including third- and fourth-generation fighter aircrafts, transport helicopters, aircraft carriers, nuclear submarines, frigates, cruise missiles, and air defenses. India signed US$15 billion in new arms contracts with Russia in the year between 2018 and 2019.

In 1998, India's Defense and Research Development Organization (DRDO) and Russia's NPO Mashinostroyenia created joint venture BrahMos Aerospace to develop a supersonic cruise missile system. Russia developed the missile's engine and seeker, while India worked on the guidance control system, airframe, and on-board electronics. Russia enabled DRDO to indigenously develop India's Agni-I missile. BrahMos propulsion technology, the most sophisticated part of the missile, is based on Russia's Yakhont SS-N-26 antiship cruise missile (Sachdeva 2010).

The Soviet Union loaned India one of its Charlie-class nuclear-powered submarines (SSN) for a period of three years between 1988 and 1991. Russia leased nuclear-powered attack submarine, the K-152 *Nerpa*, to India for a period of 10 years in 2012, and a third SSN will be leased in 2025. India also purchased Russian frigates. India purchased another three in 2013. Russia also sold India an aircraft carrier, designated INS *Vikramaditya*. The agreement for India's Hindustan Aeronautics Limited (HAL) to manufacture the Su-30MKI along with all the components of the multirole fighter aircraft, including the engine, was significant (Behera 2016). The Soviet Union and

Russia's lease of a nuclear submarine to India from 1988 to 1991 and 2012 onward demonstrates a unique willingness to share technology, and the magnitude of Russian support for India unusually generous. Russian space cooperation robustly supported India's strategic developments, such as improved navigational satellite systems. This support was the result of the 1972 agreement between the Soviet Union and the Indian Space Research Organisation. In 2004, Russian and Indian space agencies signed an agreement to partner on reestablishing and revitalizing the Russian Global Navigational Satellite System (GLONASS) for missile targeting (Sachdeva 2010; Bakshi 2006; Bedi 1998).

Russian arms sales, information sharing, collaboration, technology transfers, and hands-on technical guidance, often in the face of heavy U.S. pressure, have made significant contributions to India's defense strategy, ranging from fissile material production and reactor designs to delivery systems and space and rocket systems. However, unlike China, India has failed to take advantage of these valuable links with Russia because of its neutrality policy (Dubey 2012).

The suboptimal economic ties between India and Russia results from several bottlenecks. These include lack of physical connectivity, giving rise, in turn, to transport bottlenecks; lack of knowledge and enthusiasm on the part of the private sector; and the absence of trade facilitation mechanism and lack of banking ties (Kundu 2010).

ANALYSIS

India is now mainly a privatized economy, with declining public sector. Indian private sector owners are more interested to maintain close relationship with the United States and the United Kingdom, where they often run away without paying back their massive bank loans and deposit their ill-gotten money. They receive protection from these hosts who are also just as corrupt as these private sector owners are.

Indian politicians are highly corrupt as well. Although Chinese are not much different, they are more loyal to their country than the Indian. Chinese diaspora community is highly loyal to their country of origin and help China to obtain technology even using corrupt means. On the contrary, Indian diaspora community is highly disloyal to India.

China has the determination to enhance its power and prestige in the international arenas. China is using its close relationship with Russia to obtain every technology it needs and going to the space and moon. India in the meantime has no determination at all but wants to be neutral between the West and Russia. That is the reason India could not take advantage of its close relationship with Russia on economic and technological areas.

Chapter 12

Soft Power of India and China

Indian soft power is media propaganda of India, as India has no soft power. Various Indian-originated CEOs of the American information technology companies only are employed by these companies, but they have no effective power to determine nontechnical policy of these companies. We give two major examples. YouTube is owned by Google, whose CEO is of Indian origin, Sunder Pichai, but recently the Indian Parliament lost its account in YouTube for violating its social norms. Asad Noor is a Bangladeshi Muslim blogger in YouTube propagating the atrocities committed on the Hindu minorities in Bangladesh and in former East Pakistan by the Muslims and the governments, but his account was deleted about two years ago in 2019 and he could not put up any new blogs. Only recently, it was restored after the author of this book had drawn the attention of Sunder Pichai. However, his older blogs describing the history of serious religious discrimination against the Hindus in Pakistan since 1947 and in Bangladesh since 1971 are still unavailable on YouTube.

That is true about the politicians of Indian origin in the United States, Pramila Jayapala, Bobby Jindal, Kamala Harris, Duleep Singh, and so on, who do not support India but are either anti-Indian or against India's ally Russia. At the same time, Pakistani-origin American politicians always support Pakistan and are against India. Pakistanis today are in important position in both the United States and the United Kingdom, with most of the assistants of the Democratic Party leaders are Pakistani. A Pakistani, Khizr Khan, commissioner of the U.S. Commission on Religious Freedom, is now criticizing India on the Hijab issue ignoring the fact that it is about the school dress code for the Muslim girls not about the Muslim female dress in public in general. He will not dare to criticize France where Hijab is banned in public. Biden also gave away at least $85 billion worth of weapon and aircraft to

Taliban in Afghanistan, when Taliban was created by Pakistan. Lina Khan, another Pakistani, is now the commissioner of the Federal Trade Commission of the United States under Biden, overseeing media companies like Microsoft, Google, and Twitter, all headed by Indians. Another Pakistani, Salman Ahmed, is now the director of the policy planning in the state department of the United States under Biden. Dilwar Syed is now the deputy administrator of the Small Business Administration of the Biden administration; he will be the deputy czar of the small businesses of the Gujarati motel owners. In the United Kingdom, the mayor of London is Sadiq Khan, a Pakistani. Another Pakistani Sajid Javed is now the transport secretary and the former finance secretary of the UK government. As a result, the United States today supports the Muslims of India who are spreading hatred against India in general and Hindus in particular by saying: "Hijab bans in schools violate religious freedom and marginalize women and girls." Rashad Hussain, a Pakistani, the U.S. ambassador at Large for International Religious Freedom, criticized India on the Hijab issue, forgetting the fact that in the Koran, Hijab was not mentioned; only covering of breast of the girls was mentioned. Most schools have dress codes all over the world. There is no objection, but only in India and only by the Pakistani American politicians.

Indian multinational companies are also anti-Indian. Recently in 2022, when Air India was privatized and went to Tata Sons, an Indian multinational company with worldwide business empire, Air India appointed Ilker Ayci, the former chairman of the Turkish airlines, as the managing director and CEO, but due to the objection of Indian Ministry of Foreign Affairs that appointment was cancelled. Ayci directly helped Azerbaijan in its war against Armenia, an ally of India, and Turkey openly supports Pakistan and anti-Indian. Narayana Murthi, the founder of the multinational IT company Infosys, is financing Sheldon Pollak, a professor in Columbia University in the United States, in his massive translation works of Indian classical literature, but Sheldon Pollak is an anti-Indian and anti-Hindu. American Universities are organizing anti-Hindu campaigns, but Indian multinational companies provide finance for these entities. Jindal Steel is an Indian multinational company, which financed the University of Texas, Austin, business school. Jindal also collaborated with the former prime minister of Pakistan Nawaz Sharif in business.

The CEO of the Twitter is also of Indian origin, but Twitter, following YouTube, does not allow any anti-Chinese blogs or comments. China today effectively controls most of the international organizations. UN and its various organs regularly use Chinese-made map of the world, which shows Taiwan as a province of China and India without Jammu and Kashmir, Arunachal Pradesh, and Sikkim. WHO took no action against China for creating the deadly coronavirus. WTO takes no action against China for manipulating its exchange rate, massive subsidies for industries, agriculture, and service sector, discriminations against foreign companies, and dumping Chinese products on foreign countries.

DEPENDENCY OF AMERICAN BUSINESSES ON CHINA

Contrary to the popular perception, Apple (AAPL) generates only about 17 percent of its revenue from China. Boeing (BA), Caterpillar (CAT), General Motors (GM), Starbucks (SBUX), Nike (NKE), and Ford (F) are some other U.S. companies with a strong presence in the country. But none of them get more than 25 percent of their revenue from China (ten Brink 2019).

Topping the list is Wynn Resorts (WYNN), which operates three casinos in Macau. It also has two casinos in Las Vegas and another in Everett, Massachusetts. Wynn Resorts' Macau casinos account for 75.2 percent of its revenue. According to Tijori Finance, the Macau operations generate about 77.1 percent of its operating profits (USTR 2018)

Semiconductor giant Qualcomm (QCOM) is close behind with 66.6 percent revenue exposure. A large chunk of Qualcomm's shipments go to factories that assemble smartphones and other products. China is home to some of the world's largest smartphone vendors including Xiaomi, OnePlus, Oppo, Vivo, Lenovo, and others, most of which use Qualcomm chips in their products.

Micron Technology (MU) occupies the third spot with 57.1 percent revenue exposure to China. By comparison, the United States accounts for merely 11.9 percent of its revenue. It is one of the world's leading makers of computer data storage solutions such as USB flash drives and NAND flash memory.

Qualcomm is not the only semiconductor company in the top 10. Qorvo (QRVO) has 52 percent revenue exposure to China. It makes radio frequency systems that are used in wireless and broadband communications. Qorvo was created following the merger of TriQuint Semiconductor and RF Micro Devices (USTR 2018; Li 2019).

Broadcom gets close to 50 percent of its revenue from China, according to Tijori Finance. Broadcom is involved in designing, developing, and marketing semiconductor and infrastructure software products. Dallas-based technology giant Texas Instruments (TXN) is a leading manufacturer of semiconductors and a wide range of integrated circuits. It sells its products directly to electronics manufacturers, most of whom are concentrated in China. About 44.3 percent of Texas Instruments' revenue comes from China alone. Oxford, Massachusetts-based IPG Photonics (IPGP) is a leading maker of fiber lasers. It does not have a manufacturing facility in China, but the dragon is a huge market for the company. IPG Photonics has 43.1 percent revenue exposure to China.

AMD is another chipmaker heavily exposed to the country. About 39 percent of its revenue comes from China. The Santa Clara-based company manufactures motherboard chipsets, graphics processors, and microprocessors for both consumer and enterprise markets (USTR 2018).

Veeco Instruments (VECO) makes processing systems that are used to build semiconductors, photonics, and display technologies. Its revenue exposure to China is 35.8 percent. Maxim Integrated Products (MXIM) rounds up the top 10 with 35.7 percent revenue exposure. It designs and manufactures analog and mixed-signal integrated circuits. Intel gets 26.5 percent of its revenue from China, while Nvidia relies on the country for 23.9 percent of its revenue (USTR 2018; Rasmussen 2017).

Wall Street is the main financier of China. Companies from China and Hong Kong have raised $6.6 billion through Initial Public Offerings (IPO) in the U.S. financial market through Wall Street Banks in 2021, which is eightfold increases from the same period in 2020. The largest IPO is the $1.6 billion listing of e-cigarette maker RLX Technology Inc., followed by the $947 million offerings of the software company Tuya Inc. This is despite of the warning given by the U.S Securities and Exchange Commission that it will do financial audits of Chinese companies, which China opposes. Noncompliance could result in a delisting from the New York Stock Exchange or NASDAQ. Even then, Chinese companies raised about $15 billion through IPOs in the U.S. financial market in 2020. Alibaba, the e-commerce giant, raised $25 billion in 2014.

Didi Chuxing has filed application for U.S. IPO of $100 billion in 2021. Uber-like trucking start-up Full Truck Alliance is trying on an IPO of $2 billion in 2021. Many Chinese companies do their listings in both New York and Hong Kong. Thus, Chinese financial strength is the result of the collaboration from the Wall Street Banks. It was not a surprise that they supported *CNN*, *MSNBC*, and *New York Times* to go against Trump.

Biden Family and China

When Biden visited China as the vice president of the U.S. government of the Obama administration, his son Hunter Biden had long meetings with some major companies and the representatives of the central bank of China. The result was that Chinese central bank invested $1.5 billion in a company of Hunter Bidden. That was the beginning. Hunter Biden visited China six times when his father was the vice president of the United States. When Xi visited the United States in 2012, Yung Sun Group, close to the Communist Party of China, invested $1.2 billion in companies owned by Hunter Biden.

A Taiwanese businessman Michael Leen has acted as the middleman between Hunter Biden and the Chinese government (Areddy and Duehtrn 2020).

CEFC is a major energy company of China in the private sector with close connection with the Communist Party, which is the norm in China. It is owned by a Ye Jing Ming, who gave $4.8 million to Hunter Biden for legal consultancy so that Hunter Biden can recommend any legal firm or individual lawyer for China, in which Kamala Harris and her husband's law firm DLA Piper is a major beneficiary. Hunter Biden became co-owner of that energy company CEFC with $10 million per year as compensation. Hudson West is another Chinese company of Patrick Ho, an American Chinese company involved in transferring nuclear and other scientific secret to China. Hunter Biden used to get $1 million every year as retainer from that company. Ho was convicted in the United States in 2016. Rosemont Seneca is an American company with close link with China to manufacture military equipment with the stolen American technology. Hunter Biden and the son of John Kerry, the former Secretary of State for Obama administration, made a deal of $18 billion to help that company (Areddy and Duehtrn 2020).

John Kerry, along with Hillary Clinton, was responsible for the destruction of Libya and Syria and the creation of the ISIS, the Islamic terrorist organization, which has nearly occupied both Iraq and Syria at one time before Russia destroyed the ISIS. John Kerry also organized the coup in Ukraine to remove an elected government of Yanakovich in 2014 by giving $5 billion to different terrorists in Ukraine. The United States after the coup removed 40 tons of gold from the central bank of Ukraine and the Ukrainian government in collaboration with Bank of China invested in an investment fund controlled by Hunter Biden. Also, Hunter Biden is in the board of Ukrainian energy company Borisma. Joe Biden knew about the involvement of his son with China, according to an American-Ukrainian associate of Hunter Biden, Bobulinski. Joe Biden helped his son in that matter as the former vice president of the United States (Sonne and Grimaldi 2014; Wright 2020).

China and the Democratic Party

The national committee of Democratic Party is involved closely with China. Fox TV on August 24, 2020, declared that China financed the election campaign of Hillary Clinton in 2015–2016. Kamala Harris and her husband earned millions of dollars from China by legal support to the state-owned Chinese companies through their legal firm.

Hillary Clinton created a movement supported by the leading members of the Democratic Party including former president Obama and Nancy Pelosi, against Russia, and wasted three years of time and enormous amount of money through the useless investigation of Justice Mueller, who could not prove any Russian involvement in the U.S. election of Trump. Susan Rice, the former National Security Adviser to Obama, declared both Trump and General Flynn, the National Security Adviser to Trump, in the transitional government in 2016, as Russian agents (Clinton 2000; Sonne and Grimaldi 2014).

That Russia campaign of the Democratic Party was designed to divert attention from China, according to American journalist Sebastian Gorka in the Fox TV on March 18, 2016. Biden declared China only as a competitor not an enemy of the United States. Bill Clinton promoted China as the strategic partner. Obama had no objection against China joining the World Trade Organization as a free enterprise economy, which is totally false, as nothing can happen in China without the support of the Government of China. Kamala Harris supported in her interview in the Fox TV on September 5, 2020, the Black Lives Matter (BLM) movement. BLM created riots, looting, and chaos in cities after cities to support a known criminal George Floyd, killed by the police. That BLM movement was financed by China through some extremist organizations like Freedom Road and Liberation Road (Gonzalez 2020).

General Spalding of the Hoover Institute, Stanford University, declared that coronavirus was created by China to create chaos in the U.S. election. Nobel Prize winner French scientist who discovered the HIV virus, Luc Montagnier, said that coronavirus was created in the laboratory; it was not natural that HIV virus and malaria virus can be mixed naturally. China has created it the Wuhan Laboratory, according to Shi Ziangli Li and her associates, who published their achievement in the scientific journal *Nature* in 2015. Li Meng Yan from the Hong Kong School of Public Health knew about that. She had escaped to Britain but her mother was arrested by China (Wang 2021; Shi Zhengli Li et al. 2015).

China knew that postal ballots would be used because of the coronavirus and that would give tremendous opportunity to rig the election for Joe Biden. Most of the hardware and software used to count the votes are from China. Large number of ballot papers, which supported Trump, were discarded. Thousands of dead people voted in the election. Ballots were stamped outside the polling stations. Ballots that arrived long after the polling date were accepted, so long as these are for Joe Biden.

Dr. Shiva Ayyadurai of MIT, along with Phil Evans and Benny Smith, have analyzed the voting pattern and the Dominion System hardware, which was used along with Smartmatics-Sequila software to calculate the votes in the recent election of the United States. Most of the hardware and the software came from China. According to Ayyadurai, at least 69,000 votes in four counties in Michigan alone were switched from Trump to Biden by the software after the voting, during the counting. In 2014, Dominion System donated huge amounts to the Clinton Foundation. Just before the 2020 election, the

Dominion System donated $106 million to the governor of Georgia who employed Dominion System to count the votes in the presidential election in 2010. Both Dominion System and Smartmatics-Sequila have close contact with the Chinese government and possible fronts for the Chinese government. Facebook's owner Mark Zuckerberg donated $350 million to the Center for Tech and Civil Life, a private organization, which in turn distributed that money to various election officers in the swing states to do the alleged rigging in the election (Comment's on Shiva's election system analysis, The Intellectual Wilderness, November 20, 2020; Special Report on Dominion Voting Systems Technology, Contra Costa Herald, December 12, 2020).

To divert attention from that fraud, the Democratic Party started its campaign against Russia and its connection with President Trump. Today, new information is coming out that Hillary Clinton appointed software companies to plant fake materials in the computers of President Trump to create fake links between Russia and President Trump.

Joe Biden and the Future of India

Joe Biden will be another Bill Clinton, who created the Taliban in 1995 and sent his national security assistant Robin Rafael to Kandahar to congratulate the Taliban in 1996 when it occupied Afghanistan. Clinton also pressurized Russia not to supply the engines of India's rockets and missiles and asked Russia to cut off all arm supplies to India. Clinton declared the entire Kashmir as a disputed area. At the same time, Clinton declared China as a strategic partner of the United States. Joe Biden is supported by the leading Indians in the American politics and the corporate world, like Kamala Harris, Pramila Jayapal, and Sunder Pichai of Google, who are paradoxically anti-Indian. YouTube, owned by Google, is promoting a bunch of anti-Indian Bangladeshi Muslim journalists, who took asylum in the United States, by putting up anti-Indian videos regularly (Ashbridge 2021; Madan 2021).

China's entry into the WTO was supposed to bring it into compliance with an enforceable, rules-based regime that would require that it open its markets to imports from the United States and other nations. The United States also negotiated a series of special safeguard measures designed to limit the disruptive effects of surging Chinese imports on domestic producers. However, the core of the agreement failed to include any protections to maintain or improve labor or environmental standards and, prior to 2007, the administration rejected all requests for special safeguards protection.

China's entry into the WTO has further tilted the international economic playing field against domestic workers and firms and in favor of multinational companies from the United States and other countries as well as state- and privately owned exporters in China. This shift has increased the global "race to the bottom" in wages and environmental quality and closed thousands of U.S. factories, decimating employment in a wide range of communities, states, and entire regions of the United States. U.S. national interests have suffered while U.S. multinationals have enjoyed record profits on their foreign direct investments.

APPENDIX 1

Semiconductors, for example, are reported to have received over $150 billion in Chinese government subsidies. According to the U.S. President's Council of Advisors on Science and Technology, Chinese industrial policies in this sector pose real threats to semiconductor innovation and U.S. national security. New battery technologies have similarly received great support, with large state-owned groups like CATL now emerging as one of the largest players on the world stage. Similarly, support (and overcapacity) in wind and solar power sectors has been prominent to date.

APPENDIX 2

Here are the biggest U.S. firms to be controlled, or are soon to be controlled, by Chinese companies.

(1) Starwood Hotels

Deal size: $14.3 billion

Acquirer: Anbang Insurance

Date: March 14, 2016

The Chinese insurer bought the company that owns New York's Waldorf-Astoria. Anbang announced it was buying a number of hotels owned by Blackstone. Starwood would add 1,300 hotels around the world to Anbang's portfolio.

(2) Smithfield Foods

Deal size: $7.1 billion

Acquirer: Shuanghui International

Date: May 29, 2013

Shuanghui, a private firm based in Henan, expanded its ability to supply a fast-growing market with premium-brand pork at higher prices. Shuanghui might use Smithfield as a channel to sell its products in the United States.

(3) Ingram Micro

Deal size: $6.3 billion

Acquirer: Tianjin Tianhai Investment Development Co.

Date: February 17, 2016

No. 62 on the Fortune 500, Ingram Micro was purchased by a Chinese firm that specializes in aviation and logistics.

(4) General Electric Appliance Business

Deal size: $5.4 billion

Acquirer: Qingdao Haier Co.

Date: January 15, 2016

General Electric struck a new one with China-based Qingdao Haier.

(5) Terex Corp.

Deal size: $5.4 billion

Acquirer: Zoomlion Heavy Industry Science

Date: January 26, 2016

The 83-year-old Connecticut-based company makes machinery for construction, agricultural, and industrial purposes.

(6) Legendary Entertainment Group

Deal size: $3.5 billion

Acquirer: Dalian Wanda

Date: January 12, 2016

It is the largest China-Hollywood deal to date.

(7) Motorola Mobility

Deal size: $3.1 billion

Acquirer: Lenovo

Date: January 12, 2014

Computer maker Lenovo consolidated its phone business with Motorola's. The new handsets will go by the brand "Moto." Lenovo has downsized Motorola's old business and implemented layoffs.

(8) AMC Entertainment Holdings

Deal size: $2.6 billion

Acquirer: Dalian Wanda

Date: May 20, 2012

When Dalian bought AMC, it was the U.S. second largest movie chain.

Conclusion

What have we learned from these chapters? We have learned that there are significant differences in the economic policy of China and India. Basic microeconomic differences are as follows:

(1) In India there is no town and municipal industries or decentralized license system. In India industrial license system is highly centralized; for most industries only the central government can issue license—in some cases the state governments, but that is the limit. In China, town and municipalities can issue not only license, they also can negotiate directly with the foreign companies. As a result, there are intense competition between towns and municipalities to produce more, to have more investments including foreign investments. India has no such system.

(2) In India, there are provincial jealousy among the bureaucrats and politicians, which can destroy or delay any investments. Politicians normally want to take any investments to their state and create undue difficulties, delay the licensing or registration process, and refuse permission to import vital raw materials, or foreign exports. In 1966 there was a finance minister Morarji Desai from Gujarat-Maharashtra state, who took advantage of the IMF instruction to reduce public expenditure and cancelled most of the contracts for the large private sector industries in West Bengal, which was the leading industrialized state, and prohibited public sector industries to go to West Bengal. As a result, within a few years West Bengal lost most of its industries. Another minister for steel Kumaramangalam from Tamil Nadu transferred one special alloy steel plant from West Bengal to his home state of Tamil Nadu, although Tamil Nadu has no iron ore mines or coal-coke mines; these raw materials had to be transported at a very high

cost from West Bengal or Bihar to Tamil Nadu. In China there cannot be any such difficulties or delay or regional jealousy.

(3) In India even within a state if one political party proposes and negotiates with domestic or foreign industrial group to form a productive organization, another political party can start political agitations to destroy that proposal and negotiation. In West Bengal the Tata Motors built a factory to produce cheap motor car, but a rival political party was against it as it thought creation of the plant would create more jobs and that would make the ruling party more popular. Ultimately, Tata Motors decided to leave that state and went away to Gujarat state where there was no opposition; but as a result it lost at least 1.5 billion rupees investments. In China as there is no multiparty democracy, there is no possibility to have these types of situation.

(4) Although India has followed China to create special economic zone (SEZ), normally Indian SEZs are much smaller and not diversified enough to take advantage of the economics of scale or vertical and horizontal integrations. Both regional jealousy and jealousy among the political parties mentioned above can destroy any SEZ. In China these types of situation cannot arise; as a result, its SEZs are highly successful. In India after 1995, license, quota, and permission to imports have mainly disappeared except for some special cases; environmental objections can be still used to cancel or delay any project by the politicians or bureaucrats due to their provincialism. Haldia SEZ in West Bengal was ruined by just one political party that was jealous to destroy it. In China, that cannot happen.

(5) At the macro or national level the reason India could not take advantage of its close relationship with Russia or the Soviet Union before is due to its disastrous policy of nonalignment. India is and was always scared to go too close to Russia or the Soviet Union. When the Soviet Union built the Bhilai Steel Plant, India at the same time gave contracts to both Britain and Germany to build two other steel plants, although the financial terms of these British and German contracts were disastrous for India. Rather than giving contract to Russia to get more transport aircraft for the army, India gave contracts to the United States for transport aircrafts for the army, although the American planes are more expensive and there was no technology transfer. In the same way India purchased from France fighter aircrafts Rafale without any technology transfer but similar aircrafts from Russia with technology transfer were available to India at a much cheaper price. China has no such constraints. As a result, China took all advantages of close relationship with Russia to produce and export various products both industrial and consumption goods.

(6) India whenever there is any financial problem goes to the IMF and listen very obediently to every instructions of the IMF-World Bank,

although these recommendations have very negative effects. China had avoided the "shock therapy" recommended by the IMF-World Bank, but India embraced it. India went for privatizations of almost all public sector organizations at massive discounts. India also closed down some of the public sector plants and started importing the products they used to produce. Private owners sold part of these mines to foreign companies and sent away the money to London and other offshore financial institutions. China has not privatized its state-owned industries much. Whenever it did it transferred these to town and municipal sectors, which are also state-controlled mainly. As a result India lost its assets but China has not.

(7) India has no determination. It is going from one end to another without any direction. It had planning but in 1959 it had expelled the architect of the plan P. C. Mahalanobis from the Planning Commission because the Finance Minister Morarji Desai, a staunch conservative and anti-socialist, wanted it. At the height of the planning only 14 percent of the economy was in the public sector. The most profitable parts of the economy, the consumption goods sector, were in the hands of the private sector. With the help of various licenses, quotas for production, and permissions for imports, the scope for crony capitalists was enormous. After 1992, when India was under the control of the IMF, and most of these licenses, quotas, and permits were disappearing, India still had close relationship with Russia, and Russian scientists and engineers were eager to come to India because of their familiarity with India. However, India never invited them. India has no planning. There is no direction, no aim.

At the same time, China totally determined to replace the Soviet Union as the second most powerful nation on earth invited thousands of Russian engineers and scientists to develop all kinds of products, from electronics to rocket engines to spacecrafts. China still has a planned economy. It has progressed according to its plan to outperform the United States. India is happy to be a follower when China wants to be the leader.

However, all is not well in China either. Chinese economy is going through a declining phase. Coronavirus has destroyed the credibility of China, which is now very unpopular throughout the world. China may have overinvested. A number of Chinese construction companies are on the verge of bankruptcy. Belt and Road Initiative of China has created enemies for China as most of the recipient countries have realized that they are in the debt trap of China.

We all want both China and India to develop together peacefully but that may be a wishful thinking given the aggressive and determined behavior of China and very docile and submissive behavior of India. We think that is the root cause why China made such a rapid progress and India is still staggering.

References

Abraha, H. 2016. *To What Extent Did Ideological Differences Instigate the Deterioration of Sino-Soviet Relations*. Uppsala: University of Uppsala Press.

Acemoglu, Daron, and Simon Johnson. 2005. "Unbundling Institutions." *Journal of Political Economy* V (113): 949–95.

Aggarwal, Aradhna. 2006. "Special Economic Zones: Revisiting the Policy Debate." *Economic and Political Weekly* 41 (43/44): 74–79.

Aggarwal, Aradhna. 2011. "Promoting Agglomeration Economies and Industrial Clustering Through SEZs: Evidence from India." *Journal of International Commerce, Economics and Policy* 2 (2): 201–27.

Ahluwalia, M. S. 2002. "Economic Reforms in India since 1991: Has Gradualism Worked?" *The Journal of Economic Perspectives* 16 (3): 67–88.

Aitchison, C. U. 1929. *Convention between Great Britain, China, and Tibet, Simla: A Collection of Treaties, Engagements and Sanads*. Vol. XIV. Calcutta: Govt Printing Office.

Akamatsu, K. 1935. "Waga kuni yomo kogyohin no susei." *Shogyo Keizai Ronso* 13: 129–212.

Akamatsu, K. 1937. "Waga kuni keizai hatten no sogo benshoho." *Shogyo Keizai Ronso* 15: 179–210.

Akamatsu, K. 1956. "Waga kuni sangyo hatten no ganko keitai, tokuni kikai kigu kogyo ni tsuite." *The Hitotsubashi Ronso* 36: 514–26

Akamatsu, K. 1961. "A Theory of Unbalanced Growth in the World Economy." *Weltwirtschaftliches Archiv* 86: 196–217.

Akol, N. and Thayer, B. 2019. Why China is taking over Africa's resources one country at a time, *The National Interest*, July 31.

Alder, S., L. Shao, and F. Zilibotti. 2016. "Economic Reforms and Industrial Policy in a Panel of Chinese Cities." *Journal of Economic Growth* 21: 305–49.

Allen, R. L. 1960. "Soviet Economic Warfare." In *Indo-Soviet Relations: Problems and Prospects*, edited by V. Bhatia. New Delhi: Panchsheel Publishers

Altbach, P. 2009. "The Giants Awake: Higher Education Systems in China and India." *Economic and Political Weekly* 44 (23): 39–51.

Aoki, M., K. Murdock, and M. Okuno-Fujiwara. 1996. "Beyond the East Asian Miracle: Introducing the Market Enhancing View." In *The Role of Government in East Asian Economic Development*, edited by M. Aoki, K. Hyung, and M. Kuno-Fujiwara. Oxford: Clarendon Press.

Areddy, J. T., and A. Duehtrn. 2020. "Hunter Biden's Family Name Aided Deals with Foreign Tycoons." *Wall Street Journal*, December 22.

Arnold, L. 2001. *Britain and the H-bomb*. Basingstoke: Palgrave Macmillan.

Ashbridge, E. 2021. "US-India Relations." *The Diplomat*, March 17.

Autor, D., and G. Hanson. 2014. *Labor Market Adjustment to International Trade*. Reporter no. 2? Washington, DC: National Bureau of Economic Research

Autor, D. H., D. Dorn, and G. Hanson. 2012. "The China Syndrome: Local Labor Market Effects of Import Competition in the United States." Working Paper no. 18054, Washington, DC: National Bureau of Economic Research

Bai, C., and Z. Qian. 2009. "Who Is Squeezing out Household Income — An Analysis of the National Income Distribution in China." *Social Sciences in China (zhongguo shehui kexue)* 5: 99–115.

Bakshi, Jyotsna. 2006. "India-Russia Defence Cooperation." *Strategic Analysis* 30 (2): 467–75.

Balakrishnan, P. 2000. "Agriculture and Economic Reforms: Growth and Welfare." *Economic and Political Weekly*, March, 4–10.

Bandiera, L, and Tsiropoulos, V. 2019. A Framework to Assess Debt Sustainability and Fiscal Risks under the Belt and Road Initiative. Policy Research Working Paper No WPS 8891, Washington, DC: World Bank Group. http://documents.worldbank.org/curated/en/723671560782662349/pdf/A-Framework-to-Assess-Debt-Sustainability-and-Fiscal-Risks-under-the-Belt-and-Road-Initiative.pdf.

Bardhan, P. 2002. "Decentralization of Governance and Development." *Journal of Economic Perspectives* 16 (4): 185–205.

Bardhan, P. 2010. *Awakening Giants, Feet of Clay: Assessing the Economic Rise of China and India*. Princeton: Princeton University Press

Basu, D. 1995. *Monetary and Financial Planning for a Transitory Economy: Adaptive Control Model for India*. Brookfield, Vermont: Avebury.

Basu, D., and Victoria Miroshnik. 2015. *Dynamic Systems Modelling and Optimal Control*. Basingstoke: Palgrave Macmillan.

Basu, D., and Victoria Miroshnik. 2021. *Ethics, Morality and Business*. Cham, Switzerland: Palgrave Macmillan/Springer

Basu, D. R., and A. Lazaridis. 1983. "Stochastic Optimal Control by Pseudo Inverse." *Review of Economics and Statistics* LXV (2): 347–52

Bedi, R. 1998. "India to Sign New 10 Yr Defence Deal with Russia." *Jane Defence Weekly*, July 1, 16–22

Behera, L. K. 2016. *Indian Defence Industry: An Agenda For Make In India*. New Delhi: Pentagon Press.

Bernstein, J. 2016. "Sometimes, Your Trade Deficit Is Thrust upon You. Post Everything." *Washington Post blog*, October 31.

Bhagwati, J. 1978. *Foreign Trade Regimes and Economic Development*. Cambridge, MA: Ballinger.
Bhatia, V. 1984. "Indo- Soviet Relations: An Overall View." In *Indo- Soviet Relations Problems and Prospects*, edited by V. Bhatia. New Delhi: Panchsheel Publications.
Bitzinger, R. 2017. *Arming Asia: Technonationalism and Its Impact on Local Defense Industries*. London: Routledge.
Bitzinger, R., and N. Popescu. 2017. "Defence Industries in Russia and China: Players and Strategies." EU Institute for Security Studies. http://www.iss.europa.eu
Bivens, J. 2008a. *Everybody Wins, Except for Most of Us: What Economics Teaches about Globalization*. Washington, DC: Economic Policy Institute.
Bivens, J. 2008b. *Trade, Jobs, and Wages: Are the Public's Worries about Globalization Justified?*. Issue Brief no. 244, May 2008, Washington DC: Economic Policy Institute
Bivens, J. 2013. *Using Standard Models to Benchmark the Costs of Globalization for American Workers without a College Degree*. Briefing Paper no. 354, March 2013, Washington DC: Economic Policy Institute.
Borekov, O. B., and G. T. Koloskov. 1980. *Soviet-Sino Relationship 1945–1980*. Moscow: Tzdatelvstvo Mulv
Bosworth, B., and Susan Collins. 2007. *Accounting for Growth: Comparing China and India*. Washington, DC: NBER
Bosworth, B. and A. Maertens. 2010. "Economic Growth and Employment Generation." In *The Service Revolution in South Asia*, edited by Ejaz Ghani. Oxford: Oxford University Press.
Brandt, L., C. Hsieh, and X. Zhu. 2008. "Growth and Structural Transformation in China, 1978–2004." In *China's Great Economic Transformation*, edited by L. Brandt and T. G. Rawski. Cambridge: Cambridge University Press.
Brandt, L., J. Litwack, E. Mileva, K. Wang, Y. Zhang, and L. Zhao. 2020. *China's Productivity Slowdown, and Future Growth Potential*. Washington, DC: World Bank.
Brandt, L., and T. Rawski. 2008. *China's Great Economic Transformation*. Cambridge: Cambridge University Press.
Brandt, L., T. Tombe, and X. Zhu. 2012. "Factor Market Distortions across? Time, Space and Sectors in China." http://www.economics.utoronto.ca/xzhu/paper/BTZ0912
Branstetter, L., and N. Lardy. 2008. "China's Embrace of Globalization." In *China's Great Economic Transformation*, edited by L. Brandt and T. Rawski. Cambridge: Cambridge University Press.
Brazys, S., and K. Vadlamannati. 2018. "Aid Curse with Chinese Characteristics? Chinese Development Flows and Economic Reforms." AidData Working Paper 52, May 2018. https://www.aiddata.org/publications/aid-curse-with-chinese-characteristics-chinese-development-flows-and-economic-reforms.
Brown, Ellen. 2019. "Monsanto, Bayer, and the Push for Corporate Cannabis." Counter Punch. https://www.counterpunch.org. 29 April .
Brzezizinski, Z. 1997. *The Grand Chessboard: American Strategic Imperative*. Basic Books. New York: Basic Books.
Burns, John P. 1994. "Strengthening Central CCP Control of Leadership Selection: The 1990 Nomenklatura." *The China Quarterly* 138: 458–91

Byrd, W., and Q. Lin. 1990. *China's Rural Industry: Structure, Development and Reform*. Oxford: Oxford University Press.

Cai, D. 2008. *Xi Zhongxun Governing Guangdong (Xi Zhongxun Zhuzheng Guangdong)*. Beijing: Chinese Communist Party History Press.

Cerutti, E and Zhou, H. 2018. "The Chinese Banking System: Much More than a Domestic Giant." *VoxEU.org*, February 9. https://voxeu.org/article/chinese-banking-system

Chand, R. 2002. *Trade Liberalization, WTO and Indian Agriculture*. New Delhi: Mittal Publications.

Chand, R., and D. Jha. 2001. "Trade Liberalization, Agricultural Prices and Net Social Welfare." In *Indian Agricultural Policy at the Crossroads*, edited by S. S. Acharya and D. P. Chaudhuri. Jaipur: Rawat Publications.

Chaurey, R. 2016. "Location-based Tax Incentives: Evidence from India." *Journal of Public Economics*, 101–20.

Cheng, C. 1965. *Scientific and Engineering Manpower in Communist China (1949–1963)*. Washington, DC: National Science Foundation.

Cheremukhin, A., M. Golosov, S. Guriev, and A. Tsyvinski. 2015. "The Economy of People's Republic of China from 1953." Working Paper no 21397, Washington, DC: NBER.

Cheung, S. 2014. "The Economic System of China." *Man and the Economy* 1 (1): 1–49.

Chin, G., and K. Gallagher. 2019. "Coordinated Credit Spaces: The Globalization of Chinese Development Finance." *Development and Change* 50 (1): 245–74.

Chinese Academy of Science. 1961. "The Ten-year-work Summarization on Soviet Experts in CAS." Working Summary of Foreign Affairs, Statistics and the Ten-year-Work Summarization on Soviet Experts in CAS, 61–4 - 37, Archives of CAS, October 17.

Chow, G. 2004. "Economic Reform and Growth in China." *Annals of Economics and Finance* 5: 127–52. Beijing: Peking University Press.

Cliff, R., C. Ohlandt, and D. Yang. 2011. *Ready for Takeoff: China's Advancing Aerospace Industry*. Santa Monica, CA: RAND Corporation.

Clinton, Bill. 2000. "Expanding Trade, Protecting Values: Why I'll Fight to Make China's Trade Status Permanent." *New Democrat* 12 (1): 9–11.

Coase, R., and N. Wang. 2016. *How China became Capitalist*. New York: Springer

CSIS (Center for Strategic and International Studies, Washington D.C.). www.csis.org.

Danilin, I. 2020. "Dialogue of Russia and China in the Sphere of Innovative Technologies." https://russiancouncil.ru/analytics-and-comments/analytics/dialog-rossii-i-kitaya-v-sfere-innovatsionnykh-tekhnologiy/?sphrase_id=36438985

Davidson, J. 1903. *The Island of Formosa: Past and Present*. London: Macmillan.

Davies, C. 2018. "It Is up to China to Save the Global Trading System." Financial Times, March 10. https://www.ft.com/content/6d85636e-22ca-11e8-8138-569c3d7ab0a7

Deb, A., and S. Ray. 2014. "Total Factor Productivity Growth in Indian Manufacturing." *Indian Economic Review* XLIX (1): 1–25.

Deng, X. 1980. "On the Reform of the System of Party and State Leadership." In *Selected Works of Deng Xiaoping*, Volume II. Beijing: Foreign Languages Press.

Deng, K. 2000. "A Critical Survey of Recent Research in Chinese Economic History." *Economic History Review* LIII (1): 1–28

Dezenski, E. 2020. *Below the Belt and Road: Corruption and Illicit Dealings in China's Global Infrastructure*. Washington, DC: Foundation for Defense of Democracies, https://www.sciencedirect.com/science/article/pii/S0149718917302975)

Dhar, B. 2018. *India's Comprehensive Economic Partnership Agreements with ASEAN, Japan and Korea*. Penang: Third World Network.

Dhar, B. 2019. "India's Withdrawal from the Regional Comprehensive Economic Partnership." *Economic and Political Weekly* 54 (45): 59–65.

Dhar, B. 2020. "Political Economy of India's Trade Liberalization." In *India Rising: A Multilayered Analysis of Ideas, Interests, and Institutions*, edited by J. Plagemann, S. Destradi, and A. Narlikar. New Delhi: Oxford University Press.

Dhar, B., and R. Joseph. 2019. "India's Information Technology Industry: A Tale of Two Halves." In *Innovation, Economic Development, and Intellectual Property in India and China: Comparing Six Economic Sectors*, edited by Kung-Chung Liu and U. Racherla. Singapore: Springer.

Dhar, M. 2007. "Indo-Russia Relations are Re-energizing." *New Theme* VII (2): 26–27

Dickson, B. 2003. *Red Capitalists in China: The Party, Private Entrepreneurs, and Prospects for Political Change*. New York: Cambridge University Press.

Dollar, D. 1992. "Outward-oriented Developing Countries Really Do Grow More Rapidly: Evidence from 95 LDCS, 1976–1985." *Economic Development and Cultural Change* 40 (April): 523–44.

Dollar, D., and A. Kraay. 2004. "Trade, Growth and Poverty." *Economic Journal* 114 (493): F22–F49.

Domar, E. 1950. "The Effect of Foreign Investments on the Balance of Payments." *American Economic Review* 40 (December): 805–26.

Domar, E. 1957. *Essays in the Theory of Economic Growth*. New York: Oxford University Press.

Dong, G. B. 1997. *Chinese History of Modern Science and Technology*. Chang Sha: Hu Nan Education Press.

Doremalen, N. 2020. "Aerosol and Surface Stability of SARS-COV-2 as Compared with SARS-COV-1." *New England Journal of Medicine* 382 (April 16): 1564–67.

Dornan, M., and Philippa Brant. 2014. "Chinese Assistance in the Pacific: Agency, Effectiveness and the Role of Pacific Island Governments." *Asia Pacific and Policy Studies* 1 (2): 349–63

Drozdova N. P. 2016. "Russian Artel as an Organizational Form of Production in the Nineteenth and Early Twentieth Centuries: A Neo-Institutional Approach." Vestnik of Saint-Petersburg University. Ser. 8. Management, 2, 62–77.

Dubey, M. 2012. "Indo – (Soviet) Russian Relations." Mainstream, L, 40, September 22. http://mainstreamweekly.net/article3704.html.

Dudley, L. 2020. "Huawei Looks to Russia." Council of Foreign Relations, October 12. https://www.Cfr.org/blog/partone

Dziedzic, S. 2019. "China's 'Payday Loans' Attacked, New US Diplomat to Australia." *ABC News*, March 13, 2019. https://www.abc.net.au/news/2019-03-13/china-accused-payday-loans-pacific-us-ambassador-australia/10896280.

Edin, Maria. 2003. "State Capacity and Local Agent Control in China: CCP Cadre Management from a Township Perspective." *The China Quarterly* 173 (3): 35–52.

Edith, T. 2015. *How Asia Got Rich: Japan, China and the Asian Miracle*. London: Routledge.

Edwards, S. 1992. "Trade Orientation and Growth in Developing Countries." *Journal of Development Studies* 39 (1): 31–58.

Eldridge, P. J. 1969. *The Politics of Foreign Aid in India*. Delhi: Vikas Publications.

Eliseev I. M. 2016. "Business Incubation as Formation of Demand for Technological, Managerial and Social Innovations." *Initiatives of the XXI Century* 4–5: 7–10.

Engdahl, W. 2007. *Seeds of Destruction*. Wiesbaden: Global Research.

Engdahl, W. 2008. "The Seed Barons. How Big Ag, Big Oil & Big Government Are Hijacking the World's Food Supply." *Acres USA: A Voice for Eco-Agriculture* 38 (June): 1–8.

Engdahl, W. 2020. "AGRA and the UN Food Systems Summit." *New Eastern Outlook*. https://journal-neo.org

Estrin. S., J. Hanousek, E. Kocenda, and J. Svejnar. 2009. "Effects of Privatization and Ownership in Transition Economies." *Journal of Economic Literature* 47 (3): 699–728.

Etzioni, A. 2020. *Avoiding War with China*. Charlottsville: University of Virginia Press.

Ezell, S., and R. Atkinson. 2015. *False Promises: The Yawning Gap between China's WTO commitments and Practices*. Washington D.C.: Information Technology & Innovation Foundation.

Fan, B., X. Mao, and S. Wang. 2005. "On the Contribution of Export to Economic Growth: 1952–2003" (zhongguo chukou maoyi dui jingji zengzhang gongxianlu de shizheng yanjiu: 1952–2003). *Journal of International Trade (Guoji maoyi wenti)* 8: 5–9.

Fan, H. Y. 1999. *Zhongguo Kexueyuan Bianniansshi [The Chronicle of Chinese Academy of Sciences, 1949–1999]*. Shanghai: Shanghai Science and Technology Education Press.

Fan, X. B. 1986. *The Thirty Years of the Institute of Computing Technology of CAS (1956–1986)*. Beijing: Institute of Computing Technology of CAS.

Fan, Y. M. 1992. *Chugoku no kogyoka to gaikoku boeki*. Tokyo: Bunshindo.

Fedasiuk, R., Emily Weinstein, and Anna Puglisi. 2013. *Chinese Industrial Espionage*. London: Routledge.

Fel'dman, G. A. 1928. *On the Theory of Growth Rates of National Income*. Moscow: Planovoe khozyaistvo

Fel'dman, G. A. 1929. *An Analytical Method for Constructive Perspective Plans*. Moscow: Planovoe khozyaistvo

Filatov, A. 1980. *Economic Evaluation on the Scientific and Technological Assistance from Soviet Union to China*. Moscow: Soviet Union Science Press.

Gan, J., Y. Guo, and C. Xu. 2010. *Privatization and the Change of Control Rights: The Case of China*. Hong Kong: University of Hong Kong.

Gao, H. 2019. "Data Regulation with Chinese Characteristics." https://ssrn.com/abstract=3430284

Garnaut, R., L. Song, Y. Yao, and X. Wang. 2001. *China's Private Enterprise*. Canberra: Asia Pacific Press.

Gechev, V. 2020. "China & India: A Comparison of Economic Growth Dynamics." https://dx.doi.org/10.2139/ssrn.3578163

Gibert, S. 1970. "Soviet American Military Aid: Competition in the Third World." *Orbis* XIII (4): 1136–48.
Gidadhubli, R. G. 1999. "India- Russia economic Relations: Issues and Prospects." *Economic and Political Weekly* 34 (20): 1215–19.
Gonzalez, M. 2020. *This BLM Co-Founder and Pro-Communist China Group are Partnering up*. Washington, DC: Heritage Foundation, September 15.
Gordon, J., and P. Gupta. 2003. "Understanding India's Services Revolution." Paper prepared for the IMF-NCAER Conference, Washington, DC: IMF.
Granick, D. 1990. *Chinese State Enterprises: A Regional Property Rights Analysis*. Chicago: Chicago University Press.
Groves, T., McMilan, J., and Naughton, B. 1994. Autonomy and Incentives in Chinese State Enterprises, *Quarterly Journal of Economics*, 109, 1, 183–209.
Hannas. W., J. Mulvenon, and Anna Puglisi. 2013. *Chinese Industrial Espionage: Technology Acquisition and Military Modernization*. Milton Park: Routledge.
Hazra, S. 1985. *Capital and Technological Progress in the Indian Economy*. New Delhi: Birla Institute of Scientific Research.
Heifetz, B. A. 2020. "Technological Rise of China: New Challenges for Russia." *Voprosy Ekonomiki* 6: 104–20.
Herd, D. 2020. *Estimating Capital Formation and Capital Stock by Economic Sector in China*. Washington DC: World Bank.
Herd, R., and S. Dougherty. 2007. "Growth Prospects in China and India Compared." *European Journal of Comparative Economics* 4 (1): 65–89.
Heston, A., and T. Sicular. 2007. "China and Development Economics." In *China's Great Transformation: Origins, Mechanism, and Consequences of the Post-Reform Economic Boom*, edited by L. Brandt and T. Rawski. Oxford: Oxford University Press.
Hewson, R. 2010. "Fighter Club." *Jane's Defence Weekly* 47 (28): 73–78
Hillman, J. 2018. "Game of Loans: How China Bought Hambantota." *CSIS Briefs*, March. https://www.csis.org/analysis/game-loans-how-china-bought-hambantota.
Hoeffding, O. 1963. "Sino-Soviet Economic Relations, 1959–1962." *The Annals of the American Academy of Political and Social Science* 349: 94–105.
Hopewell, K. 2019. "US-China Conflict in Global Trade Governance: The New Politics of Agricultural Subsidies at the WTO." *Review of International Political Economy* 26 (2): 207–31.
Horesh, N., and K. Lim. 2017. "China: An East Asian Alternative to Neoliberalism." *Pacific Review* 30 (4): 425–42.
Horn, S., C. Reinhart, and C. Trebesch. 2019. "China's Overseas Lending." NBER Working Paper No 26050. https://www.nber.org/papers/w26050.
Huang, Y. 1996. "Central–local Relations in China during the Reform Era: The Economic and Institutional Dimensions." *World Development* 24 (4).
Hurley, J., S. Morris, and G. Portelance. 2018. "Examining the Debt Implications of the Belt and Road Initiative from a Policy Perspective." CGD Policy Paper, Center for Global Development:, Washington, DC. https://www.cgdev.org/sites/default/files/examining-debt-implications-belt-and-road-initiative-policy-perspective.pdf.
Imai, Y. 1990. "The Artel' and the Beginnings of the Consumer Cooperative Movement in Russia." In *Land Commune and Peasant Community in Russia: Communal*

Forms in Imperial and Early Soviet Society, edited by R. Bartlett. New York: St. Martin Press.

Indurthy, R. 2016. "India and China: Conflict, Competition, Cooperation, and Prospects for Peace." *International Journal of World Peace* 33 (1): 43–108.

Jain, R. 2021. "Privatization and Indian State." *Economic & Political Weekly* 56 (18): 695–722

Jefferson, G., T. Rawski, and Y. Zhang. 1996. "Chinese Industrial Productivity: Trends, Measurement Issues, and Recent Developments." *Journal of Comparative Economics* 23 (2): 146–80.

Jefferson, G., T. Rawski, and Y. Zhang. 2008. "Productivity Growth and Convergence across China's Industrial Economy." *Journal of Chinese Economic and Business Studies* 6 (2): 1–40.

Jin, S., H. Ma, J. Huang, R. Hu, and S. Rozelle. 2010. "Productivity, Efficiency and Technical Change: Measuring the Performance of China's Transforming Agriculture." *Journal of Productivity Analysis* 33 (3): 191–207.

Johnson, R. 2017. "Shenyang Continues Prototype Development of FC-31." *Jane's Defence Weekly* 54 (19): 8–10.

Kanbur, R., and X. Zhang. 2005. "Fifty Years of Regional Inequality in China: A Journey Through Central Planning, Reform, and Openness." *Review of Development Economics* 9 (1): 87–106.

Kaple, D. 2016. "Agents of Change: Soviet Advisers and High Stalinist Management in China." *Journal of Cold War Studies* 18 (1): 5–30

Karmakar, A. 2012. "Development Panning and Policies under Mahalanobis Stagey." *International Journal of Business and Social Research* 2 (2): 122–29.

Katyrin S. 2019. "On the Development of Bilateral and Multilateral Cooperation with the Countries of the Asia-Pacific Region." https://rg.ru/2019/09/02/u-59-regionov-rossii-est-soglasheniia-o-sotrudnichestve-s-knr.html.

Kaushal, G. 2004. *Economic History of India*, 1757–1966. New Delhi: Kalyani Publishers.

Kesling, B., and J. Emont. 2019. "How the U.S Is Countering China's Empire Building Plan." *Wall Street Journal*, April 9, New York: Wall Street Journal.

Khosla, S. S. 2020. "How India Helped China to Steal Its Industry and Jobs." *Times of India*, July 17.

Kimball, W., and R. Scott. 2014. "China Trade, Outsourcing and Jobs: Growing U.S. Trade Deficit with China Cost 3.2 Million Jobs between 2001 and 2013, with Job Losses in Every State." Briefing Paper no. 385, December 2014. Washington, DC: Economic Policy Institute.

Kohli, A. 2006. "Politics of Economic Growth in India, 1980–2005, Part II: The 1990s and beyond." *Economic and Political Weekly* (April 8): 1361–70.

Korolev, A. 2016. "Systematic Balancing and Regional Hedging: China Russia Relations." *Chinese Journal of International Politics* 9 (4): 375–97.

Koves, A., and P. Marer. 1991. *Foreign Economic Liberalization: Transformation in Socialist and Market Economies*. Boulder, CO: Westview Press.

Kregel, J. 2008. *Financial Flows and International Imbalances*. Annandale-on-Hudson, NY: Bard College.

Kroeber, A. R. 2016. *China's Economy: What Everyone Needs to Know*. New York, NY: Oxford University Press.

Krueger, Anne. 2002. *Economic Policy Reforms and the Indian Economy*. Chicago: University of Chicago Press.

Kumar, S. 2008. "SEZs in India." Paper presented in the National Seminar on Special Economic Zones, Sri Adichunchanagiri College of Arts, Commerce and Science, India.

Kundu, Nivedita. 2010. *India- Russia Strategic Partnership: Challenges and Prospects*. New Delhi: Academic Foundation.

Kundu, Nivedita. 2016. "India-Russia Relationship: Past, Present and Future." *Valdai*, June 14. http://valdaiclub.com/a/highlights/india-russia-relationship-past-present-future/.

Lang, L. H. 2010. *The New Imperialism in China II*. Beijing: Dong fang Press.

Lary, H. B. 1946. "The Domestic Effects of Foreign Investment." *American Economic Review* 36 (2): 672–85.

Lau, L.J., Qian, V., Roland, G., 2000, Reform without losers. *Journal of Political Economy*. 108, 1, 120–143.

Lau, L. J., and H. Zheng. 2015. "How Much Slack Was There in the Chinese Economy Prior to Its Economic Reform of 1978?" Working Paper No. 34, The Institute of Global Economics and Finance, Hong Kong: The Chinese University of Hong Kong

Li, F. 2019. "Why Have All Western Internet Firms (WIFS) Failed in China? A Phenomenon-Based Research." *Academy of Management Discoveries* 5 (1): 13–37.

Li, J. 2003. "An Empirical Study on Export's Contribution to GDP Growth." *World Economy (shijie jingji)* 4: 31–34.

Li, R. 2008. "Li Rui's Reflections on Reform and Open-up" (Li Rui dui gaige kafang de yizhong huigu). *Yanhuang Chunqiu* 11: 48–59

Li, S. Y. 1994. "Japanese Direct Foreign Investment and Trade Flows in the Asia-Pacific Region." Economic Research Center, International Economic Conflict Discussion Paper No.72, Nagoya: Nagoya University.

Liang, Qiao, and Wang Xiangsui. 1999. *Unrestricted Warfare*. Beijing: PLA Literature and Arts Publishing House.

Lin, J. 1992. Rural Reforms and Agricultural Growth in China. American Economic Review, 82, March, 34–51.

Lin, J., and Y. Li. 2003. "Export and Economic Growth in China: A Demand-oriented Analysis." *China Economic Quarterly* 3: 779–94.

Lo, B. 2016. *The Illusion of Convergence; Russia, China and the BRICS*. Paris: IFRI

Lu, F. 2010. *Labor Productivity and Macroeconomic Cycles in China*. Beijing: China Economic Observer of Peking University.

Lu, H., and X. Xu. 2005. "Reexamining the Impact of Export on China's Economic Growth." *Quantitative Economic Methods and Econometric Research (shuliang jingji yu jiliang jingji)* 2: 136–42.

MacFarquhar, R. 1974. *The Origins of the Cultural Revolution*. Vols. I, II, III. New York: Columbia University Press.

MacFarquhar, R., and M. Schoenhals. 2006. *Mao's Last Revolution*. Cambridge: Harvard University Press.

McKinsey Survey, *Economic conditions*, https://www. mckinsey.com/capabilities/2017

Madan, T. 2021. *India and the Biden administration; Agenda 2021*. Washington, DC: Brooking Institution.

Maddison, A. 1998. *Chinese Economic Performance in the Long Run*. Paris: OECD.

Maddison, A. 2001. *The World Economy: A Millennial Perspective*. Paris: OECD.

Maddison, A. 2007a. *Chinese Economic Performance in the Long Run, 960–2030*. Paris: OECD.

Maddison, A. 2007b. *Contours of the World Economy, 1–2030 AD: Essays in Macroeconomic History*. Oxford: Oxford University Press.

Mahalanobis, P. C. 1952. "Some Observations on the Process of Growth of National Income I." *Sankhya* XII: 307–12.

Mahalanobis, P. C. 1953. "Some Observations on the Process of Growth of National Income II." *Sankhya* XIV: 3–62

Mahalanobis, P. C. 1955. "The Approach of Operations Research to Planning." *Sankhya* XVI: 63–89

Mahalanobis, P. C. 1956. "Draft Plan-Frame for the Second Five-Year Plan." *Sankhya* V16: 3–62.

Malykh, O. E., and E. A. Gafarova. 2019. "High-tech Sectors of the Russian Economy: Opportunities and Resources for Development." https://cyberleninka.ru/article/n/vysokotehnologichnye-otrasli-rossiyskoy-ekonomiki-vozmozhnosti-i-resursy-razvitiya.

Markevich, A., and Zhuravskaya, E. 2009. *Career Concerns in a Political Hierarchy*, working paper no 134, Moscow: New Economic School.

Marshall, Julie. 2004. *Britain and Tibet: 1765–1947*. London: Routledge.

Martin, G. J. 2013. *General de Gaulle's Cold War*. New York: Berghahn Books.

Mastney, V. 2010. "The Soviet Union's Partnership with India." *Journal of Cold War Studies* 2 (3): 50–90.

McMillan, J., and B. Naughton. 1992. "How to Reform a Planned Economy: Lessons from China." *Oxford Review of Economic Policy* 8 (1): 130–43.

McMillan, J., J. Whalley, and L. Zhu. 1989. "The Impact of China's Economic Reforms on Agricultural Productivity Growth." *Journal of Political Economy* 97: 781–807.

Mehta, V. 1975. *Soviet Union and India's Industrial Development*. New Delhi: Manas Publications.

Mellor, J. 1976. *The New Economics of Growth: A Strategy for India and the Developing World*. Ithaca: Cornell University Press.

Millward, J. 2007. *Eurasian Crossroads: A History of Xingjiang*. New York: Columbia University Press.

Narlikar, A. 2019. "Regional Powers' Rise and Impact on International Conflict and Negotiation: China and India as Global and Regional Players." *Global Policy* 10 (2): 22–28.

Naughton, B. 2007. *The Chinese Economy: Transitions and Growth*. Cambridge, MA: MIT Press.

Nölke, A., T. ten Brink, C. May, and S. Claar. 2019. *State-permeated Capitalism in Large Emerging Economies*. Abingdon: Routledge.

Norris, R. 1996. "French and Chinese Nuclear Weapon Testing." *Security Dialogue* 27 (1): 39–54

North, D. 1981. *Structure and Change in Economic History*. New York: W.W. Norton & Co.,.

O'Neill, D. 2018. *Dividing ASEAN and Conquering the South China Sea*. Hong Kong: Hong Kong University Press.

Oi, J. C. 1999. *Rural China Takes Off: Institutional Foundations of Economic Reform*. Los Angeles: University of California Press

Prat, A., Yu, B., and Fan, S. 2008. The Total Factor Productivity in China and India, *China Agricultural Economic Review*, 1, 9–22.

Peng, M. 1989. *Dangdai Zhongguo De Jiben Jianshe* [The Capital Construction in Contemporary China]. Vol. 1. Beijing: China Social Science Press.

Perkins, D. 1977. *Rural Small Scale Industry in the People's Republic of China*. Los Angeles: University of California Press.

Pierce, J., and P. Schott. 2016. "The Surprisingly Swift Decline of U.S. Manufacturing Employment." *American Economic Review* 106 (7): 1632–62.

Pinkus N. 1902. "Artels." *The Economic Journal* 12 (48): 485–500.

Pradhan, M. 2019. "Soviet Union in India's Industrialization." *International Journal of Research and Analytical Reviews* 6 (1): 243–48.

Pradhan, P., A. Pandey, A. Mishra, P. Gupta, P. Tripathi, M. Menon, J. Gomes, P. Vivekanandan, and B. Kundu. 2020. "Uncanny Similarity of Unique Inserts in the 2019-nCoV Spike Protein to HIV-1 gp120 and Gag." https://doi.org/10.1101/2020.01.30.927871

Puglisi, Anna. 2020. "The Myth of the Stateless Global Society." In *Beyond Espionage: China's Quest for Foreign Technology*, edited by W. Hannas and D. Tatlow. Milton Park: Routledge.

Qian, Y., and C. Xu. 1993. "Why China's Economic Reform Differ: The M-form Hierarchy and Entry/Expansion of the Non-state Sector." *Economics of Transition* 1 (2): 135–70.

Rajan, R. 2014. *Address at the 20th Lalit Doshi Memorial Lecture on August 11, 2014*. Mumbai: Reserve Bank of India.

Rajshekhar, M. 2020. "Crony Capitalism on Modi's Watch Means Invisible Hands Ensure You Never Go Bankrupt." *The WIRE* 29 (7).

Ramesh, S. 2017. *China's Lesson for India*. New York: Springer

Rao, C., and B. Dhar. 2018. *India's Recent Inward Foreign Direct Investment: An Assessment*. New Delhi: Institute for Studies in Industrial Development.

Rasmussen, C. 2017. *Jobs Supported by Exports 2016: An Update*. U.S. Department of Commerce, Washington, DC: International Trade Administration.

Ravallion, Martin, and Shaohua Chen. 2007. "China's (Uneven) Progress against Poverty." *Journal of Development Economics* 82: 1–42.

Rearden, M. 2012. *Council of War, a History of the Joint Chiefs of Staffs*. Washington, DC: NDU Press.

Reed, T., and D. Stillman. 2009. *The Nuclear Express*. Minneapolis: Zenith Press.

Richardson, H. E. 1984. *Tibet and Its History*. Boulder: Shambala.

Riordan, P. 2018. "Coalition Attack on China over Pacific Aid." *The Australian*, January 10. https://www.theaustralian.com.au/nation/foreign-affairs/coalition-attack-on-china-over-pacific-aid/news-story/29eb518cae5b114272a664aa56a67166

Rodis, R. 2012. "China's Mining Occupation of the Philippines." *Philippines Daily Inquirer*, December 12, Manila.

Rodis, R. 2014. What did Estrada and Arryo promise China, *Philippines Daily Inquirer*, March 21.

Rodrik, D. 2006. "Goodbye Washington Consensus, Hello Washington Confusion?" *Journal of Economic Literature* XLIV (December): 969–83.

Rodrik, D. 2012. *The Globalization Paradox*. Oxford: Oxford University Press.

Rodrik, D. 2016. *Straight Talk on Trade*. New York: WW Norton.

Rothermund, D. 1969. "India and the Soviet Union." *Annals of the American Academy of Political and Social Sciences* 386: 78–88.

Roy Chaudhury, D. 2017. "India-Bangladesh Russia Civil Nuclear Cooperation on the Cards." *The Economic Times*, March 23. http://economictimes.indiatimes.com/news/politics-and-nation/india-bangladesh-russia-civil-nuclear-cooperation-on-the-cards/articleshow/57782501.cms.

Rubin, A., A. Omar, L. Martinez, J. Dow, and Anna Puglisi. 2022. "The Huawei Moment." Center for Security and Emerging Technology. https://doi.org/10.51593/20200079

Rudra, A. 1995. *Indian Plan Models*. Bombay: Allied Publisher.

Rudra, A. 1982. *Indian Agricultural Economics*. Bombay: Allied Publisher

Rudra, A. 1992. *Political Economy of Indian Agriculture*. Calcutta: KP Bagchi.

Sachdeva, G. 2010. "Indo- Russia Economic Linkages: A Critical Assessment." In *India Russia Strategic Partnership Challenges and Prospects*, edited by N. Kundu. New Delhi: Academic Foundation.

Saha. S. 2014. "Total Factor Productivity Trends in India." *NEHU Journal* XII (1): 95–106.

Scarlett, Z. 2013. *The Sino-Soviet Split*. Boston: Northeastern University.

Scott, R., and H. Wething. 2012. "Jobs in the U.S. Auto Parts Industry Are at Risk Due to Subsidized and Unfairly Traded Chinese Auto Parts." Briefing Paper no. 336, Washington, DC: Economic Policy Institute.

Scott, Robert E. 2013. "Trading Away the Manufacturing Advantage: China Trade Drives Down U.S. Wages and Benefits and Eliminates Good Jobs for U.S. Workers." Briefing Paper no. 367, Washington, DC: Economic Policy Institute

Scott, Robert E. 2017a. *Growth in U.S.–China Trade Deficit between 2001 and 2015 Cost 3.4 Million Jobs: Here's How to Rebalance Trade and Rebuild American Manufacturing*. Washington, DC: Economic Policy Institute.

Scott, Robert E. 2017b. *We Still Haven't Recovered Well-Paying Construction and Manufacturing Jobs*. Washington, DC: Economic Policy Institute

Scott, Robert E., and Elizabeth Glass. 2016. "Trans-Pacific Partnership, Currency Manipulation, Trade, and Jobs: U.S. Trade Deficit with the TPP Countries Cost 2 Million Jobs in 2015, with Job Losses in Every State." Briefing Paper no. 420, Washington, DC: Economic Policy Institute.

Sen, A. 1996. "Economic Reforms, Employment and Poverty: Trends and Options." *Economic and Political Weekly*, Special Number, 35 (36): 2459–78.

Sengupta, A. 2008. *Report on Conditions of Work and Promotion of Livelihoods in the Unorganised Sector*. New Delhi: National Commission for Enterprises in the Unorganised Sector.

Shaikh, A. 1974. "Laws of Production and Laws of Algebra, the Humbug Production Function." *Review of Economics and Statistics* 56 (1): 115–20.

Shen, L., and Z. Wu. 2003. "The Contribution to Economic Growth from Export in China: An Empirical Analysis Based on the I-O Table." *Economic Research (jingji yanjiu)* 11: 3–41.

Shi Zhang Li. 2015. "Isolation and Characterization of a Novel Bat Coronavirus Closely Related to the Direct Progenitor of Severe Acute Respiratory Syndrome Coronavirus." *Journal of Virology* 90 (6) (December 30): 3253–56

Shi Zheng Li. 2017. "Discovery of a Rich Gene Pool of Bat SARS-related Corona Viruses Provides New Insights into the Origin of SARS Corona Virus." *PLoS Pathog* 13 (11): e1006698. doi: 10.1371/journal.ppat.1006698.?

Shi Zheng Li. https://www.nature.com/articles/nm.3985/

Shi Zheng Li, V. D. Menachery, and B. Yount. 2015. "A SARS Like Cluster of Circulating Bat Corona Viruses Shows Potential for Human Emergence." *Nature Medicine* 21 (November 9): 1508–13.

Shi, Jingxia. 2010. "China's Indigenous Innovation and Government Procurement." *Bridges* 14 (3): 19–20.

Shi, Z., V. D. Menachery, B. Yount, and R. Baric. 2015. "A SARS Like Cluster of Circulating Bat Corona Virus Shows Potential for Human Emergence." *Nature Medicine* 21: 1508–13

Solow, R. M. 1957. "Technical Change and the Aggregate Production Function." *Review of Economics and Statistics* 39 (3): 312–20.

Sondhi, N., M. Pang, and R. Chatterjee. 2021. *Comparative Development of India & China*. New Delhi: Sage.

Sonne, P., and J. V. Grimaldi. 2014. "Biden's Son, Kerry Family Friend Join Ukrainian Gas Producer's Board." *Wall Street Journal*, May 16.

Spulber, N. 1964. *Foundations of Soviet Strategy for Economic Growth*. Bloomington: Indiana University Press.

Srinivasan, T. N., and J. Bhagwati. 1999. *Outward Orientation and Development: Are Revisionists Right*. New Haven: Yale University.

Starr. F. 2004. *Xingjiang: China's Muslim Borderland*. New York: ME Sharpe.

Stephen, M. D., and M. Parízek. 2019. "New Powers and the Distribution of Preferences in Global Trade Governance: From Deadlock and Drift to Fragmentation." *New Political Economy* 24 (6): 735–58.

Stichele, M. 1997. *Globalisation, Marginalisation and the WTO*. Amsterdam: Transnational Institute.

Surnin A. A. 2020. "The Role of Business Incubators in the Development of Innovative Business." *Young Scientist* 2018.25 (211): 88–89. https://moluch.ru/archive/211/51612/

Svensson, J. 2005. "Eight Questions about Corruption." *Journal of Economic Perspectives* 19 (3): 19–42.

Takekoshi, Y. 1907. *Japanese Rule in Formosa*. London: Longmans, Green and co.

Talbot, Cynthia. 2015. *The Last Hindu Emperor*. Cambridge: Cambridge University Press.

Taylor, L. 1979. *Macro Models for Developing Countries*. New York: McGraw-Hill.

Tembekar, C. 2015. "Tata Power Signs a Pact with Russia for Investment in Energy Sector." December 29. http://timesofindia.indiatimes.com/business/india-business/Tata-Power-signs-a-pact-with-Russia-for-investment-in-energy-sector/articleshow/50372636.cms.

ten Brink, T. 2019. *China's Capitalism. A Paradoxical Route to Economic Prosperity*. Philadelphia: University of Pennsylvania Press.

Tian, J. 2008. "How Economic Reforms Started" (Jingji Gaige Shi Zenyang Gao Qilai de). *Yanhuang Chunqui* 1.

Todhunter, Colin. 2019a. "On Independence Day, India's New Rulers Are the World Bank, IMF, WTO and Monsanto." *The Ecologist*. https://www.the ecologist.org

Todhunter, Colin. 2019b. "Poisoned Agriculture: Depopulation and Human Extinction." *Counter Punch*. https://www.Counterpunch.org. 29 April.

Todhunter, Colin. 2019c. "Monsanto In India: Meet The New Boss – Same As The Old Boss?" *Counter Currents*. https://www. countercurrents.org. 30 April 2019.

Toh, H. S. 2017. *Is China an Empire*. Singapore: World Scientific.

Torgoviy, U. 1903. *Svod zakonov Rossiyskoy Imperii [The Digest of Laws of the Russian Empire]*. XI, part II. (In Russian). Moscow: Kustare Soyuz.

Tsui, K. Y., and Y. Wang. 2004. "Between Separate Stoves and a Single Menu: Fiscal Decentralization in China." *China Quarterly* 177: 71–90.

Ushimura, K. 2003. *Beyond the Judgment of Civilization: The Intellectual Legacy of the Japanese War Crimes Trials, 1946–1949*. Tokyo: International House of Japan.

Van Walt van Praag, M. 1987. *The Status of Tibet, History, Rights, and Prospect in International Law*. London: Wisdom

Vittori, J. 2021. *Illicit Financial Flows in Authoritarian States*. Washington, DC: Carnegie International.

Wädekin, K. 1992. "Verlustminderung als zentrale Aufgabe der Nahrungswirtschaft in Russland und der GUS (SNG)." *Osteuropa*, November, 938–50.

Wallach, L. 2019. "What Should Replace It? Two decades after Seattle, It Has Failed to Deliver on Its Promises." *New York: The New York Times*, November 28.

Wang, J. 1988. "Choose the Right Long-term Development Strategy — A Framework for 'the Great International Circulation'." *Economic Development Strategy. Economic Daily*, January 5.

Wang, J. 2013. "The Economic Impact of Special Economic Zones: Evidence from Chinese Municipalities." *Journal of Development Economics* 101 (March): 133–47.

Wang, Y. 2021. "China's Dangerous Game around Covid-19 Vaccines." *Human Rights Watch*, 4 March.

Weber, Isabella. 2021. *How China Escaped the Shock Therapy*. London: Routledge.

Webster, T. 2013. "Paper Compliance: How China Implements WTO Decisions." *Michigan Journal of International Law* 35 (3): 534–35.

Whiting, N., C. Zhou, and K. Feng. 2019. "What Does It Take for China to Take Taiwan's Pacific Allies, Apparently, $730 Million." *ABC News*, September 19. (https://www.abc.net.au/news/2019-09-20/kiribati-to-switch-diplomatic-ties-from-taiwan-to-china/11532192).

Wong, Christine. 1987. "Between Plan and Market: The Role of the Local Sector in Post-Mao China." *Journal of Comparative Economics* 11 (3): 385–98

Wright, T. 2020. "The Risk of John Kerry Following His Own China Policy." *The Atlantic*, December 23.

Wroe, D. 2018. "China Eyes Vanuatu Military Base in Plan with Global Ramifications." *The Sydney Morning Herald*, April 9. https://www.smh.com.au/politics/federal/china-eyes-vanuatu-military-base-in-plan-with-global-ramifications-20180409-p4z8j9.html.

Wu, M. 2016. "The 'China, Inc.' Challenge to Global Trade Governance." *Harvard International Law Journal* 57 (2): 261–324.

Xing, Y. 2010. "Processing Trade, Exchange Rates, and China's Bilateral Trade Surpluses." Paper presented at the Beijing Forum, November 6.

Xu, C. 2011. "The Fundamental Institutions of China's Reforms and Development." *Journal of Economic Literature* 49 (4): 1076–151.

Xu, C., and X. Zhang. 2009. "The Evolution of Chinese Entrepreneurial Firms: Township-Village Enterprises Revisited." In *China's Economic Transformation*, edited by Ronald Coase. Chicago: University of Chicago Press.

Xu, Q. 1995. *Theory and Practice of Mao Zedong in His Late Years, 1956–76 (Mao Zedong wannian de lilun yu shijian, 1956–1976)*. Beijing: China Encyclopedia Press,

Xu, X., X. Wang, and Y. Shu. 2007. "Local Officials and Economic Growth." *Economic Research (Jingji Yanjiu)*, September.

Young, A. 2003. "Gold into Base Metals: Productivity Growth in the People's Republic of China during the Reform Period." *Journal of Political Economy* 111 (1): 1220–61.

Zaderskov, G. 2003. *Soviet Experts' Role on Forming Military Industry in China*. St. Petersburg: St. Petersburg State University.

Zhang, B. C., Z. Q. Zhang, and K. L. Huang. 2000. "Jixie Fazhan Gaishu" [A Survey of the Development of Machinery]. In *Zhongguo?Jinxiandai Jishu Shi [A History of Technology in Modern China]*, edited by W. Xijing. Beijing: Science Press.

Zhang, B., J. Zhang, and Y. Yao. 2006. "Technology Transfer from the Soviet Union to the Peoples Republic of China, 1949–1966." *Comparative Technology Transfer and Society* 4 (2): 105–71.

Zhang, J. C., and B. C. Zhang. 2003. "20 Shiji 50 Niandai Zhongguo Jisuan Jishu? De Guihua Cuoshi Yu Sulian Yuanzhu" [China's Plan and Measures for Computing? Technology and Soviet Assistance in the 1950s]. *Zhongguo Keji Shiliao?[China Historical Materials of Science and Technology]* 24 (3): 189–251.

Zhang, L., and A. Ong. 2008. *Privatizing China: Socialism from Afar*. Ithaca: Cornell University Press.

Zhang, Z. 1995. "International Trade and Foreign Direct Investment: Further Evidence from China." *Asian Economic Journal* 9: 153–68.

Zhao, Z. 2009. *Prisoner of the State – the Secret Journal of Zhao Ziyang*. New York: Simon & Schuster, 2009.

Zhong, T. 2016. "Analysis of the US Challenge against China's Grain Support Policies." *China Daily*, September 28. http://www.chinadaily.com.cn/opinion/2016-09/28/content_26927610_2.htm

Zhu, N., D. Zhang, and W. Wang. 2020. "A Novel Corona Virus from Patients with Pneumonia in China in 2019." *New England Journal of Medicine* 382 (8): 72733. doi: 10.1056/NEJMoa2001017.?

Zhu, X. 2012. "Understanding China's Growth." *Journal of Economic Perspectives* 26 (4): 103–24

SOURCES OF DATA

2018. https://www.exportfinance.gov.au/resources-news/news-events/world-risk-developments/2018/world-risk-developments-october-2018/.

ABC News. "Papua New Guinea Asks China for Help with $11.8b National Debt." August 7, 2019. https://www.abc.net.au/news/2019-08-07/png-to-ask-china-for-help-refinancing-national-debt/11391186.

ABC News. 2018. "Tonga Gets Five Years' Grace on Chinese Loan as Pacific Nation Joins Belt and Road Initiative." November 19. https://www.abc.net.au/news/2018-11-19/china-defers-tongas-loan-payments-as-nation-signs-up-to-bri/10509140

ADB. 2017. *Meeting Asia's Infrastructure Needs*. Manila: Asian Development Bank. https://www.adb.org/sites/default/files/publication/227496/special-report-infrastructure.pdf.

ADB. 2018. "Pacific Economic Monitor." December. https://www.adb.org/sites/default/files/publication/471196/pem-december-2018.pdf.

AFL-CIO, https://aflcio.org/search?=right to work&[0]=issue:2102

AidData. "What's Included in China's Official Finance?" https://www.aiddata.org/china-official-finance.

AmCham China. 2018. "Business Climate Survey Report." January 2017. http://www.amchamchina.org/

Asia Maritime Transparency Initiative. 2020. "Chinese Investment In The Maldives: Appraising The String Of Pearls | Asia Maritime Transparency Initiative." https://amti.csis.org/chinese-investment-in-the-maldives-appraising-the-string-of-pearls/

Asian Development Bank. 2007. "Purchasing Power Parity: Preliminary Report 2005." International Comparison Program in Asia and the Pacific, Manila; Asian Development Bank.

Bureau of Economic Analysis (BEA). 2018. "Industry Data: GDP-by-Industry." https://www.bea.gov/data/gdp/gdp-industry

Bureau of Labor Statistics (BLS). 2018a. "Displaced Workers Summary: Worker Displacement: 2015–17" (news release). August 28.

Bureau of Labor Statistics (BLS). 2018b. "Employment, Hours, and Earnings from the Current Employment Statistics Survey (National): Manufacturing Employment, Seasonally Adjusted." https://data.bls.gov/cgi-bin/surveymost?ce.

Bureau of Labor Statistics (BLS). 2018c. “Employment Level” [Labor Force Statistics from the Current Population Survey Data Series LNS12000000].

Bureau of Labor Statistics, Employment Projections program (BLS-EP). 2017a. “Chain-Weighted (2009 Dollars) Real Domestic Employment Requirements Table for 2001.” In Historical Employment Requirements Tables, 1997–2016.

Bureau of Labor Statistics, Employment Projections Program (BLS-EP). 2017b. “Domestic Industry Output Chain Weighted Deflator, 2009 = 1000.”

Bureau of Labor Statistics (BLS). 2018c. “Employment Level” [Labor Force Statistics from the Current Population Survey Data Series LNS12000000].

Chatham House – International Affairs. 2020. “Debunking the Myth of ‘Debt-Trap Diplomacy’.” https://www.chathamhouse.org/2020/08/debunking-myth-debt-trap-diplomacy.

“China | Data.” data.worldbank.org.

Chinese Academy of Sciences. 2018a. “China and Russia jointly established the US$100 million Sino-Russian Science and Technology Fund.” Chinese Academy of Sciences, October 22.

Chinese Academy of Sciences. 2018b. “Chinese Academy of Sciences and Russian Academy of Sciences Signed a Cooperation Agreement.” Chinese Academy of Sciences, June 10.

Conference Board. 2010. “Long-term Wage Trends in China.” https://www.conference-board.org/research/economy-watch-china

Cordaid. 2021. UN Food Systems Summit, September 20.

China. 2012. *Statistical Yearbook*. China.2012. Statistical Yearbook, Beijing: China Statistical Press.

China Statistical Yearbook. China Statistical Year Book, various years, Beijing: China Statistics Press.

China-U.S. Trade Issues. 2021. *Report RL33536*. Washington, DC: Congressional Research Report.

Deloitte. 2016. “Global Manufacturing Competitiveness Index.” https://www2.deloitte.com/content/dam/Deloitte/us/Documents/manufacturing/us-gmci.pdf.

Economist Intelligence Unit, Data Tool, June 2019.

Embassy of India in Moscow. “Bilateral Relations: India-Russia Relations.” Embassy of India in Moscow. http://indianembassy.ru/index.php/bilateral-relations/bilateral-relations-india-russia.

Economictimes. http://economictimes.indiatimes.com/news/economy/foreign-trade/india-russia-to-put-in-place-a-green-corridor-to-enhance-bilateral-trade/articleshow/54355281.cms.

Ernst & Young. 2017. “Debt in the Steel Sector.” http://www.ey.com/Publication/vwLUAssets/ey-debt-in-the-steel-sector-august-2016/$FILE/ey-debt-in-the-steel-sector-august-2016.pdf

ESCAP Comparisons of Real Gross Domestic Product and Purchasing Power Parities. 1993. (ST/ESCAP/1918), Bangkok.

Export Finance Australia. 2018? “PNG—Sovereign Bond Issue Bodes Well; but FX Shortages Remain.” World Risk Developments, October

Financial Express. 2016. “India Discussing Natural Gas Swap with Russia, Involving China.” December 8. http://www.financialexpress.com/india-news/india-discussing-natural-gas-swap-with-russia-involving-china/467819/.

Financial Times. 2018. "Global Greenfield Investment Trends: The fDi Report 2018." https://www.fdiintelligence.com/Landing-Pages/The-fDi-Report-2018/The-fDi-Report-2018.

FT.com. 2020. "China'S Belt and Road Projects Drive Overseas Debt Fears." https://www.ft.com/content/e7a08b54-9554-11e8-b747-fb1e803ee64e

FutureRussia.gov.ru. 2019. "Huawei Launched 5G Pilot Area in Luzhniki." *Future-Russia.gov.ru*, September 13.

Government of India. 2006. "The National Strategy for Manufacturing." National Manufacturing Competitiveness Council.

Government of India. 2011. "National Manufacturing Policy." Press Note 2 (2011 Series), Ministry of Commerce and Industry.

Government of India. 2016. "India and Mauritius Sign the Protocol for Amendment of the Convention for the Avoidance of Double Taxation and the Prevention of Fiscal Evasion with respect to Taxes on Income and Capital Gains." Press Information Bureau Press Release dated May 10, 2016. http://pib.nic.in/newsite/PrintRelease.aspx?relid=145185.

Government of India, Committee on Public Undertakings. 1969. *Forty-Sixth Report: Indian Drugs and Pharmaceuticals Limited.* Fourth Lok Sabha. New Delhi: Lok Sabha Secretariat.

Government of India, Committee on Public Undertakings. 1976. *Eightieth Report on Hindustan Antibiotics Limited.* Fifth Lok Sabha. New Delhi: Lok Sabha Secretariat.

Government of India, Ministry of Finance. Economic Survey (Various annual issues). New Delhi.

Government of India, Ministry of Finance and Company Affairs. *Reports of the Task Force on Direct Taxes (2002–2006)*. New Delhi: Government of India, Ministry of Finance and Company Affairs.

Government of India, Ministry of Petroleum and Chemicals. 1975. "Report of the Committee on Drugs and Pharmaceutical Industry." Hathi Committee Report.

Harbin Institute of Technology. 2017. "Intelligent Manufacturing China–Russia Bilateral Doctoral Forum Convened." October 12.

"Haval Plant Adapts Chinese Cars to the Russian Climate." https://iz.ru/945088/2019-11-19/zavod-haval-adaptiruet-kitaiskie-avtomobili-pod-rossiiskii-klimat

"Huawei and Skolkovo Will Develop an Innovation Centre." 2018. *Telecomtimes.ru*, October 18.

"Huawei Strengthens Its Russian Development Centre." 2019. *Vedomosti.ru*, August 15.

IMF Debt Limits Policy. https://www.imf.org/external/np/spr/2015/conc/index.htm.

"India – from Soviet Ally to Russian Trading Partner." *The BRICS Post*, October 20, 2013. http://thebricspost.com/india-from-soviet-ally-to-russian-trading-partner/#.WQbeH0WGMdU.

International Energy Agency. "India Energy Outlook." International Energy Agency. https://www.gita.org.in/Attachments/Reports/IndiaEnergyOutlook_WEO2015.pdf.

International Food Policy Research Institute, China: Shadow WTO Agricultural Domestic Support Notifications (IFPRI Discussion Paper 793, 2008), Washington, DC.

International Monetary Fund (IMF). 2006. "Methodology for CGER Exchange Rate Assessments." Prepared by the Research Department, Washington, DC: International Monetary Fund.

International Monetary Fund. 2009. *Balance of Payments and International Investment Position Manual*. Washington, DC: International Monetary Fund.

International Monetary Fund. 2017. "World Economic Outlook." October.

International Monetary Fund. 2018. "World Economic Outlook Database." April 2018 Edition. Data extracted September 2018.

International Monetary Fund. 2019. "World Economic Outlook Database." April.

"Interstate Relations between Russia and China." 2020. https://ria.ru/20191113/1560810249.html.

"Invest in Innovation, Forum in Shanghai Will Feature AI." 2019. *DKNews.kz*, September 15.

Joint Russian-Chinese laser laboratory opened in Shanghai. 2020. https://ria.ru/20191104/1560554111.html.

"Lenta.ru China Purchases Russian Engines for Its Fighter Jets." *Lenta.ru*, October 7, 2011

McKinsey Global Institute. 2001. *India: The Growth Imperative*. India: The Growth Imperative, 2001, San Francisco: McKinsey Global Institute.

McKinsey Global Institute. 2019. *Globalization in Transition*. New York: McKinsey.

MHRSS (Ministry of Human Resources and Social Security). 2009. *Chinese Labor Statistical Yearbook*. Beijing: Statistical Press.

Ministry of Commerce of the People's Republic of China. http://fec.mofcom.gov.cn/article/tzhzcj/tzhz/.

Ministry of Commerce People's Republic of China (MOFCOM). 2019. "MOFCOM Department of Foreign Investment Administration Comments on China's Absorption of Foreign Investment in January-December 2018." http://english.mofcom.gov.cn/article/newsrelease/policyreleasing/201901/20190102827255.shtml.

Report on Tibet, 1992. *Ministry of Information: People's Republic of China*. Xinhuanet.com/English/2021-05/C_139959978.htm

Ministry of Commerce, Government of India. "Export Import Databank." Ministry of Commerce, Government of India. http://commerce.gov.in/EIDB.aspx.

Ministry of External Affairs, Government of India. 1971. "Treaty of Peace, Friendship and Co-operation." Ministry of External Affairs, Government of India, August 9. http://mea.gov.in/bilateral-documents.htm?dtl/5139/Treaty+of+.

Ministry of External Affairs, Government of India. 2014. "Strategic Vision for Strengthening Cooperation in Peaceful Uses of Atomic Energy between the Republic of India and the Russian Federation." Ministry of External Affairs, Government of India, December 11. http://pib.nic.in/newsite/PrintRelease.aspx?relid=113165.

Ministry of External Affairs, Government of India. 2015. "Joint Statement between the Russian Federation and the Republic of India: Shared Trust, New Horizons." Ministry of External Affairs, Government of India, December 24. http://mea.gov.in/bilateral-documents.htm?dtl/26243/Joint_Statement_between_the_Russian_Federation_and_the_Republic_of_India_Shared_Trust_New_Horizons_December_24_2015.

Ministry of Science and Technology (MOST). 2017. "The First Sino-Russian Innovation Dialogue Was Held in Beijing." June 14.

MOFCOM. 2016a. "Statement of the head of the Trade Relief Investigations Department of the Ministry of Commerce on the EU's Final Anti-dumping Measures on

Cold-rolled Steel Sheet Products from China." August 4. http://www.mofcom.gov.cn/article/ae/ag/201608/20160801372689.shtml

MOFCOM. 2016b. "Statement of the Head of the Treaty and Law Department of the Ministry of Commerce on the U.S. Suing China for Agricultural Support Policies at the WTO." September 13. http://www.mofcom.gov.cn/article/ae/ag/201609/20160901392733.shtml

MOFCOM. 2017. "Director of Trade Remedy and Investigation Bureau of MOFCOM Wang Hejun Comments on US Final Ruling on Anti-dumping and Countervailing Investigation against Stainless Steel Plate Imported from China." February. http://english.mofcom.gov.cn/article/newsrelease/policyreleasing/201702/20170202513073.shtml

MOST. 2016. "China and Russia Formally Establish an Innovative Dialogue Mechanism." July 12.

National Accounts Statistics. 2000–2007. *National Accounts Statistics is the name of the book*. New Delhi: Government of India, CSO, Ministry of Statistics.

National Bureau of Statistics (NBS) (various years [a]). *China Foreign Economic Statistical Yearbook*. Beijing: China Statistics Press.

National Bureau of Statistics (NBS) (various years [b]). *China Trade and External Economic Statistical Yearbook*. Beijing: China Statistics Press.

National Bureau of Statistics. 2009. "New China 60th Anniversary Report Series No. 5" (xin zhongguo chengli 60 zhounian xilie baogao zhiwu). http://www.stats.gov.cn/tjfx/ztfx/qzxzgcl60zn/t20090911_402586311.htm.

National Bureau of Statistics of China. 1999. Beijing: China Statistics Press.

National Commission for Enterprises in the Unorganised Sector. The Report of the National Commission for Enterprises in the Unorganized Sector. 2022, New Delhi: Planning Commission.

National Sample Survey. 2001–2006. *National Sample Survey is the name of the book*. New Delhi: Government of India, Ministry of Statistics.

National Statistical Bureau. 2006a. *China Statistical Yearbook, 2006*. Beijing: China Statistics Press.

National Statistical Bureau. 2006b. *China Industrial Economy Statistical Yearbook, 2006*. Beijing: China Statistics Press.

National Statistical Bureau. 2006c. *China Regional Economy Statistical Yearbook, 2006*. Beijing: China Statistics Press.

New York Times. 2010. "Mao's Great Leap to Famine." December 15.

Observer. 2017. "Shanghai Jiaotong University and Moscow Aviation Institute Jointly Established Sino-Russian Joint Aviation Academy." *Observer*, April 10.

OECD. "Official Development Assistance — Definition and Coverage." https://www.oecd.org/dac/stats/officialdevelopmentassistancedefinitionandcoverage.htm.

OECD *Economic Survey*, 2006. Paris: OECD.

OECD *Economic Survey*, 2007. Paris: OECD.

OECD.2019.EconomicOutlook,May.https://www.oecd-ilibrary.org/docserver/b2e897b0-en.pdf

Oxfam Report on WTO. "Eight Broken Promises." file:///G:/WTO%205%20OXFAM%20report.pdf

Peterson Institute of International Economics. 2010. "Renminbi Undervaluation, China's Surplus, and the US Trade Deficit." Policy Brief, August 2010.
RBI, Goyal, Rajan. 2012 "Sustainable Level of India's Current Account Deficit." RBI Working Paper Series No. WPS (DEPR: 16/2012, Reserve Bank of India.
"RCVF Announce Their First Investment to Support the Russian Substrate Producer Rusalox." Russia-China Investment Fund, June 6, 2019. https://rdif.ru/Eng_fullNews/4098/.
Report on Conditions of Work and Promotion of Livelihoods in the Unorganised Sector, 2008. 2008. https://ruralindiaonline.org/en/library/resource/report-on-conditions-of-work-and-promotion-of-livelihoods-in-the-unorganised-sector/
"Report on the Implementation of the 2019 Plan for National Economic and Social Development and on the 2020 Draft Plan for National Economic and Social Development." http://english.www.gov.cn/news/topnews/202005/30/content_WS5ed24e81c6d0b3f0e9499215.html
Handbook of Statistics on Indian Economy, 2002. Mumbai: Reserve Bank of India.
Annual Report, 2002–2003. Mumbai: Reserve Bank of India.
Annual Report, 2015–2016. Mumbai: Reserve Bank of India.
Annual Report, 2017–2018. Mumbai: Reserve Bank of India.
Ria.ru. 2019a. "Huawei and the Siberian Branch of the RAS Agree on Cooperation." *Huawei Ria.ru*, May 21.
Ria.ru. 2019b. "Expert Evaluated the Cooperation between Russia and China in Medical Robotics." *Ria.ru*, August 23.
Ria.ru. 2019c. "Preparing the 'FEDOR' Robot for Space Flight." February 27.
Roscosmos and Chinese National Space Administration (CNSA). 2020. "Joint Lunar Research." https://www.roscosmos.ru/24772/
Rural Statistical Yearbook of China, various years, Beijing: China Statistical Press.
Russian-Chinese Scientific Laboratory of Radiation Control and Inspection. 2020. https://tpu.ru/university/structure/department/view?id=7433
RVC.ru, II Sino-Russian Forum. 2017. "Investments in Innovation." official forum page, RVC.ru, June 2017.
Sina. 2019. "Russia Assists China in Building a Missile Warning System? Ministry of Foreign Affairs Responds." *Sina*, October 8.
"Sino-Russian Silk Road Hi-tech Innovation Park Explores New Path of Open Economy." Shaanxi Province Department of Commerce, June 13.
Sistema. "CapitalBio Technology and RCIF to Create the Largest Innovative Biotechnology Laboratory in Russia." *Sistema.com*, September 11, 2018.
Sputnik International. 2016. "India's Biggest Pharmaceutical Company Enters Russian, CIS Markets." November 23. https://sputniknews.com/asia/201611231047755695-india-drug-maker-russia/.
Standard & Poor. 2001–2007. *Asia Business Scorecard*. Singapore: McGraw-Hill.
State Council. 1986. *The Seventh Five-year Plan for Economic and Social Development, The People's Republic of China (zhonghua renmin gongheguo jingji he shehui fazhan diqige wunian jihua)*. Beijing: The Remin Press, 1986.
Tass.ru. 2019a. "Russian Scientists Created a Supercomputer for AI." *Tass.ru*, January 17.
Tass.ru. 2019b. "Russia and China Will Sign Military and Military–technical Agreements." *Tass.ru*, September 4.

Tass.ru. 2019c. "Kremlin: Russia, China to Create Missile Attack Warning System for China on Time." *tass.com*, October 4.

Tass.ru. 2019d. "Best Russian AI Startups to Present Projects at SPIEF-2019." *Tass.com*, April 22.

Tass.ru. 2019e. "Chinese and Russian Scientists Identified Six Areas for Cooperation." *Tass.ru*, July 19.

Tass.ru. 2019f. "Huawei May Install the Russian Operating System on Its Smartphones." *Tass.ru*, June 10.

Tass.ru. 2020. "RAS Intends to Open a Representative Office in China to Develop Joint Projects." https://tass.ru/obschestvo/7086959

Tibet Support Group, www.dalailama.com

UNCTAD. 2017. *Trade and Development Report*. New York: UNCTAD

UNCTAD. 2019. "World Investment Report." https://unctad.org/en/PublicationsLibrary/wir2019_en.pdf

UNDP. 2009. "Human Development Report." UNDP. https://hdr.undp.org/content/human-development-report-2009

United Nations. 2009. *System of National Accounts 2008*. New York: United Nations Organisation.

United Nations Conference on Trade and Development. 1995. https://en.wikipedia.org/wiki/United_Nations_Conference_on_Trade_and_Development

United Nations Conference on Trade and Development. 1997. https://www.bing.com/search?q=United+Nations+Conference+on+Trade+and+Development+(1997).&cvid=2787e6790ef04dd8a198356612cb73ea&aqs=edge..69i57j69i64.210j0j4&FORM=ANAB01&PC=DCTS

United Nations Economic and Social Commission for Asia and the Pacific. 1999. www.Unescap.Org

United Nations, Food Systems Summit. 2021. https://www.un.org/en/food-systems-summit/news/un-food-systems-summit

U.S. Census Bureau. 2018a. "Advanced Technology Product Code Descriptions" (web page). Accessed September 2018. www.census.gov

U.S. Census Bureau. 2018b. "ATP Data—Imports and Exports by ATP Group" [data set]. Accessed September 2018.

U.S. Census Bureau. 2018c. "U.S. Trade in Goods and Services—Balance of Payments (BOP) Basis, 1960–2017." Foreign Trade: Historical Series. Published June 6, 2018.

U.S. Census Bureau. 2018d. "U.S. Trade in Goods by Country." https://www.census.gov/foreign-trade/balance/index.html

U.S. Census Bureau. 2018e. "Trade Definitions." Accessed October 18, 2018. www.census.gov

U.S.–China Business Council. 2014. "USCBC: EPI Study on US Jobs, Trade Deficit, and China Currency is Wrong." U.S.–China Business Council, December 12. https://www.uschina.org/media/press/uscbc-epi-study-us-jobs-trade-deficit-and-china-currency-wrong

U.S.-China Economic and Security Review Commission. 2011. "An Analysis of State-owned Enterprises and State Capitalism in China." October 26. https://www.bing.com/search?q=U.S.-China+Economic+and+Security+Review+Commission

%2C+An+Analysis+of+State-owned+Enterprises+and+State+Capitalism+in+China%2C+October+26%2C+2011.&cvid=974b6e4d3ec9421ca0fd053cf96fbf70&aqs=edge..69i57.205j0j4&FORM=ANAB01&PC=DCTS

U.S. International Trade Commission (USITC). 2014. "A Note on U.S. Trade Statistics." August 2014. https://usitc.gov/publications/332/note_us_trade_statistics.htm

U.S. International Trade Commission (USITC). 2018. "USITC Interactive Tariff and Trade DataWeb." https://www.usitc.gov/

USTR. 2016a. "United States Challenges Excessive Chinese Support for Rice, Wheat, and Corn." September 13. https://ustr.gov/about-us/policy-offices/press-office/press-releases/2016/september/united-states-challenges

USTR. 2016b. "The United States Challenges China's Non-compliance at the WTO on Behalf of American Farmers." May 10. https://ustr.gov/about-us/policy-offices/press-office/press-releases/2016/may/us-challenges-china-non-compliance-at-WTO

USTR. 2017. "Report to Congress on China's WTO Compliance." January. 2018. https://ustr.gov/sites/default/files/files/Press/Reports/China%202017%20WTO%20Report.pdf

USTR. 2018. "Findings of the Investigation into China's Acts, Policies, and Practices Related to Technology Transfer, Intellectual Property and Innovation under Section 301 of the Trade Act of 1974." Washington, DC, p. 10. https://ustr.gov/sites/default/files/Section301

USTR. 2019. "Statement on WTO Appellate Report on China Countervailing Duties." July 16. https://ustr.gov/about-us/policy-offices/press-office/press-releases/2019/july/statement-wto-appellate-report-china

Wharton, Knowledge@Wharton. 2020. "China's Belt and Road Initiative: Why The Price Is Too High." https://knowledge.wharton.upenn.edu/article/chinas-belt-and-road-initiative-why-the-price-is-too-high/.

World Bank. "Country Snapshot: India." World Bank. http://wits.worldbank.org/CountrySnapshot/en/IND.

World Bank. "World Development Indicators." World Bank. http://devdata.worldbank.org/AAG/chn_aag.pdf

World Bank. "IDA Lending Terms." http://ida.worldbank.org/financing/ida-lending-terms

World Bank. "Non-Concessional Borrowing Policy." http://ida.worldbank.org/debt/non-concessional-borrowing

World Bank. 1993. *China Trade Policy*. Report No.11568-CHA, Washington, DC: World Bank.

World Bank. 1996. *India: Country Economic Memorandum; Five Years of Stabilization and Reform; The Challenges Ahead* (Report no 15882-IN). Washington, DC.

World Bank. 2002a. *China: National Development and Sub-National Finance*. Washington, DC: The World Bank.

World Bank. 2002b. "World Development Indicators 2002." Washington, DC. https://openknowledge.worldbank.org/handle/10986/13921

World Bank. 2003. "World Development Indicators 2003." Washington, DC. https://openknowledge.worldbank.org/handle/10986/13920

World Bank. 2006. "World Bank Indicator (WDI)." CD-Rom.

World Bank. 2007. *Cost of Pollution in China: Economic Estimates of Physical Damages*. Washington, DC: The World Bank.

World Development Indicator, various years, Washington D.C: World Bank https://datatopics.worldbank.org/world-development

World Bank. 2017. "China Overview." March 28. http://www.worldbank.org/en/country/china/overview

World Bank. 2018a. "IBRD Financial Products: Lending Rates and Fees." https://treasury.worldbank.org/en/about/unit/treasury/ibrd-financial-products/lending-rates-and-fees#1;

World Bank. 2018b. "Migration and Remittances: Recent Developments and Outlook." Migration and Development Brief No. 30 (December), Washington, DC.

World Bank. 2019. *Doing Business 2019: Training for Reform*. Washington, DC: The World Bank Group.

World Bank, Data. https://data.worldbank.org/indicator/NV.IND.MANF.CD.

World Bank Databank: World Development Indicators; Updated on December 20, 2019. https://www.gktoday.in/gk/license-raj-in-india/; https://www.gktoday.in/gk/dutt-committee/18; http://www.yourarticlelibrary.com/industries/dutt-committee-on-industrial-licensing/23446; http://www.yourarticlelibrary.com/policies/the-industrial-licensing-policy-1970/23448; http://www.preservearticles.com/notes/brief-notes-on-industrial-licensing-policy-1970/1974421

The Global Competitiveness Report, 2016, Geneva: World Economic Forum. https://www.weforum.org/reports/the-global.

World Economic Forum. 2017. "China's $900 Billion New Silk Road. What You Need to Know." June 26. https://www.weforum.org/agenda/2017/06/china-new-silk-road-explainer/

World Investment Report, various years, New York: United Nations https://worldinvestmentreport.unctad.org/world

World Risk Report. 2018. *Berlin: Bündnis Entwicklung Hilft and Ruhr University Bochum — Institute for International Law of Peace and Armed Conflict*. 40. https://reliefweb.int/sites/reliefweb.int/files/resources/WorldRiskReport-2018.pdf.

World Trade Organization (WTO). 1996. "Ministerial Declaration on Trade in Information Technology Products." WT/MIN(96)/16. Singapore, December 13. https://data.worldbank.org/.

World Trade Organization (WTO). 1998. "Trade Policy Review—India." Geneva. https://www.wto.org/english/tratop_e/tpr_e/tp071_e.htm

World Trade Organization (WTO). 2002. "Trade Policy Review—India." Geneva. https://www.wto.org/english/tratop_e/tpr_e/tp195_e.htm

Annual Reports, various years, Geneva: World Trade Organization. https://www.wto.org

World Trade Organization (WTO). 2017. "Schedules of Tariff Concessions to the General Agreement on Tariffs and Trade 1994 — Certification of Modifications: Schedule XII — India." WT/LET/181. October 2.

World Trade Organization (WTO). 2018c. *Trade Topics: Anti-dumping*. Washington, DC: WTO. www.wto.org/english/tratop_e/adp_e/adp_e.htm.

World Trade Organization (WTO). 2018b. *World Trade Statistical Review 2018*. Geneva: World Trade Organization.

World Trade Organization (WTO) Secretariat. 2016. *Trade Policy Review: China*. October 12. Washington, DC: WTO.

Xinhuanet. "China Signs Cooperation Agreements with 86 Entities under Belt and Road." http://www.xinhuanet.com/english/2017-12/23/c_136846221.htm; http://www.xinhuanet.com/english/2019-01/16/c_137749000.htm

Index

www.ingramcontent.com/pod-product-compliance
Ingram Content Group UK Ltd.
Pitfield, Milton Keynes, MK11 3LW, UK
UKHW041835031026
15587UKWH00002B/773

9 781666 921922